THE REUNION OF
THE CHURCH

" God forbid that I should glory, save in the cross of our Lord Jesus Christ "

GALATIANS vi. 14

THE REUNION OF THE CHURCH

A DEFENCE OF THE SOUTH INDIA SCHEME

J. E. LESSLIE NEWBIGIN

General Secretary of the International Missionary Council; formerly Bishop in Madhurai and Ramnad of the Church of South India

Revised edition 1960

WIPF & STOCK · Eugene, Oregon

Wipf and Stock Publishers
199 W 8th Ave, Suite 3
Eugene, OR 97401

The Reunion of the Church
A Defence of the South India Scheme
By Newbigin, Lesslie
Copyright©1948 by Newbigin, Lesslie
ISBN 13: 978-1-61097-512-4
Publication date 6/1/2011
Previously published by SCM, 1948

CONTENTS

Foreword to the 1948 edition		vii
Introduction to the 1960 edition		ix

PART I

| I | THE BASIS OF UNION IN THE LIFE OF THE CHURCH | 9 |

PART II

The Nature of the Church's Unity and Continuity

II	THE PROBLEM	23
III	THE ISRAEL OF GOD	27
IV	THE SPIRIT, THE BODY AND THE FLESH	44
V	THE EXTENSION OF THE INCARNATION?	55
VI	JUSTIFICATION BY FAITH	84
VII	THE METHOD OF REUNION	104

PART III

Heads of Agreement

VIII	THE STANDARD OF FAITH	124
IX	THE MINISTRY	148
X	THE SACRAMENTS	170

PART IV

XI	SOUTH INDIA AND THE ECUMENICAL MOVEMENT	181
	Index	191

To the Reverend Dr J. J. Banninga and the Reverend J. S. M. Hooper, Secretaries successively of the Joint Committee on Church Union in South India, from the beginning of its work in 1920 to its completion in 1947

FOREWORD TO THE 1948 EDITION

THIS book has been written during the last few months of a crowded furlough when I was necessarily separated from my own books. It bears, I am afraid, the marks of the haste with which it has been produced. My only excuse for writing is that this is a living issue for the whole Church, and that during all the recent controversies about the South India Scheme—in books and in Committee meetings and Assemblies—I have been compelled to try to think out the theological questions involved. So much is involved for the future of the Church that one cannot altogether avoid a somewhat sharply controversial tone in writing about the South India Scheme, but if I have been unfair in criticism of its opponents I ask to be forgiven. I am especially compelled to say this because I am deeply grateful for personal contacts which I have had in recent months with some of those whose writings I have criticized in the following pages.

It is perhaps necessary to say that what I have written is the expression of my own belief only, and is not to be taken as a statement of the belief of the Church of South India.

I have to express my gratitude to many friends who have most generously helped me: to the Rev. Professor Donald Baillie of St. Andrews and to the Rt. Rev. Michael Hollis, Bishop in Madras, who have read through the typescript and saved me from many mistakes; to the Rev. R. G. Macdonald, Edinburgh, who has undertaken responsibility for correcting the proofs and for providing the index; and to Dr. Hugh Martin of the S.C.M. Press who has spared no pains to ensure the early publication of the book. I have also to thank the Christian Literature Society, Madras, for permission to reproduce the substance of two or three pages previously published by them. Biblical quotations are generally from the Revised Version. References to the Scheme of Union are to the seventh edition.

While this book was being written one could speak only of a Scheme. Since 27th September, 1947, we have been members of the Church of South India, and the glow of that unforgettable day is still with us. I am sure that there are many things in our Scheme of Union which need to be corrected; but none who has lived through these days can doubt that God has sealed our union with His Spirit, and that even in our weakness and foolishness He will reveal His wisdom and His strength.

LESSLIE NEWBIGIN
Bishop

Madura
South India
November 1947

INTRODUCTION
TO THE SECOND EDITION (1960)

IN the summer of 1946 I was on furlough after seven years absence in India. Church union in South India was still very much an open question. The main decisions were still to be made, and it was doubtful whether union would actually take place. I was in a London bookshop and asked the assistant to give me what they had on South India. It was clear that I had come to the right shop. I came away with an armful of books and pamphlets, most of them bearing on their cover the information that they were for the defence of Church principles. The authors clearly believed that the best method of defence was attack. In the course of the next few weeks I received a liberal education in ecclesiastical polemics. The effect was "as it were a fire shut up in my bones" which could not be contained. The Foreign Mission Committee of the Church of Scotland was good enough to give me a spell of free time, and the result was *The Reunion of the Church*. The book has now been out of print for a number of years, and the publishers have decided that the demand justifies a second edition. The question arises whether re-publication after so long an interval is justified. The book was part of an argument, and the argument has now moved on. Neither the writer nor the subject are what they were ten years ago. Of the former, it is sufficient to say that he was then a Presbyterian minister writing from the point of view of a Church looking forward to union. No one could have lived through the experience of being a bishop in the Church of South India from 1947 till to-day without having his mind and spirit profoundly changed. There are things which I would now desire to put differently, and I have in fact tried to do so in a later book.[1] Nevertheless, in its main substance what was said here is still what I would want to say. More important are the changes in the ecclesiastical situation. Three may be especially referred to.

Firstly one must put what happened at Amsterdam in 1948.

[1] *The Household of God.* S.C.M. Press 1953.

The existence of the World Council of Churches has become so immensely important for the whole work of the Church in the world, that it is hard to believe that it is only ten years since it was formally constituted.   The existence of the Council, and especially the elucidating of its significance for the life of the Churches in the famous "Toronto Statement" and the subsequent discussion thereof, puts Church relations in a new light for all of us.   The Churches which are members of the Council are now bound to one another in a covenant relation which is something quite new. In the light of this, some of what is said in the last chapter of the book has to be corrected.

Secondly one must refer to the various Anglican actions on the subject of the Church of South India.   The book was written in reply to those who were urging Anglicans to reject completely the South India approach to unity and to sever communion even with Anglicans who had entered the united Church.   Since then not only have several provinces of the Anglican Communion taken official action to recognize the ministries of the C.S.I., but the Lambeth Conference of 1958 has made most generous and unequivocal statements regarding the development of the C.S.I. in the first decade of its life.   Does it not therefore seem ungracious to republish a work directed against counsels which have not prevailed?

Thirdly there is the development of the C.S.I. itself.   In many respects the Church is not to-day precisely what we thought, twelve years ago, that it would be.   It has become more of a unity than we expected.   Many of the passages of the Bases of Union read oddly now.   They are so obviously drafted by people still afraid of one another!   Is it necessary at this stage to republish a defence of them?

These are weighty questions.   And yet, upon reflection, I have decided that there are sufficient grounds to justify republication. Perhaps I can indicate them by taking up again precisely these three points and examining them more closely.

I. *The World Council of Churches and the Shape of the Ecumenical Movement*

The coming into existence of the World Council of Churches constitutes a new fact in the history of Christianity.   It was one

INTRODUCTION

thing for Churches to collaborate for limited periods and for limited purposes—for example, for missionary work, for social witness, and for the exploration of their agreements and differences in faith and order; it was quite another thing to bind themselves together in a solemn covenant, confessing that "Christ has made us one, and He is not divided." The spiritual reality which then came into existence—and here I am thinking not only of the World Council itself, but also of the vast development of national and local councils of Churches—was something new, and we do not yet know completely what it is. The Churches of which it is formed themselves came into existence as separate entities because it was judged that the others were either no true churches, or lacked something essential of churchliness. Apart from that judgment there could be no justification for separation. Nor does the formation of the Council imply a reversal of that judgment. The Council has made it clear in the famous "Toronto Statement" that membership does not imply mutual acceptance of one another as, in the full sense, churches. And yet, in some sense or other, they have accepted one another and are working together more and more effectively, thinking together as Christians with growing mutual confidence, and worshipping and praying together with growing freedom. What, then, is this thing—and again I am thinking both of the World Council and the many national and local councils of Churches? What is this form of being-together in Christ which is not the Church and strenuously denies that it intends to be?

What is the outward form which corresponds to the inward reality of being-together in Christ? Our various Churches are the answers to that question which have been bequeathed to us from the past. But the World Council is also an answer to that question; what is its relation to the older answers? It is not sufficient to say that it is a neutral meeting-ground where rival ecclesiologies can meet and debate; of course it aims to be such a neutral meeting-place, but the idea of permanent neutrality is here (as so often elsewhere) an illusion. The Council is itself a form of being-together in Christ. It is therefore not ecclesiologically neutral. A single conference or a limited group of conferences is in a different category; it can legitimately claim neutrality. But an on-going council, with such an immensely strong corporate spiritual life as the World Council now has, cannot continue to

THE REUNION OF THE CHURCH

pretend that it has no character of its own. It is a form—an immensely effective and impressive form—of visible unity in Christ.

Those who have a strongly articulated Churchmanship will at this point interject: "Yes, but the Council is protected from appearing to claim a churchly character by the fact that it does not itself administer sacraments or authorize any person to do so." That is a solid and impregnable fact; but like other impregnable fortifications which have played a prominent part in history, it is liable to be rendered useless by an enveloping movement before the garrison realizes it. The World Council (and again we are thinking also of smaller councils of Churches) provides a place where Christians can do together most of the things which Churches ought to do, *except* the administration of the sacraments. Worship, prayer, the preaching of the Word, witness, service, prophecy—these all form part of the regular common life which is expressed in ecumenical meetings. It would be no exaggeration to say that the organized ecumenical movement is becoming the focus of much of the most spiritually vigorous Christian thought and life in the modern world—always excepting sacramental fellowship. But what will be the long-term consequences of this situation? From the point of view of any traditional understanding of Christianity, and surely from the point of view of the New Testament, being "in Christ" must mean belonging together to a totally committed fellowship in life, prayer, service, worship, and witness—all finding its centre and focus in common participation in the one loaf and the one cup, therein we are united as branches in the Vine Himself. What will be the long-term effects of a situation in which everything is there except the centre, in which the most significant relationships we have are those with "Christians not in communion with us"? I would not venture to try to answer those questions, but I cannot doubt that there is already discernible a shift of the centre of gravity for many of the most serious Christians, from the total sacramental and congregational life of the Church, to the conference room and the programme, from the priest or pastor to the "secretary," from the sermon to the "agreed statement," from Church to "movement." It is already difficult in many places to secure the services of the ablest young men for the ministry, because it appears that opportunities more spiritually significant (and more

INTRODUCTION

financially rewarding) are open to the secretary of some branch of ecumenical activity than to the pastor of a congregation. Without any attempt to be more precise, it can surely be agreed that there is here a profound change in the traditional understanding of what our being-together in Christ means.

If one draws attention to these dangers, it is certainly not in order to belittle the great achievements of the ecumenical movement, or to join with those who already think that we have gone too far in the direction of co-operation. On the contrary, it is to insist that we must go farther, because the place where we now stand is a stepping-stone which will not permanently bear our weight. There can be no going back. Our traditional forms of denominational life are already being brought under judgment. In some respects they have become irrelevant to the real requirements of faithfulness to Christ in our twentieth-century world. More especially is it important to state that the traditional denominational structures have become almost irrelevant to the real evangelistic issues that face the world mission in Asia and Africa. I am sure that God is pressing upon us in our day the question, What is the proper form of our being-together in Christ and for Christ to-day? The World Council, and its related councils, provide a place where we can together wrestle with this question. But it is an illusion to suppose that, simply because we keep the celebration of the sacraments out of the life of the ecumenical movement, we thereby secure for ourselves a place of permanent ecclesiological neutrality. Whether we acknowledge it or not, the on-going life of the ecumenical movement embodied in such structures as the World Council and national and local councils of Churches, is a form of being-together in Christ, and as such is not ecclesiologically neutral. And faithfulness to the New Testament requires us to state plainly that—except as a transitional stage from disunity to unity—it is the wrong form.

There is no way of escaping the issue of full churchly unity. An attempt to take refuge in permanent neutrality will only mean that we are shut up to the wrong form of unity. There is a tendency even among serious churchmen to speak of this question as though it was one on which there was no real urgency, on which we were free to construct our own timetable of study and to proceed entirely at our own pace. It is, in fact, common to hear churchmen speak as though they did not really regard Christian unity as a serious question this side of the End. This is a disastrous illusion. Christians cannot behave as though time were unreal. God gives us time, but not an infinite amount of time. It is His purpose that the Gospel should be preached to all nations, and that all men should be brought into one family in Jesus Christ. His purpose looks to a real End, and therefore requires of us real decisions. If we misconstrue His patience, and think that there is an infinity of time for debate while we perpetuate before the world the scandal of our dismemberment of the Body of Christ, we deceive ourselves. In an issue concerning the doing of the will of God there is no final neutrality.

I believe, therefore, that the development of the ecumenical movement and its organizational embodiment in growingly effective councils of Churches, makes it not less but more necessary to press the question of churchly unity. The Church of South India is—of course—very far from being the only example of the reunion of churches in our time. There have been many others, and some very significant ones have taken place in the ten years since the C.S.I. was inaugurated. But it is generally conceded that there is as yet no other union of Churches quite comparable with that in South India in respect of the variety of traditions which it incorporates. The theological arguments which have centred round its formation are of great importance for the further progress of reunion. The Churches most concerned have—for the most part—been willing with varying amounts of hesitation to recognize the newly formed Church, but they have made it clear that they have no present intention of following its example. In the minds of the South Indian negotiators it was always hoped that union in one area would lead the way to similar action in others. As the years since 1947 pass by, it becomes more necessary to ask whether this is going to happen, or whether the Church of South India is to be condemned to become just one more oddity among the infinite fissiparations of Christendom.

If this is not to happen there is need to press upon all who are concerned with the ecumenical movement the questions, What form of unity does God will for His people? and What is the method by which we are to move from our present disunity to unity in that divinely willed form? Both questions are urgent for our time; this book deals primarily with the second. The

INTRODUCTION

argument of the book is directed to the defence of the particular method followed in South India, but the theological issues involved are urgent for all who care for the unity of Christendom. The unity of the Church will not be distilled out of a process of pure academic theological study, necessary as this is. It will arise through the bringing to bear of sound theological thinking upon the making of practical decisions in concrete cases. The actual developments in South India provide as good a focus as any available for the theological thinking that is needed.

The question of the method of reunion, that is to say, the question how do we move from our present situation of disunity to the divinely willed form of unity, has to be posed first as a theological problem. Each of our ecclesiastical traditions has articulated a doctrine of the form of the Church which is integral to its whole understanding of the Gospel and cannot be treated as a detachable or replaceable part. These doctrines have been articulated in explicit opposition to those of the other Churches which share in the ecumenical movement. The articulation and defence of them has been understood as an integral part of obedience to the truth of the Gospel. This being so, how can a Church theologically understand the task of redefining them so as to include those whom they were defined precisely to exclude? Is not this asking for an impossibility? There are two ways in which, in fact, this impossibility is side-stepped. On the one hand there are those whose real conviction (however courteously muffled) is that reunion can only come about when the others are brought to the point of repudiating in effect the position of their ecclesiastical forbears and accepting the position from which they formerly dissented. On the other hand there are those who solve the problem by relativizing all ecclesiologies and denying that anything of the absolute claims of the Gospel is involved in the rival claims of different church orders.

It is not necessary to spend time commenting on these two positions. They have only to be clearly stated to be rejected, by those who have any experience of the ecumenical movement. (Those who stand outside it do, of course, generally take the first position.) The ecumenical movement exists because Christians have been obliged to recognize elements of true churchliness in the bodies from which they are separated. They have therefore come to see that it is impossible to ask the members of other

Churches simply to repudiate the very heritage through which they have been made Christians. On the other hand you cannot agree to treat all ecclesiology as merely relative without endangering the absoluteness of the claim of the Gospel itself. The Church faces the unbelieving world with the absolute claim that Christ is the truth, and her whole mission to the world becomes meaningless if it is accepted that her Gospel is merely one of the possible opinions. But the Church's understanding of her own nature is part of her understanding of the Gospel, and while Christians must always be penitently aware of the possibility of their being wrong, they cannot honestly allow that their doctrine of the Church is in principle a mere matter of opinion. That would be to sever Churchmanship from the Gospel, and eventually to sever being from thinking and to leave us with only what van der Post has called "a pale cerebral Christianity."

Is there, then, any other honest way of understanding theologically the issues involved in moving from disunity to unity? It is the main purpose of this book to argue that there is, and that the heart of it is to be found in the Christian doctrine of justification by faith. This doctrine, so central to the teaching of St. Paul, has for a long time and in many contexts been expounded as though it referred primarily to the individual Christian and only derivatively, and at a long remove, to the Church. I do not find any grounds in St. Paul's own writing for this view. If one begins one's thinking about Christianity with the individual, then it is natural that one begins one's reading of St. Paul with the same bias. But if one begins by thinking of the fellowship, the group, the Church, then St. Paul's language is equally relevant. It is the central purpose of this book to argue that the theological clue to the problem of the method of reunion lies in the fact that the Church has its being from the God who justifies the ungodly, raises the dead, and calls the things that are not as though they were.

When the book was first published no reviewer noticed the argument about justification by faith, except one—who complained that it was out of place in a book on the Church. That is surely a measure of my failure to make my purpose clear, but it is—I hope—also a good reason for approving of the reprinting of the book in the hope that the argument, for what it is worth, may be seriously weighed. If the argument is found wanting, I can only hope that someone more competent than I will give his

INTRODUCTION

mind to wrestling with this central question: "What is the theological meaning of the attempt of a Church to move from disunity to unity?" Not in spite of, but because of the vast development of the ecumenical movement in the years since this book was written, this question is urgent to-day.

II. *The Lambeth Conference and the Church of South India*

I have suggested that it may seem ungracious to republish a defence of the South India Scheme against its critics when the Lambeth Conference of 1958 has just placed on record such generous testimony to the spiritual blessings which the C.S.I. has received, and when so many provinces of the Anglican Communion have taken official action to recognize the ministries of the C.S.I. One can only express gratitude for these things, coupled with a penitent recognition of the fact that a critic of C.S.I. can still find plenty of material for a negative judgment. But something much more than the C.S.I. is involved. What is involved is the whole future of the movement for Christian reunion, and it is here that something still needs to be said. The Lambeth Conference has coupled its kind references to C.S.I. with a very firm instruction that others must not follow its example. The Churches in West Africa, which had just made a promising fresh start with union negotiations on the South India model, are "strongly recommended" to look rather to the Ceylon scheme, and similar advice is given to the Churches of the Middle East. The two points of difference upon which this preference is based are the statement of faith and the method of unification of ministries. Both of these matters, but especially the second, involve issues which may be of great importance for the future.

I confess that I embark upon this discussion with hesitation, and even with some distaste. The duty of working and praying together for the unity of the Church is of such supreme importance that one wishes very much to avoid mutual criticism among those working for the same end. I know that it is terribly easy, even when one is engaged on the noblest of tasks, to develop a possessive and selfish spirit in relation to one's own particular methods. I hope to be kept free of such a spirit. But there are issues of truth involved on which it is important that we should be able to speak to one another frankly. I hope and believe that this discussion can be used to forward and not to hinder the cause of Christian unity.

1. *The Statement of Faith*

The two statements are as follows:

Ceylon	South India
The uniting Churches hold the Faith which the Church has ever held in Jesus Christ, the Redeemer of the world, in whom men are saved by grace through faith; and in accordance with the revelation of God which He made, being Himself God incarnate, they worship one God in three Persons, Unity in Trinity and Trinity in Unity. Under the guidance of the Holy Spirit, the Church has handed down the Holy Scriptures of the Old and New Testaments. The uniting Churches receive and accept these Scriptures as containing all things necessary to salvation, and as the standard of Faith. They accept the Creeds commonly called Apostles' and Nicene, as witnessing to and safeguarding that Faith which is continuously confirmed in the spiritual experience of the Church of Christ; and as containing a sufficient statement thereof for a basis of union.	The Church of South India accepts the Holy Scriptures of the Old and New Testaments as containing all things necessary to salvation and as the supreme and decisive standard of faith; and acknowledges that the Church must always be ready to correct and reform itself in accordance with the teaching of those Scriptures as the Holy Spirit shall reveal it. It also accepts the Apostles' Creed and the Creed commonly called the Nicene, as witnessing to and safeguarding that faith; and it thankfully acknowledges that same faith to be continuously confirmed by the Holy Spirit in the experience of the Church of Christ. Thus it believes in God, the Father, the Creator of all things, by whose love we are preserved; It believes in Jesus Christ, the incarnate Son of God and Redeemer of the world, in whom alone we are saved by grace, being justified from our sins by faith in Him; It believes in the Holy Spirit, by whom we are sanctified and built up in Christ and in the fellowship of His Body; And in this faith it worships the Father, Son and Holy Spirit, one God in Trinity and Trinity in Unity.

INTRODUCTION

It will be recalled that in the earlier drafts of the South India Scheme the statement of faith was along lines similar to those of the Ceylon Scheme except that there was no reference to the Church "handing down" the Scriptures. The reasons for which the change was made were clearly explained in the official answer given by the Church of South India to the Archbishop of Canterbury in 1950, with reference to the request of the Lambeth Conference for a re-drafting. (Lambeth 1948 Res. 53; and Committee Report II, p. 44.) They may be summarized as follows:

1. The Ceylon statement defines the "faith which the Church has ever held" as faith in Jesus Christ, the Redeemer of the world. This is not a statement of the orthodox Christian faith, which is faith in God, Father, Son and Holy Spirit.

2. The title "Redeemer of the world" does not safeguard the Christian faith in Christ as God. It could be used by a Hindu for the god of his worship. It is inadequate for the purposes of a credal statement of this kind. South India has corrected this by speaking of Him as "incarnate Son of God and Redeemer of the world," and by adding the important (and in certain contexts essential) word "alone"; so as to read "by whom *alone* we are saved by grace."

3. The statement that the Faith is "continuously confirmed in the spiritual experience of the Church" is open to question. The Faith does not depend upon our experience for its confirmation. It is the work of the Holy Spirit Himself to confirm the faith in our experience, and this should be explicitly stated.

4. The old statement began with a (very inadequate) credal summary and then went on to speak of Scriptures and Creeds. The revised statement begins with Scripture and Creeds, which are the source and standards and then—in subordination to these, and with the explicit statement that the Church holds itself ready to correct itself in the light of Scripture—adds a brief statement of Trinitarian faith. This is more logical.

5. The old statement did not appear to give to Scripture the absolutely decisive place which it must have as the standard of faith. (The Ceylon statement diverges widely from the old South India statement at this point, and has never been officially considered in South India. It seems to make Scripture entirely the creature of the Church, and one wonders if the full implications of this were faced before the Lambeth Conference decided to

press this statement upon other Churches. Is it really possible that a reformed Church can accept this statement as adequate?)

Perhaps the crux of the matter lies in the phrase "the faith which the Church has ever held." If that is so, then I submit that the arguments on that point contained in Chapter VIII of the present book have sufficient importance to justify reprinting. In the context of a Scheme of union for divided Churches "the faith which the Church has ever held" cannot be regarded as a standard unless the word "Church" is first defined. And that means begging the all-important question. There are quite a number of bodies calling themselves "churches" whose faith we do not hold. Of course one can well understand, and share, the anxiety which prompts this insistence; it is the anxiety to ensure that what is intended is not schism. That is indeed a proper concern. But the Church does not remain in the orthodox faith merely by proclaiming that it does not intend to leave it. It remains in that faith only by a continually renewed laying hold upon God's revelation of Himself in Christ, and this means preserving the right relation of the Church to its standards of faith. One may be sure that neither in Ceylon nor in North India is there any intention to depart from the historic faith, and yet question the wisdom of asking Nigeria to return to so defective a statement of it.

2. *The Unification of the Ministry*

The plans for union in North India and Ceylon both contain (with some important differences in detail) provisions by which—at or near the inauguration of the union—all ministers shall receive, with prayer and the laying on of hands, commission for their ministry in the united Church. It is undoubtedly this element in these two schemes which has led the Lambeth Conference to commend them to others as models, rather than the South India scheme which deals with the unification of the ministry upon different principles.

During the period before 1948 proposals of this kind were widely discussed under the title "supplemental ordination." The book which is now republished contained a theological and practical criticism of the whole idea. The Lambeth Conference report of 1948 contained an Appendix entitled "The Theory of 'Supplemental Ordination.'" The first part of this was an exposition and defence of the theory. The second was an attack

INTRODUCTION

upon it which—to one reader at least—seemed unanswerable. The Committee on Unity added a final paragraph: "We, without identifying ourselves with either of the two theological attitudes towards the conception of 'Supplemental Ordination' which have been outlined, have been content to state them both, side by side and unreconciled, in the belief that further consideration and study will need to be given to the subject by theologians before a decision can be reached with regard to the possibility of bringing peace to the Church, by means of a procedure based theologically on the conception of 'Supplemental Ordination' in any of its forms."

Since that date I do not think that anyone has attempted to defend the theory of supplemental ordination *by that name*. Nor do I know of any serious theological study of the subject such as the Lambeth Conference desired. I speak subject to correction. What has happened is that the name has been dropped, but the article (with slight modifications) is now commended for universal use in healing the wounds of Christendom. It is because I think this to be a very serious matter for the future of the movement for Christian reunion that I think the theological argument must be reopened.

The Lambeth Report of 1958 devotes much careful attention to an examination of the plans for the unification of the ministry in North India and Ceylon. It defines the purposes which must be fulfilled by any service for the unification of the ministry as threefold:

"1. Negatively the liturgical form must be such as to raise no question as to the relative sufficiency, reality, or effectiveness of the various ministries which are brought to be unified;

"2. Positively, the liturgical form must be one appropriate to the essential function of seeking from God through prayer and laying on of hands a continuance and increase of spiritual gifts already received and possessed by each Minister for the work of the Office and Order of Ministry in the Church of God to which he is now freshly called in the United Church;

"3. In order that the intention of removing all ground for doubts or scruples may be fulfilled, the liturgical form must also be appropriate for its function of seeking from God that he will 'endue each according to his need' with whatever of grace, gifts, character or authority may in the sight of God be needed for the

Office and Order of Ministry referred to. Thus every Church may be satisfied that all of its inheritance has been faithfully conveyed to and shared by the ministry of the United Church."

One enters upon controversy on this matter with real trepidation. All concerned have been anxious to avoid precise statements as to what is intended to be achieved by these rites, and to insist that the intention is that all should humbly submit themselves to God asking that He will do what is needed. Why not leave the matter there? The answer is that we cannot do so because the Church's prayers are acts which have consequences. If we do not define exactly what we ask for, we do define beforehand what we expect. We expect that "all doubts and scruples will be removed." It is the simple truth that these doubts and scruples exist on the Anglican side, but not on the other. For serious theological reasons the non-episcopal churches concerned accept episcopal ordination as valid, whereas—for equally serious reasons—the reverse is not so. The scruples to be removed are Anglican scruples. The purpose to be achieved is that all ministers of the united Church may be free to minister in all—including Anglican Churches. Lambeth has advised all the Provinces that they should be willing to enter into full communion with a Church whose ministry has been so unified (Resolution 23). "Full communion" has been defined by the Conference itself as complete *communio in sacris* such as exists to-day, for example, between provinces of the Anglican communion.

The declared intention of the Conference therefore is that a presbyter from the Church of Lanka who had been ordained before the union as (for instance) a Methodist, and who has received the commission proposed in the rite for the unification of the ministries, will be free to minister in an English parish church. Now it is laid down both in the Book of Common Prayer and in the Colonial Clergy Act of 1874 that no person shall so minister unless he has been ordained by a Bishop. Two possibilities, therefore, are open if the intention of Lambeth is to be fulfilled: either the Book of Common Prayer and the Colonial Clergy Act will have to be altered so as to permit the relaxing of the rule of episcopal ordination; or the commission received at the unification of the ministries will have to be declared by competent authority to be ordination by a bishop. The first alternative would certainly involve a most radical revision of the traditional

INTRODUCTION

position of Anglicanism. It does not seem likely that such a revision is contemplated. The second alternative involves consequences which must be examined.

Let us consider the case of a priest of the Church of England proceeding to Ceylon as a missionary. At present he would of course be received immediately as a priest in the Church of India, Pakistan, Burma, and Ceylon without any question of his ordination. In the united Church this will not be so. He will have to be received with a service similar to that which is to take place at the inauguration (Const. XV 7 (b)). His own Church will have already officially defined this service as an episcopal ordination. The United Church has itself stated that it is not re-ordination. I do not see how the conclusion can be avoided that, by accepting admission on these terms, he will be concurring in an official denial of the reality of his own ordination in the Church of England, or else condoning a profanity.

The consequences are, however, even more far-reaching than this. It is provided that ministers from other churches are to be received with a like service to that provided for at the inauguration. There is no reason to think that this can be other than a permanent feature of the united Church and of other united Churches formed on the same principles. These are the principles which the Lambeth Conference urges other negotiators to adopt. If they were extensively followed what would be the result? Not a series of regional churches enjoying full communion among themselves. On the contrary, any ministers going from one of these churches to the other would require to be received with a service which Anglicans are bound to define as ordination—even though they were already episcopally ordained. Thus the intention of the Conference that there should be full communion between the Church of Lanka and the Churches of the Anglican Communion appears to be incapable of realization upon the basis of the method of unification which the Conference recommends.

These arguments will provoke an impatient retort. There are many with whom I can only disagree with extreme reluctance, who will say: "Let us not try to define everything! Let us humbly pray God to give us what He sees we need, and then let us go ahead trusting that He will do so." It would be a great sin to put any obstacle in the way of any promising plan of unity among Churches. But even in the most hallowed things we are called upon to think as clearly as we can. Confusion in fundamental matters eventually works itself out in the life of the Church. The kind of mood referred to could well carry one through the inauguration of the union. But is it not inevitable that questions should be raised as the years go on? There will be those who will be bound to make an official declaration that the rite *is* episcopal ordination, since otherwise its purpose will not be achieved. There will inevitably be others who will feel bound in conscience to reply in an equally public manner that it is not. Will it be possible for the Church itself to remain untouched by these pronouncements? And will it not be inevitable that—as I have argued in the body of the book—the whole idea of ordination will be weakened. Each new accession to the united Church will (if we are to be fair and logical) involve the repetition of the rite for the whole ministry. This (if our experience in South India is a guide) might well happen two or three times in a decade. How will it be possible for men to go through a service which is in all essentials an ordination several times in their lives without thereby losing some sense of that which ordination has always been believed to convey? Moreover when the Church gathers to administer the rite of admission to its ministry to a new missionary already ordained (for instance) in the Church of England, are questions not bound to arise as to what it is precisely that is being done? The prayers and formulae proposed for these rites are in all essentials those of an ordination service; can the same words be regularly used by the same church at one time to mean the quite precise act of ordination, and at another with no precise meaning at all?

The Appendix to the Lambeth Report of 1948 has these trenchant sentences: "A man has either received the commission of Christ by ordination, or he has not. The Church can only recognize the fact, not supplement it, since the efficacy of ordination comes from Him, and not merely from the Church's administration." I submit that those words need to be seriously considered. Proposals for supplemental ordination tend to involve a way of thinking and talking about ordination as though it were purely a matter of transmitting the Church's authority. Of course this is one aspect of ordination, but it is not the whole. The central act of ordination is a prayer that God may endue the ordinand with that which he requires for the form of ministry in

INTRODUCTION

question. The faith of the Church is that God hears this prayer and bestows these gifts, and thereafter the Church acts in the faith that He has done so. I have attempted in the body of the book to discuss the relation of this faith that God is Himself the true ordainer to the undoubted fact that the divisions of the Church limit both the unanimity of the prayer which is offered, and the recognition of the authority of the orders conferred. Here I would only raise the following question: has not much thinking on this subject been led astray by the late mediæval distortion of the western ordination rites, which removed the prayer from the centre of the action and substituted the words addressed by the Bishop to the ordinand: "Receive the Holy Ghost"? If ordination is understood primarily as an act in which something is conferred by a Bishop or Presbytery upon the ordinand, then the idea of supplemental ordination is intelligible. But if—as the ordinals of the undivided Church plainly imply—ordination is an act of God in response to the prayers of the Church, then the idea of supplemental ordination becomes impossible. There may be need to enlarge the sphere of a minister's jurisdiction: there can be no question of adding to the reality of his ordination.

It is true that the phrase "supplemental ordination" has been abandoned in the proposals now before us. But the substance of them is the same—the attempt to combine a recognition of an existing ordination with the addition to it of something which also has the character of ordination. The Lambeth Conference of 1948 was surely wise in saying that this proposal requires much more thorough theological scrutiny before it can be recommended as the medicine for the healing of the Church. I feel bound to submit that the Conference of 1958 was not wise in deciding, without that scrutiny, to advise all concerned to take only that medicine.

If the matter at issue were simply the proposals for union in North India and Ceylon, one would wish to remain silent. The Churches there have wrestled together with these problems for many years; they have had to face situations different in some respects from that in South India; they have been led into a remarkable measure of agreement and there is a fair prospect of unity being achieved. All who care for the healing of the Church's divisions will surely pray that union may be achieved, and that if there be any defect in the basis of union, God Himself may in due course set it right. It would be very much better that union should go forward even on a defective basis than that there should be no union at all. God will not abandon those who are honestly trying to do His will. If Lambeth had simply given the blessing that it has given to these schemes, surely no one—certainly no one from the Church of South India—ought to cavil. What does, however, call for comment is the action of the Conference in advising negotiators in West Africa to abandon the South Indian pattern and follow that of Ceylon. The former has in fact been found to provide a workable basis for union; the latter has yet to be tried in practice, and is based upon principles which the previous Lambeth Conference judged to require further study before they could be generally recommended. It is this action which justifies a reopening of the study which Lambeth 1948 desired. It will surely be wise to consider the question again before concluding that the method of supplemental ordination is to be the basis for all future unions in which Anglicans are involved.

If the plan of union as proposed in North India is to go through, I hope the phrase "It is not re-ordination" will be removed. There is no such thing as re-ordination, as there is no such thing as re-baptism. One has the unhappy suspicion that it has found a place in the Plan because some people are simple-minded enough to believe that it safeguards the reality of the ordination previously received. It does nothing of the kind and it would be the honest course to delete it.

The sentences I have quoted from the Lambeth Appendix on Supplemental Ordination really raise the ultimate question "What are we doing when we set about the reunion of the Church?" Probably the authors of those sentences, and of that section of the Appendix, would be among those who would settle the whole question simply along the following lines: Episcopal ordination is necessary for a valid ministry; persons who have received "ordination" otherwise are not ordained and therefore require not "supplemental ordination" but ordination *simpliciter*. Proposals for supplemental ordination have arisen because Anglicans engaged in unity negotiations have found themselves unable to accept that position, unable to deny reality to the ministries of non-episcopal Churches. How can one combine a belief that episcopacy is God's will for the Church with a belief that non-episcopal Churches are fully and really Churches? The proposal

INTRODUCTION

for supplemental ordination has emerged out of that dilemma; but it does not resolve it; it only confuses vital issues, concerning the Church and the ministry. The dilemma is insoluble if one's thinking is on the two-dimensional surface of a legalistic doctrine of the Church. Only in terms of the mystery of justification by faith, of the God who calleth things that are not as though they were, is the dilemma to be resolved. The central purpose of this book was to place the discussion of the question of Church union in that perspective. My hope in issuing a reprint is that this purpose may be served.

III. *Developments in the Life of the Church of South India*

Perhaps the most serious difficulty about republishing this defence of the South India Scheme after an interval of more than a decade arises from the development of the Church of South India itself. When the book was written there was no Church of South India. There was a scheme, prepared in all essentials during the 1920's, by representatives of three Churches divided from one another by deep and ancient differences of faith and practice. There are things in it which—as I have said—read rather oddly now. They were written by those who still faced each other as negotiators across the conference table. Now we look at one another as fellow-members in one Church, and we have learned to trust each other in a way that is scarcely possible in any relationship short of full organic unity. And yet, as one reads the Basis of Union now, the thing that strikes one most forcibly is the fact that it was proved to be such a sound and workmanlike basis. The authors of it were writing in the midst of a climate of theological opinion vastly different from that in which the inauguration actually took place. They were trying to envisage something which had never yet existed and for which there were no models or pilot projects. And yet they were able to put down on paper something which has stood the test of actual use, and has provided at every essential point a thoroughly sound basis of union. There are a few matters on which amendment has been found necessary, but none of them touches any of the fundamental features of the Scheme. Perhaps the one point at which the Constitution as it stands seems to be rather remote from what has actually happened is in the sections dealing with the relation of the Bishops to the Synod. That provides for an elaborate procedure to safeguard the special duties of the Bishops in regard to faith and worship, and to safeguard also the final responsibility of the Synod as a whole. But in fact, partly because the Synod has never proceeded by the method of majority voting on any vital matter, and partly because there has been from the beginning a relation of mutual trust and affection between the Bishops and the rest of the Church, there has never been any occasion when it was felt necessary for the Bishops to act separately over against the Synod. In fact I find it almost impossible to imagine now a situation in which the elaborate procedure of the Constitution would be used. The Bishops sit and speak as part of the Synod. They do not always take the same side in a debate! But they are always listened to with the respect due to their office. And they, with the other members of the Synod, have always been able to come away from the meetings with a real conviction that they could say together: "It seemed good to the Holy Spirit and to us . . ."

If, therefore, I were re-writing this book to-day, I should be less inclined to apologize for the Scheme than I was twelve years ago. Of course it is not perfect, but if I were sitting down to-day to write a defence of it, I would defend it more unreservedly than I did then. And yet, since the book is re-issued after these years of actual experience, it is right to say something about what we have learned in these years together, for this has a bearing on the argument of the book.

In the first place, there has been a quite vigorous development of theological reflection in the Church itself. For this we have in large measure to thank our brethren of the Lutheran Churches in South India. At the first Synod an invitation was extended to other Christians in South India to engage in conference with a view to the possibility of wider union. This resulted in the starting of conversations with representatives of the Lutheran and Baptist Churches. After a short time the Baptist participation ceased and we settled down to a rather thorough and extended process of discussion with the Federation of Evangelical Lutheran Churches in India. These involved questions completely different from those which had engaged the attention of the Joint Committee prior to 1947. The theologians of the C.S.I. had been accustomed for two decades to discussion which centred almost entirely in the matters which divide Anglicans from "free churchmen."

INTRODUCTION

Now they were called upon to discuss a quite different set of questions—the Law and the Gospel, Election, the Holy Spirit, the Lutheran doctrine of the Lord's Supper, and others. This was wholly to the good for the C.S.I. It revealed a much greater measure of theological unity amongst us than we had expected; it compelled us to do some vigorous thinking; and it cemented our unity in doctrine. It was often remarked by visitors to the discussions that there was a greater theological unity in the C.S.I. delegations than there was among the Lutherans. But this was a unity which arose out of quite vigorous discussion and not from mere passivity.

In the second place, we have found that our coming together in one Church, faced with the practical tasks of evangelism and pastoral care in the conditions of India to-day, has precipitated a vigorous process of self-criticism in regard to the methods of life and work which we have inherited. The union necessarily began with an act of comprehension. It was agreed that, as far as possible, all the existing patterns of work should be continued until the united Church took order otherwise. But this comprehension was only a starting point. When we began to sit down together in councils and synods to think about our tasks, we found ourselves compelled to examine critically the various patterns that we had inherited. As long as each of us was continuing to run in the grooves that had been provided for us, we were not forced to ask these questions. Precedent settled most matters. But when there were three or four different kinds of precedent to be considered, then deeper questioning became inevitable. We found ourselves looking afresh at the forms of congregational life, of ministry, of lay service which we had inherited; and asking of them "Is this what God wants us to do in South India to-day? It may have been right in Europe or America in the eighteenth or nineteenth centuries; is it right for India in the twentieth?" The asking of such questions took us back to the New Testament, and compelled us to begin changing many things that we had taken for granted. We have been forced to think more seriously than we had done before about the congregation as the fundamental unit of Church life, about the diaconate, about the ministry of the laity and especially of women, and about the need for an ordained non-professional ministry of the kind that seems to have been common in the early Church and is still common in some parts of Christendom to-day. If one were re-writing this book to-day, much of this thinking about the pattern of the Church's life would find a place.

In the third place, and perhaps more difficult to explain briefly, there has been the development in the C.S.I. of what one might call a theology of the Church-in-motion. There are several places in the Constitution at which the idea of development is expressed. The section on the faith of the Church speaks of the Church being ready to correct and reform itself in accordance with the teaching of Scripture as the Holy Spirit shall reveal it. The section of the Governing Principles which deals with "The Purpose and Nature of the Union" says that the final aim in any such plan of union must be "the union in the Universal Church of all who acknowledge the name of Christ." The Church thus confesses an aim which has not been reached. And in the very important (and much misunderstood) section dealing with the famous "Thirty Year Period," the idea of development is quite explicit and determinative. As the united Church has begun to reflect upon its own nature and calling, these passages have assumed a larger significance. It has become more and more obvious that the process of reunion cannot stop at the point reached in 1947. One cannot therefore imagine that development will be something which takes place for thirty years and then stops. There have been those who found it hard to accept the anomalies of the thirty-year period, but comforted themselves with the thought that after thirty years all would be trim and tidy again. But if union goes on, if—for instance—during the next twenty years there are unions with Lutheran and Baptist Churches, and if they proceed on the same principles as have been accepted in the present union, it is obvious that the "period of growing together" will be extended. Is this, we have been compelled to ask ourselves, something to be deplored or something to be welcomed? The answer has been given with growing assurance that it is something to be welcomed. If the Church is the sign and fruit and instrument of Christ's purpose to draw all men to Himself; if it is the embassage sent into all the world to beseech men "Be ye reconciled to God"; and if the ultimate purpose is the union in one fellowship of all who accept Christ as Lord; then movement belongs to the very nature of the Church. It is, in its very nature, a pilgrim people. Therefore we must not imagine that the Church can

INTRODUCTION

here settle down to a static existence. Of course this has always been recognized where the missionary obligation has been accepted. It has been understood that the Church is—in this sense—*in via*, in that she must be always pushing out beyond her frontiers to draw in new members into fellowship with Christ. But what is now becoming plainer is that mission and unity cannot rightly be separated from each other, and that the task of drawing all God's people into one fellowship, so that there may be one flock as there is one Shepherd, is something that belongs to the intrinsic nature of the Church until the End.

I do not pretend that this is explicitly understood and accepted throughout the Church, though in one form or another it finds increasingly frequent expression. But what is certain is that the Church has in fact become much more "open" to other Churches than the Basis of Union might have led us to expect. One could summarise a good deal of evidence about the development of the C.S.I. during its first decade by saying two things: on the one hand the Church is far more unified round the bishops than many of us expected. Undoubtedly many in the non-episcopal churches accepted episcopacy simply because it was one of the things without which union could not be had. To-day I think it would hardly be possible to get a vote anywhere for a proposal to drop episcopacy, even as the price of a wider union. The position of the Bishop as the Chief pastor of the flock in each area has become something that hardly anyone would wish even to think of abandoning. But, on the other hand, the Church has a far more open door to the non-episcopal communions than the written text of the Basis of Union suggests. Not only have ministers of the parent Churches been received freely and without question to minister in the C.S.I., whether episcopally ordained or not; ministers of other non-episcopal communions have also been received, and there has been no desire even to consider the question of ordaining them. This goes beyond the provisions of the Basis of Union. I can only interpret these two facts to mean that episcopacy is seen and valued as the visible centre of the process by which the Good Shepherd gathers together His own; and that the desire to see this unifying and reconciling work extended and strengthened overmasters any desire to make claims for episcopacy which would exclude those who are willing to come into the one fellowship.

THE REUNION OF THE CHURCH

The picture which these years of living together in the united Church have begun to open out for us is thus of a continuing process of reunion among Churches, with the historic episcopate as the visible centre round which the fellowship of the Church is gathered. This is a process to which we cannot put a term short of "the union in the Universal Church of all who acknowledge the name of Christ." The end of the thirty-year period will mark an important moment in the life of the C.S.I., for it will be the point at which we are required by our constitution to determine the rules which are to govern admission of ministers from other Churches. But it can hardly be believed that at that date the C.S.I. would wish to take an action which arrested the further development of union, if that development had not already been arrested by other factors. If the prayers and labours which are at present devoted to the effort to find a way of reconciliation with Lutherans and others in South India are not to go without fruit, then it is hard to believe that in 1977 the C.S.I. will be willing to have the same kind of rules about admission of ministers from other Churches that Anglican Churches have to-day.

I know that the objection will at once be raised: this means that the anomalies of the thirty-year period, instead of being temporary, will be—to all intents and purposes—permanent. Is that not an intolerable conclusion? I do not think so. The word "anomaly" is used by our friends outside the C.S.I., but it does not occur to us to use it ourselves. We have lived very happily with these anomalies for over a decade! In what do they consist? Ministers not episcopally ordained work with ministers episcopally ordained in one diocese. They are all under the jurisdiction and pastoral care of one bishop. So far as concerns their relation to him, to one another, and to the Church, they are one brotherhood. It is true that there are those (many in some places, few in others) who are unable on ground of conviction to receive sacramental ministrations from those not episcopally ordained. This is accepted and respected; so far as my own experience is concerned it does not destroy the real spiritual unity of the ministry. And all the time they are living together in one episcopally ordered church wherein the bishop is accepted by all without question as father in God, and as the minister who properly presides at an ordination.

But does not this mean that in fact episcopal ordination is made a matter of merely relative importance? Does it not create

INTRODUCTION

a position intolerable for those who believe that episcopacy is God's will for the ordering of the Church? I answer No; it is precisely the implementation in practice of the belief that episcopacy is God's will for the Church. It is a method—so far as the evidence so far available goes, the only method—by which Christians of the non-episcopal communions may be brought together in one communion and fellowship with their episcopal brethren in an episcopally ordered Church. Which is the more faithful expression of the doctrine that episcopacy is God's will for the Church, a policy which actually draws Christians together in an episcopally ordered fellowship, or one which hardens the divisions between episcopal and non-episcopal communions to the point where there is no reasonable hope of their reconciliation?

But, it will be replied, these merely pragmatic considerations cannot outweigh the fundamental theological argument: if one believes that episcopal ordination is essential for a true ministry, then one cannot—even for the highest reasons—accept as ministers those who are not so ordained. I leave aside the question whether pragmatic arguments are to be wholly ignored, without, however, admitting that a Christian can be indifferent to the question whether or not God's will is actually done in the world. I will come to the central point, and I will state it as plainly as possible. It is possible to believe (as I do) that it is God's will that the Church should be episcopally ordered, and yet deny absolutely that episcopal ordination is essential for a valid ministry. For the being of the Church, and therefore the validity of its ministry, rest not upon the conformity of the Church to God's will, but upon the grace of God who justifies the ungodly. Once again we come to the doctrine of justification by faith. If episcopal ordination is essential to a valid ministry, then that ministry which is not episcopally ordained is not a valid ministry and has no way of becoming such except by receiving the ordination which it lacks. But if the true secret of the Church's being is that it is the place where God's supernatural grace takes hold of those who were no people and makes them His people, takes the prodigal and makes him a beloved son, takes the sinful man and the sinful body of men and makes them verily members incorporate in the Body of Christ for no worthiness of theirs but for His own infinite mercy; then one can *both* insist that episcopacy is God's will for the Church *and* at the same time acknowledge without any hedging

THE REUNION OF THE CHURCH

or double-talk that non-episcopal bodies are truly churches. That is the root of the matter. Conformity to God's will is not the pre-condition of fellowship with Him, but the fruit of it. God justifies the ungodly through Jesus Christ. That is the secret of the being of the Church as it is of the Christian man. Those who know that will rightly resist any plans for reunion which appear to found the being of the Church upon any other foundation. Those who believe, as I do, that God wills His Church to be one body, united not only in word and sacrament but also in visible fellowship with a universal ministry credibly representative of that apostolic ministry which was its first foundation, must also listen to the apostolic teaching about justification by faith as our only standing ground in the presence of God. If they will do so, then we can look forward to a growing visible re-integration of Christendom, a re-integration having the historic episcopate as its visible ministerial focus, a re-integration not in some distant hypothetical future but now in the decades immediately before us. This concern that the bearing of the doctrine of justification by faith upon the practical tasks of Christian reunion should be more seriously considered is the main reason for agreeing to the re-issue of this book.[1]

Those who are rightly concerned about anomalies and irregularities in the life of the Church should reflect that, in regard to any anomaly, one must always ask: Does it arise from the neglect of the law, or from the fact that the law is being applied with discretion in order to fulfil its purpose? The main thing is that the purpose of the law should be fulfilled. In this case, the purpose is that all Christ's people should be kept in a recognizable unity with one another and with the undivided Church. The fact of division is itself the great anomaly. The process of reunion must involve adjustments which, from the point of view of the divided Churches, are anomalous. The question is: Are they anomalies which necessarily arise in the process of restoring the broken unity? If they are, they must be gladly accepted. There

---

[1] It is noteworthy that it is a Roman Catholic writer who has noticed the significance of the development which I have tried to indicate in this section. "The C.S.I. cannot be appraised only from the peculiarities of its organization; the implications of its theology must also be considered. For it is giving rise to a relatively new conception of the Church. According to this view the Church should be defined in terms of what it is becoming rather than in terms of what it is. This dynamic approach may eventually open a way of escape from the difficulties that beset the World Council itself." George H. Tavard: *The Catholic Approach to Protestantism*, Harper, 1955, pp. 81–82.

is a vast difference between the untidiness which arises from neglect and erosion and the untidiness which arises at the point of new growth. The "anomalies" in South India are part of the untidiness that we must expect to appear at a fresh growing edge. The main point is that it is growing, that the area of visible unity centred in the historic episcopate is being extended.

IV

I venture to quote in closing a paragraph from the official reply of the Church of South India to the question formulated by the Derby Committee and put by the Lambeth Conference of 1948 on the subject of the future relations of the C.S.I. with other Churches:

"We are united in one Church; our parent Churches are divided. If it is now insisted that we state what our permanent relation with them is to be, we can only say that we can be content with nothing except that they should be united as we are. So long as they remain divided our position must remain anomalous from the point of view of any one of the divided Churches. But from the point of view of the historic faith of the Church we must surely judge that the real anomaly, the real scandal, is that the Church should be divided. We have promised at the end of thirty years to give equal weight to two principles; that our own ministry shall be one and that we shall maintain and extend full communion with our parent Churches. As things stand, these two principles are irreconcilable. They can only be reconciled when the parent Churches now divided are united. Our act of union is an act of faith in the Holy Spirit that He will bring this about. We cannot therefore say more than the Constitution has said about what our successors will do in circumstances which we pray may be profoundly different from those in which we now are."

For the Church of South India, the progress of reunion among the Churches is a matter almost of life and death. If at the end of thirty years the lead which was given in Madras in 1947 has not been followed up, if the relations between the Churches remain substantially as they are now, the union in South India will have failed in one of its great purposes, even though so much will have been gained in South India itself. The C.S.I. will be just one more denomination. Surely if that happened one would have to say that a great and God-given opportunity had been wasted. For us, therefore, the question of the reunion of Christendom cannot be a merely academic one; it is one in the solution of which our whole being is bound up. If, in what I have written, there is detected a note of stridency or impatience, I ask that the charitable reader may remember the background from which it is written.

But there are grounds for urgency more important than these. The more one studies the situation of the Christian mission in the great nations of Africa, Asia and Latin America, the more urgent does it appear that its fragmentation should be ended. What is said in the first chapter of the present book is relevant to the situation of the world mission everywhere. Here again one must protest against the idea that there is an infinity of time. Failure to deal with our denominational differences at this stage in the development of the missionary enterprise may well preclude altogether a transition from the colonial pattern of last century to a genuinely ecumenical pattern relevant to the realities of this. There is not space here to justify that statement in detail. But surely it is clear that no pattern of missionary strategy can meet the needs of the world in which we live save one in which men everywhere can recognize the lineaments of one universal fellowship, transcending the divisions that scar our world, and holding out to all men the secret of reconciliation with God. And men will not see that except in a Church which has dealt far more seriously than it yet shows signs of doing with its denominational divisions. It is my prayer that the argument of this book, even though it was formulated at an earlier stage in the ecumenical discussion, may yet help towards the healing of these divisions by which we so grievously contradict our Gospel, and hide from men the all-sufficiency of Christ's redemption.

PART

I

CHAPTER ONE

THE BASIS OF UNION IN THE LIFE
OF THE CHURCH

IT is a matter of common remark that the movement towards Christian reunion has received its chief impulse from the Churches of what used to be called the " mission field." Everyone sees it to be natural that when Christians find themselves in a small minority facing an ancient and powerful religious system they should feel themselves instinctively drawn together and should emphasize what they hold in common rather than what divides them. From this point of view the greater enthusiasm of the younger Churches for reunion might be dismissed as merely a matter of perspective. It might be argued that since the Christians of the younger Churches certainly do not fully understand the importance of the principles for which Christendom has split into so many fragments, their impatience with these divisions can in reality teach us nothing about how we are to heal them.

It is easy for a churchman of the older Churches thus to dismiss the attitude of the younger Churches as simply the natural result of a different point of view, but it would be unfortunate if the matter were left there. What is much more difficult is for the younger Churches to understand the astounding complacency of the Churches of the West regarding a situation which so plainly and ostentatiously flouts the declared will of the Church's Lord. That Christians should desire to be united ought not to cause surprise. What requires explanation is that they should be content to be divided. There is certainly a difference of viewpoint. What has to be challenged is the tacit assumption that the viewpoint of " the older Churches " is the true one.

To probe the difference would take one back to those decades which saw the birth of the modern missionary movement of the non-Roman Churches. The partial failure of the Reformation shattered the conception of the ecumenical Church, and left Europe with the stalemate represented by regional and national Churches. The Protestant Churches of the eighteenth century had almost totally lost the conception of the mission of the Church to the whole world. A study of the arguments which were used against the early pioneers of the missionary movement shows that the idea that the Gospel was for all men, while doubtless not theoretically denied, was in influential quarters regarded as having no bearing on the Church's actual duty. The project of world evangelization was opposed with contempt and ridicule. The missionary movement—itself the result of fresh re-discovery of the Bible and a consequent new movement of the Spirit in the Church—expressed itself mainly in extra-ecclesiastical channels. As so often happens, the correction of a deformity in the Church was itself deformed by its opposition to that which it sought to correct. The New Testament knows of only one missionary society—the Church. The eighteenth century knew Churches which had totally ceased to be missionary societies and saw the birth of missionary societies which made no claim to be Churches.

The missionary societies set the patterns upon which the great missionary expansion of the following decades proceeded. They carried the Gospel to every part of the globe, and thereby put back again into the consciousness of Christendom some sense of the ecumenical character of the Church. Their character as missionary societies governed the character of the native Christian communities which their preaching called into being. Their life was dominated by the idea of mission. They were but the first fruits, the advance guard. They existed to bring the rest of their peoples to the Redeemer's feet. Evangelism was their life-blood. As was to be expected, the missionary societies often brought with them an inadequate doctrine of the Church. The main emphasis in all the thinking of the younger Churches to-day is towards the remedying of that defect. The words " devolution," " integration " and the like remind us of the struggles which the younger Churches are having to reassert the truth that it is the Church which is the mission because it has the commission to represent Christ to men. From the opposite side, the Churches of the old Christendom, conscious of the paganism of their lands, are painfully struggling back to the truth that mission is the task of the Church, and that

THE BASIS OF UNION IN THE LIFE OF THE CHURCH

a Church which is not a mission is not a Church. There are many signs in the Churches of the West of a striving towards a truly missionary relation between the Church and its environment. Nevertheless, these are only signs. An ordinary congregation in a Western city or village does not regard itself as a mission. It would, in fact, repudiate the appellation as an insult. The Church carries on missions at home and abroad. But its ordinary congregational life is not oriented towards its pagan environment or dominated by the missionary aim. The life of the younger Churches is, on the other hand, much more influenced by the missionary impulse which produced them and by the enormous evangelistic task which confronts them. It is true, of course, that there are many exceptions. There are congregations which have practically lost all sense of responsibility for the evangelization of their neighbourhoods and have become introverted religious clubs interested only in their own survival. But there is, nevertheless, a real contrast at this point between the older and younger Churches. The main life of the latter still remains under the domination of that missionary impulse which produced them. They face outwards to the world.

I believe that it is this difference in character which accounts for the difference in attitude to the question of reunion. It is not possible to account for the contentment with the divisions of the Church except upon the basis of a loss of the conviction that the Church exists to bring all men to Christ. There is the closest possible connection between the acceptance of the missionary obligation and the acceptance of the obligation of unity. That which makes the Church one is what makes it a mission to the world. The study of the connection between these two things can be introduced in a concrete way by indicating one very important feature of the development of church life in many parts of the mission field, a feature which has profoundly affected the movement towards unity in South India and elsewhere. I refer to what is known as the principle of mission comity. When the modern missionary movement began among the non-Roman Churches of Europe and America there was a general desire to avoid overlapping and competition among the different Churches. The fields to be occupied were so vast, and the forces available so infinitesimally small, that it seemed natural that each Church or Society should choose a distinct area in which to begin its missionary work, and that competition which would be wasteful of effort and harmful to the work should be avoided. This principle was not always followed and there were and are examples of overlapping and competition, but over very wide areas this principle of " comity " was accepted, and when in due course the machinery of consultation and common action was developed, one of the first subjects dealt with by the National Christian Councils was the regularizing of this practice and the laying down of definite rules about comity.

It will be easily understood that the acceptance of this principle had a profound effect upon the churchmanship of those who were begotten and nurtured as Christians under it. It means that in any one place—town or village—there is *normally* but one Christian congregation, and upon this congregation rests the responsibility for the evangelization of the area allotted to it under the principle of comity. Several important consequences result from this. The outsider is presented with a clear and simple choice between Christ and no-Christ, unconfused by conflicting interpretations of what to be " in Christ " means. The proper connection between the Gospel and the Church is visibly preserved, for the Church stands in the pagan community as a clearly marked society founded upon the Gospel in such a way that faith in the Gospel and membership in the Church obviously and naturally belong together. The Church stands as a visible and distinct community possessing the secret of reconciliation and offering this secret to men in its evangelism. As Christians move about from place to place in the course of their employment they are commended to the congregation in the place to which they go and are invited to identify themselves with it. This means that in a large town congregation there will be Christians coming from every sort of background of caste, class and denomination. There may be in one such congregation in South India men and women whose original affiliation has been Syrian, Lutheran, Anglican, Methodist, Presbyterian, Congregational, Baptist. There may be representatives of the highest and the lowest castes of Hinduism. There will be an immense range of wealth and education. In a typical Western city with its multitude of different denominational Churches each of these groups would find its own group of like-minded people with whom to associate. In a South Indian country town they have all to face the choice between accepting member-

THE BASIS OF UNION IN THE LIFE OF THE CHURCH

ship of the one congregation which is there and being outside the visible membership of the Church in the place altogether. In other words, the question is raised with absolute simplicity and in a way which requires an answer one way or the other: "Is it sufficient for men divided on every other ground to have in common their redemption in Christ?" It would have been easy—it would still be easy—for the Church in South India to answer "no," and to consent to the establishing in each major centre of a number of different congregations, each reflecting one particular type of piety, of economic background or—most powerful of all divisive forces—of caste. It would be easy, and it would save the Church many of those painful strains and stresses, those party disputes and struggles for power which now often disfigure its congregational life. It would perhaps make possible at once a more dignified and orderly congregational life. But all this would be easy because the Church would have accepted defeat on the main issue. It might develop into an admirable series of religious clubs, each designed to satisfy to the full the particular religious interests of its members. It might be able to show to the world a splendid variety of activities and services. But one thing it would not be able to do. It would not—in common honesty—be able to stand before those outside and offer to them the secret of reconciliation with God through Christ. Having confessed to itself that common membership in Christ is not *by itself* enough to hold men together in one fellowship, how could it confess to the world that Christ is its only redeemer?

But the Church in South India has clung stubbornly to the conviction that to have Christ in common is enough. It has refused to accept the necessity to cater for varieties of tradition, caste and class by setting up a variety of congregations in each place. The principle of comity has meant this, that the typical congregation in a South Indian country town consists of men and women who have nothing in common save their redemption in Christ. That means, as has been said, strain and stress within the congregation. It means that quarrels are frequent and often bitter. It means that party spirit often disfigures the conduct of church business. But it does also mean that men are driven back to Christ and compelled to ask themselves again and again how much it matters to them that Christ died for them. If congregational life is not to dissolve altogether, men have to allow themselves to be driven back to this fundamental fact, that Christ died for them and for their friends and for their enemies—for on no other fact can the common life of the congregation hold together. The divisions between Christians are seen vividly for the sinful things they are, for a quarrel in a Christian congregation is such a plain and open contradiction of the Gospel by which it lives that so long as it lasts the members can only hang their heads in shame before the outsider. It is sometimes asked whether the average church member in South India really understands the issues involved in the Scheme of Union. If it be asked whether the typical member could take part in a disputation between Episcopalian and Presbyterian theologians of the West, the answer is No; in that sense he does not adequately understand the points at issue. But in another sense I suspect that he understands the point at issue extremely well. He is familiar with the spectacle of a quarrel in the Church, of real or imagined issues being made the occasion for party spirit, of the slow and difficult process of repentance and reconciliation as the village elders or the pastor plead again to both warring parties the sacrifice of Christ. He regards the issue of union as the problem of bringing to an end a particularly long and stubborn quarrel in the Church, and in that light he prays for reconciliation. Is he wrong?

This point requires to be pressed a little further. It is a frequent charge against the South India scheme that it seeks unity on merely pragmatic grounds and that it attempts to find the basis of unity in what the Churches hold in common without seriously facing the issues on which they differ. The result, it is held, will be an unstable union incapable of bearing any real stress, and it will have been achieved by treating as optional matters which are in fact vital to the faith and life of the Church. It is impossible, of course, either to prove or disprove this charge except by detailed examination of the Scheme, but in this preliminary chapter something must be said about it in general. With regard to the first part of the charge, it is true that the desire of the South Indian Churches for union cannot be understood except on the basis of their concern for the task of evangelism. I have already suggested that it was the acceptance of the principle of comity which laid the foundation for the movement towards unity, because it produced a situation in which the normal form of the Christian Church in any locality was not a series of rival congregations, but one congregation facing one area. But this principle of comity was itself dictated by an over-mastering concern for the evangelization of the world, a concern which drove those who were possessed by it to accept an arrangement which was not warranted by the theological principles to which they had grown accustomed within the frontiers of the old Christendom. And the effect of the principle of comity was to keep the Church constantly aware of its evangelistic task. Where there is only one Christian congregation in a town or village or district, its members can never forget the fact that the responsibility for making known the Gospel in that area rests upon them alone. If they do not do it, no one else will. If they behave unworthily, their neighbours will have no other epistle in which they may read the truth of Christ. Where, on the other hand, there is a multitude of competing congregations it is wellnigh impossible for their members to feel resting upon themselves the full responsibility for their neighbours. Inevitably each congregation becomes more concerned with the maintenance of its own distinctive life. But where there is only one congregation it is impossible for its members to escape from the solemn recollection that on the day of judgment it is they and they alone who can be questioned about their neighbours who had never heard the good news. And where that sense of obligation has become determinative of the character of churchmanship, when men's minds both inside and outside the Church are being constantly directed to the central message of the Gospel, the message of redemption through Christ, when men are constantly going out to tell others the news of what God has done for men in Christ, and constantly reminding themselves of the unpayable debt which their redemption lays upon them, it is inevitable that the things which divide Christians from one another, however real and important, should drop into a secondary place. It is not possible to continue steadily testifying to men that the one thing that matters to them is their relation to Christ and at the same time steadily to maintain that many of the things on which Christians differ matter so much that even the common bond of redemption in Christ is not big enough to transcend them.

But what is involved in the answer to this criticism is not merely the proper sense of proportion which can distinguish between primary and secondary matters—important as this is. It is a question of the nature of the Church's unity itself. This has to be discussed more fully in what follows, but here it is necessary to say a word about it in dealing with the background of the Scheme of Union in the life of the Church. I have already suggested that the position of the Church under the arrangement known as "mission comity" has tended both to force the Church to face the question whether the common fact of redemption in Christ is by itself a sufficient basis of outward unity, and also to lay upon the Church a vivid sense of its evangelistic responsibility. All of this can be put in another way by saying that the Church has been forced to consider what is the real basis of its unity, and what it is that marks it off from the pagan world. In this situation it has been easy to remember the truth, which is often disastrously obscured in a situation where a number of small congregations exist together in one locality, that the Church is not primarily an association constituted by the agreement of its members on a number of points of belief and practice, but simply humanity reconstituted by its redemption and regeneration in Christ. That which is constitutive of the Church is this fact of redemption and regeneration, this new relationship with God effected by the atonement wrought by Christ on the Cross. Credal and dogmatic statements are for the purpose of protecting the statement of this fact from distortion by various tendencies of human thought. The fact itself is something of the utmost simplicity which an illiterate villager can make his own. The danger inherent in all the (necessary) work of theological statement is that it may go beyond the task of protecting the gospel and become a series of additions to the gospel. This danger is accentuated when there is a number of rival denominations, for in this situation each group tends to accentuate the matters on which it is divided from the others and which justify its continued existence as a separate group. The force of its group egotism is thrown behind the particular emphasis of doctrine or practice which has led to its separate existence, and while all the members of all the groups will doubtless agree that the faith they hold in common is more fundamental than the points of disagreement, yet the fact remains that what constitutes each group as a separate group is not what it holds in common with the others, but what it holds alone. The situation then created is that there is a whole variety of groups each having more and more the character of a particular association based on a particular type of belief and practice, and it is more and more

THE BASIS OF UNION IN THE LIFE OF THE CHURCH

difficult to see either in any one of the groups, or in all of them collectively, the lineaments of the Church in the New Testament sense, the reconstituted human race, the new man in Christ. The separate groups are marked off from one another and from the world outside not simply by the fact of redemption and reconciliation in Christ, but by a whole variety of different shades of belief and piety. Looking at them the outsider sees, not simply humanity true to the purpose of its creation, not simply man remade in Christ, but a series of particular associations based on a series of beliefs and practices which largely contradict each other and, taken together, cancel each other out.[1]

On the other hand, as I have tried to suggest, where the Church has been led into a position such as is normal in South India; where, that is to say, the Church in any one place is normally one body which has to include within itself, somehow or other, all the varieties of intellectual and emotional type, all the varieties of class, caste and culture, then either it visibly disintegrates into warring factions, or else it stands before men as a society constituted by nothing else than its relation to God through Christ, facing fallen humanity not as a series of particular associations but simply as humanity restored to itself in Christ. What lies behind the movement towards unity in South India, and what has sustained it through the long painful years of apparently barren negotiation, is the fact that the Church has found in experience that in spite of quarrels and factions and grievous failures of fellowship, there is that in the Gospel which can hold together men of every kind in one fellowship founded upon what God has wrought for all men in Christ, and that to deny publicly that this is so would be to contradict the very Gospel by which alone the Church lives. There is a way of trying to bring men together by ignoring the matters on which they are divided, and when this is attempted among Christians it is apt to produce a kind of tasteless slush devoid of any power to salt the earth. Differences of belief have to be faced with the fullest seriousness and realism. But the point surely is that there is that in the nature of the Church which can endure very profound differences of belief because that which constitutes the Church is something which, from the human point of view, concerns a far deeper level of personality than that

[1] Cf. M. J. Congar, O.P., *Divided Christendom*, p. 32. "Catholicism keeps its anti-Protestant face to the world."

which is concerned with intellectual agreement. It is true, of course, that—as has already been said—credal statements are required to safeguard the true statement of the Gospel itself. But there is an experience of living together in which deep differences of tradition are overcome not by being ignored, but by being held in relation to the fundamental fact of a common debt to the Redeemer. Within the bond of mutual love which that creates, the differences become creative of new understanding and new action—not without pain and stress. When, however, the grounds of difference are made the ground of *separation*, when rival factions and ultimately rival denominations are organized on the basis of these differences, then what has come into existence is a society of a different order, a society not spiritual but carnal (1 Cor. iii. 3-4), not founded upon the work of the Spirit but on some work of man—some system of ideas or some tradition of practice or piety. These two things go together and mutually reinforce one another—the development of separated groups, and the addition to the Gospel of other things which do not belong to its essence. The Church in its true nature is founded on the Gospel alone, because the Gospel is not a human construction but the news of what God has done. To add anything to the Gospel is to corrupt the sources of the Church's life and to reduce it to the level of a human association based on some identity of belief or practice. In that sense every movement towards reunion must involve a process of simplification, a stripping away of things which are not of the essence of the Gospel itself in order that the Gospel may be apprehended afresh in all its simplicity. I have sought to suggest that the South India Church has been forced to some such simplification by the circumstances of its life under the arrangement of mission comity.

Again, just as the arrangement of comity was the result of an evangelistic impulse, so this process of simplification is intimately related to the maintenance of a truly evangelistic character in the whole life of the Church. That which makes the Church the Church is at the same time the thing which gives it its mission. That which reduces the Church to a series of associations is at the same time that which destroys the possibility of evangelism in its true sense and transforms it into the proselytizing effort of some human enthusiasm. That which constitutes the Church is the act of God in Christ by which men are reborn in Him and made sharers through the Holy Spirit in that divine life which the Son shares with the Father. But it is this same fact which gives to those who have been so reborn into Him their mission to the world. That same divine grace which reconciled them in one body also sends them out as ministers of reconciliation, beseeching men on behalf of Christ to be reconciled to God. That same death and rebirth in which every human ground of confidence is destroyed, and a new life of union with Christ is created, makes them sharers in His mission to the world, rejoicing in every opportunity to fill up that which is lacking of the sufferings of Christ for His body's sake which is the Church. Everything, in other words, which drives men away from confidence in their own intellectual constructions and their own traditions of piety, back to that one central fact which is the substance of the Gospel, has the effect both of making the Church more truly the Church, and of making it more truly a mission to the world. The connection between the movement for Christian reunion and the movement for world evangelization is of the deepest possible character. The two things are the two outward signs of a return to the heart of the Gospel itself.

The fact, therefore, that the movement for reunion has received so large a part of its impetus from the younger Churches must not be dismissed as merely the natural effect of minority status upon the outlook of a Church. Rather we must surely see here a very deep and significant movement of the Spirit in the life of the Church. The missionary movement of the last two hundred years was the slow, painful and often reluctant obedience of the Churches of the West to the fundamental demand of the Gospel. To re-read the story of the early years of that movement, of the mass of hostility and contempt which it had to face within the Church, of the staggering magnitude of the tasks to which the few pioneers set themselves, and of the terrible toll which death took of them in the early decades of the movement, is to realize afresh both how great is the work which has been done within these two hundred years, and also how very much remains to be done if the Churches of the old Christendom are to accept seriously the missionary obligation which the Gospel lays upon them. One cannot read the story without feeling again and again that the obedience of those few early pioneers has been the human instrument of a mighty divine purpose for the Church. It is in that context that the movement for reunion in the younger Churches is to be understood. Obedience is the condition for further understanding, and the obedience of the Churches of the West—partial and halting as it has been—to the divine command to preach the Gospel to every creature, has been the means by which new understanding has been granted to them, and has opened the way by which they are groping back to a true sense of what the Church is. The enthusiasm of the younger Churches for reunion is not merely the particular point of view of a minority movement: it is the fruit of an act of obedience to the Gospel.

As far as South India is concerned there is an issue to be faced in the life of the Church which must be put as clearly and sharply as possible. Under the conditions of mission comity Churches have grown up each of which has accepted the responsibility of being the Church in that area, the responsibility of being the household of God in that place, a home for all of every sort who have been begotten again as God's children, and the responsibility of being the embassy of Christ to all the people of that region.[1] But because the Churches belong to different denominations the cause of Christ is represented in one place by Episcopalian, in another by Presbyterian, in another by Baptists, and so on, each denomination having its own rules regarding church membership and church government. Because in each place there is, normally, no rivalry of different groups, each local Church tends to regard its neighbours in the adjoining area as its partners and fellow workers, and when Christians go from one area to the others they are commended to the fellowship of the Church to which they go. But as such contacts multiply, the illogicality of the situation becomes more and more apparent. A Methodist who comes into an Anglican area is not, by the rules of the latter Church, entitled to receive communion. A Presbyterian baptized in infancy will not count as a full member of the Church if he goes to live in a Baptist area. In practice what frequently happens is that the

---

[1] The picture which I have given is over-simplified because I have omitted mention of the Roman Catholic Church, which has very widespread work in South India and which does not observe " comity." This qualifies, but does not invalidate, the points I have tried to make in the text. In the villages—which is where the Church has its roots—it is normal to have only one congregation; and where—as in larger towns—the Roman and non-Roman Churches are side by side, their methods of expansion and their customs of life and worship are so different as to make them appear to the common man both inside and outside their membership as almost two separate religions.

THE BASIS OF UNION IN THE LIFE OF THE CHURCH

rules of the different Churches are simply not applied. But it is a sure way to corrupt sound church life to have rules on paper which are not kept, and the Church cannot be content to leave things as they are. What, then, is to be done? Two ways only are open. One is to work for the establishment in every centre of the full range of denominational Churches, so that any Christian, as he moves about the country, may find wherever he goes a congregation which abides by the ecclesiastical rules and practices in which he has been brought up. The other is to seek for reunion.

That is the issue which the Church in South India has faced. It has chosen the second alternative and the result is the Scheme of Union. It is certainly a very imperfect scheme. It bears on it many marks of hasty work by men not able to spare for the necessary work the hours and days that were needed. It bears on it scars received during long and arduous passages through many committees and councils and synods. At some points it may be radically wrong. But it is an answer to the situation which I have described, and when judgment is passed on it, the judge must be able at the same time to state what better alternative he has to offer. For this is a matter of practical decision in a situation where decision cannot be delayed without harm to the Church. It would be possible to adopt the other alternative which I have suggested, to abandon the principle of comity and to work towards a type of denominational church life such as the West has grown accustomed to. But I believe that to do so would be to turn our backs upon the great illumination which has been given to us through the obedience of those who went before us in the missionary expansion of the Church. It would be the corrupting of that by which the Church lives and by which it is sent out on its mission to the world. It would be the public denial of the Gospel which we preach, the good news of Him who, being lifted up, will draw all men to Himself. To the multitude in India, weary of everlasting division and distrust and turning longing eyes to the Church as the place where men of all castes and classes can be made one, it would be a plain announcement that they will look to the Church in vain.

The Scheme of Union must be judged on theological grounds, and in what follows I shall try to say something in justification of it from a theological point of view. But it is also a plan of action which must be judged in the light of the possible alternatives. I am sure it is very far from perfect. But I am driven to the belief that it is substantially a plan of action into which the Church has been led by obedience to the commission which gives it its existence: "As the Father hath sent me, so send I you."

PART

2

The Nature of the Church's Unity and Continuity

CHAPTER TWO

THE PROBLEM

IF the Church—or rather the "Churches"—were a series of voluntary associations for the culture and practice of the religious life, their disunity might be deplorable but it would not be scandalous, and the problem of uniting them would be fundamentally a matter of mutual understanding and adjustment. But every body of Christians which calls itself a Church and accepts the New Testament as the final authority as to what that word means must believe itself to be, not a voluntary association based on the decision of the members to unite, but in some sense the *ecclesia* of God, the new Israel, the Body of Christ, the Vine, the Temple of the living God of which the New Testament speaks. Our problem is that there is a plurality of bodies each claiming to be that *ecclesia*. It is true that both honesty and charity have compelled most of us to abandon the claim to be exclusively the Church, but that very abandonment has radically corrupted our churchmanship, for it is very certain that the word *ecclesia* in the New Testament is an exclusive word, describing the Body of Christ in the world, something of which it is unthinkable to predicate plurality except in the sense of the plurality of local Churches. The fact that for the majority of Churchmen disunity does not appear to be an intolerable offence against the very nature of the Church is due to the fact that we do not seriously believe that the Church is what the New Testament says it is. A somewhat crude and imperfect analogy will perhaps illuminate the point. It may be unfortunate to have two rival temperance societies in the same town, but it is not scandalous. If the members are reasonable people they will avoid occasions of friction and may, in fact, find that friendly rivalry has an invigorating effect on their work. But a temperance society whose members are habitually drunk is generally regarded as scandalous. The existence of a plurality of "Churches" (in the modern sense of the word) is scandalous in the same sense, for the Church's unity in Christ is of its very essence. The degree to which it has ceased to appear scandalous is the measure of the extent to which the word "Church" has been evacuated of its New Testament meaning. A divided Church in the New Testament sense of the word Church is something illogical and incomprehensible—as illogical and incomprehensible as human sin. Perhaps nothing is more important than to state that clearly at the outset. We are familiar with theories of sin and of how it is to be dealt with which achieve logical coherence just in proportion to their failure to grasp the dimensions of the issue. They have their counterparts in the discussions that centre in the task of Christian reunion. If we have—in Anselm's famous phrase —considered of what weight sin is, we shall be prepared for an element of the illogical, prepared to recognize and discard superficial explanations of the Church's disunity and correspondingly superficial proposals for its reunion.

The attempts to achieve a logical explanation of the Church's disunity are of two types. Both amount to a denial that there is in truth disunity at all. Both are characteristic products of a theology which has failed to take adequate account of the fact of sin, failed to understand how deep and universal is the irrationality which sin introduces into all things human. The first type, represented in its most unambiguous form by the Roman Catholic Church, identifies one existing Church exclusively with the Church of the New Testament and regards other "Churches" as congeries of baptized persons to which God in His mercy has granted many of the gifts and graces of His Spirit, but which are not parts of the Church. On this view the Church is not divided. What has happened is that members have fallen away from it. The way of reunion is simply that they should return to it. The second type, represented by many Protestants, affirms that the unity of the Church is a spiritual unity, that outward unity of organization is not of the essence of the Church, and that true Christians are in fact united already. It sings with determination:

THE PROBLEM

*We are not divided,
All one body we,*

and regards questions of "ecclesiastical joinery" as belonging to a lower level of spirituality than that upon which it becomes possible to make this affirmation. On this view what is required is primarily an increase of cordiality among Christians, and the question whether or in what way this is to lead to institutional unity is a relatively minor matter.

Each of these types of theory does justice to one aspect of the New Testament teaching about the Church—the first to the fact that the Church in the New Testament is one visible society, the new Israel, the holy temple in the Lord, in whom Christians are builded together for a habitation of God in the Spirit; the second to the fact that the Church in the New Testament is Israel after the Spirit, created and constituted by the union of its members through the Spirit in the ascended life of the Lord. Both fail, as it seems, to do justice to the effect of sin in severing the two things that God has joined, and both, therefore, in fact deny the existence of the real problem.

Continuing to speak only in crude outline we may perhaps set the terms of the problem by examining a little further these two ways of thinking about the Church's unity. The unity of the Christian with Christ, and of Christians with one another, in Christ, is quite clearly in the very centre of the New Testament message. But what exactly is the nature of this unity? One type of Christian will answer, "It is a spiritual unity. God is spirit, and the bond of faith is a spiritual bond. The unity of the Church is not constituted by or determined by any outward organization. The fundamental unity of spirit will express itself in variety, not uniformity of organization, in freedom, not in rigidity. In contrast to the old temple of Jerusalem, the Church is the invisible temple not made with hands. No actual historical institution can be simply identified with the Body of Christ, nor is the relation of the Christian with Christ settled by his place in the historically continuous existence of any ecclesiastical body. His relation with Christ is in the spirit, constituted by faith. The Church is not intended to be one huge all-embracing organization. It is a fellowship in the spirit, and its life may often be best nurtured by the existence of a number of smaller, freer units, provided always that these recognize one another and maintain with one another relations of brotherly concord."

To this another Christian will reply in William Temple's phrase, "Christianity is the most materialistic of the world's great religions." "The heart of the Christian message," he will say, "is the Incarnation, the Word made flesh. At the heart of the Gospel there is not merely an idea, nor a spiritual experience, but a Man who lived, died and rose again at a certain place in the world and a certain point in time. Something concrete, visible and tangible (1 John i. 1) is the burden of the Christian message. And just as it was by actual meeting with the Incarnate Christ that the first disciples became apostles, built as living stones into the new temple, so no one in subsequent generations becomes a member incorporate in Christ except through contact with the visible historical society which sprang from the Incarnation and is its continuation. The material and institutional is not, therefore, peripheral or secondary, but is a vital part of what it means to be in Christ. The Church's unity is not merely spiritual. It is the unity of one divine organism, the Body of Christ, existing in time and space, yet showing the life of eternity. Visible unity and continuity are of its essence."

These rough-and-ready summaries may serve in a preliminary way to remind us of the problem with which we are concerned. Those who adopt the first point of view will see no necessity for preserving in any scheme of union the historically continuous order of the Church. They will require only that any system of church order which it is proposed to adopt should be such as will adequately express and minister to the Church's spiritual unity. Those who hold the second point of view will put first the requirement that the continuous historic order be understood and preserved, and will insist that reunion, whatever else it may include, is primarily the return to that continuous order of those who had left it.

Because the method of reunion adopted in South India satisfies neither of these schools of thought it is often regarded as an unworthy compromise between them. I hope to show reasons for believing that it deserves more serious consideration as an attempt to do justice to the truth in both.

CHAPTER THREE

THE ISRAEL OF GOD

THE Bible is not the story of ideas about God, but the story of the people of God. It is impossible to stress too much the importance of this fact. Men are not redeemed from sin by having right ideas about God. They are redeemed when they meet God in His judgment and mercy. But men can only meet God on this plane of history where they live. The Bible is the story of God's action in history, of His setting apart a people, one of the numerous branches of the human race, to be the bearers of His revelation, to be the means whereby humanity might be reconciled to God. The Bible describes conflicts as to the nature and constitution of the people of God and as to its relation to the rest of humanity. The New Testament especially records the decisive conflicts by which it became clear that the people of God according to His will is not constituted by Jewish birth or by circumcision, but by incorporation in Christ. But it is fundamental to the teaching of the Bible throughout that God's purpose of redemption is wrought out through a people of His choice. This people is likened collectively to a child whom God has adopted and brought up, a wife whom He has chosen, a vine or an olive which He has planted, a building which He is erecting. It is never a society (or series of societies) which men have founded to express their obedience to God or their aspirations after Him. It is always the society which He has called into being and to which men are called in His Name. "Ye did not choose me but I chose you, and appointed you that you should go and bear fruit," might have been said to God's people at every stage.

This people—God's people—is the Church of the twentieth century no less than of the first. If that were not so, then the Bible would become again to us simply a record of ideas. It is important to stress this point. It is possible to take the record of the Bible and expound its meaning in terms of general concepts applicable to our life to-day. Indeed it is necessary to do so. It is even possible—in so doing—to lay great stress on the fact that what is spoken of is not a series of myths or symbols, but the record of actual historical events. It is possible to emphasize—as one is bound to do in preaching to Hindus—that the life, death and resurrection of Jesus are not illustrations of eternal truths which, when we have once grasped them, we can hold in our minds apart from the illustration, but events by which something irreversible was effected for humanity. But even the idea of historical actuality is only an idea. Even the idea of something irreversible effected in human history is still only an idea, until one meets the actual effect here in the twentieth century. Perhaps the idea of concreteness is the most abstract idea there is, and hence one of the most useful to theologians! But God meets us through His people here and now, in the form of an actual invitation into the fellowship of a body of people calling themselves one Church. The invitation is, of course, meaningless and inexplicable apart from the record which the Bible contains, for the Church derives its existence from the revelation of which the Bible is the record. But the Bible would not be the means of God's actual meeting with me here and now and reconciling me to Himself if it were not that it comes to me in the hands of His reconciled people. The Gospel comes to men not only as a set of ideas; it does not even come only as a set of ideas which includes the idea of historical actuality. It comes in the concrete actuality of an encounter with God's people. The redemption which God has wrought in Christ is for the world. Its purpose is a new humanity, mankind made one in Christ, converted from that egocentricity which cuts man off from God and his neighbour, and restored to that life of communion for which mankind was created. The first fruits and the instrument of that purpose is the Church, the fellowship of those who have received the reconciliation. There is no reconciliation to God apart from reconciliation with the fellowship of His reconciled people.

This indissoluble connection of a Gospel claiming to be the final truth of human existence with a particular human society is nowhere more offensive than in the eyes of the cultured and spiritually minded Hindu. But there is that in all of us which resents it. We are all inclined to say in our hearts, "Why should I have to go there, or do that, in order to receive God's grace? Cannot God deal with me direct instead of by this roundabout and arbitrary way? Why can I not find Him in my own soul, in the culture or religion of my own tradition? Are not Abanah and Pharpar, the rivers of Damascus, better than all the waters of Israel? May I not wash in them and be clean?" The answer to all this is, of course, that the purely inward and spiritual may be the purely private and selfish. What is needed to break through the pride which is the fundamental form of sin is something that comes to us from outside, the fact or the person who, being outside of us, cannot be adjusted to suit us, or confused with the motions of our own spirit. We all know the type of man who loves humanity in general but cannot get on with any of his neighbours in particular. "Humanity," being a mere abstraction of our own minds, does not take us a hair's breadth beyond the circle of our own selfhood. But the man next door is outside of me, and I cannot love him and receive his love except when that circle is broken. Thus it is that God's approach to us is through the concrete fact or person outside us, the beggar in the street, the actual concrete organization of the Church, the concrete, unique, unrepeatable fact of a Jewish Messiah. Much so-called spirituality is really an attempt to escape from this method of God's dealing with us into a mystical and private type of experience which, being purely private, is wholly self-centred. The Gospel does not come to each of us in isolation. It comes to us through a particular book and through a particular fellowship, whether that fellowship be represented in parent, teacher, preacher, or friend. And that fellowship, like all human fellowships, has maintained its existence in history as a visible organization with visible tests of membership, with officers, rules and ceremonies. There is no other way by which the Gospel comes to us. It is a false spirituality, divorced from the whole teaching of the Bible, which regards this visible and continuing Church as of subordinate importance for the life in Christ. "Those who have God as Father must have the Church as Mother."[1]

But the very use of that quotation from Calvin (following Cyprian) brings us right up against the question with which we are concerned—what *is* the Church? What, in other words, is the thing that constitutes this people of God? What are the distinguishing features which make it possible to say of one body of people, this is the Church of Christ, and of another, this is not? What constitutes the Church? That is the fundamental question, and we have to turn to the Bible for our answer.

The Bible is the story of the people of God. Within that story it records conflicts as to who in truth are God's people. The story

[1] Calvin, *Institutes* IV, I, 1.

begins with the promise to Abraham and his seed. But from the beginning there is a process of elimination. Physical descent alone does not confer membership in the chosen people. Nor does circumcision. There is a covenant between God and Israel, and those who flout the terms of the covenant are no part of the chosen people. In the time of Elijah we read of an apostate people, in which, however, there is a minority which remains faithful to the covenant. The anointed heads of the people are therefore to be destroyed and new leaders from among the faithful are to be set up (1 Kings xix. 15-18). In Amos there seems at times to be no light beyond the gloom of complete apostasy, even though all the outward organs of the people's life are intact. But from Isaiah onwards the ideas of a faithful remnant, the true People within the people, and of a true King in contrast to the false and apostate kings who had led the people so far from the Covenant, come into prominence. These ideas are further developed in the visions of the Servant of the Lord who shall be the means both of restoring Israel to its true allegiance and also of bringing all nations to the worship of the true God in Zion. In the Gospels we find a marked cleavage between "the people who know not the Law," the publicans and sinners, and those who are seeking both to live in strict obedience to the letter of the covenant and to win proselytes to the same obedience.

Jesus does not found a new people of God, a new society. He announces the advent of the Kingdom and leads those who follow Him to faith in Himself as Christ, Lord and God. He chooses twelve (significant number) and admits them to His most intimate fellowship, making them witnesses of His deeds and words of power, and above all preparing them for His sacrificial and redeeming death and resurrection. His mission is to Israel, but His contacts with Gentiles are made the occasion for prophecy of the drawing together of all nations into the Messianic Kingdom, and for teaching about the primacy of faith (Matt. viii. 5-13; xv. 21-8; John xii. 20-32). When He comes to His Cross He is utterly alone, He is tried and condemned by the highest tribunal of Israel. The final offering of perfect obedience and perfect holiness is made not by a People, but by Him alone. He alone on that day is Israel.

But this is not the end of the story of Israel. It is the beginning of the story of the true Israel. "Except a grain of wheat fall into the earth and die it abideth by itself alone; but if it die it beareth much fruit." " I, if I be lifted up, will draw all men unto myself." The perfect obedience of mankind is offered proleptically to God by Him whose solitary obedience alone has power to create it.

The meaning of these events is not at once understood. At first they appear to mean only the final shattering of the hope of Israel. But the astounding facts, first of the empty tomb and then of the risen Lord, slowly convert despair into faith—faith of a new kind. During the days that follow the resurrection the risen Jesus interprets to the disciples in all the Scriptures the things concerning Himself. He prepares them both for His departure from them in bodily presence and for His coming to them again through the Spirit.

Then comes the mighty event of Pentecost, the birthday of the new Israel, when what had been a body of men gathered round the Incarnate Christ, and depending for their intercourse with Him upon the ordinary organs of human communication, becomes the community indwelt by the Holy Spirit of God, having communion at all times and in all places with the Father through the Son in the Spirit. Immediately its spokesman, Peter, proclaims a message which begins with a reference to God's ancient promise to pour out His Spirit upon " all flesh," and ends: " To you is this promise and to your children, and to all that are afar off, even as many as the Lord our God shall call unto Him." The message is for all men; now at last the ancient promise that Israel shall be a light to the Gentiles and salvation to the ends of the earth is to be fulfilled. In a very short time the uncircumcised Gentiles, "alienated from the commonwealth of Israel and strangers from the covenants of the promise," begin to hear and believe. The Church is faced at once with a question that affects decisively its whole nature and constitution; the question " Upon what terms are Gentiles to be incorporated into the Church? " Of the controversy that centred in this question the New Testament bears abundant evidence and the study of it concerns the very heart of our problem.

One thing which is clear is that neither side in this controversy questioned the fact that the Church is the Israel of God, not a newly founded society. In his most sustained discussion of the relations between the Church and the Jews who had rejected Christ, Paul strains his metaphor to the breaking-point in his insistence that Gentile Christians are not a new and independent growth, but slips cut out of a wild olive tree and grafted, contrary to nature, into a good olive tree. "It is not thou that bearest the root," he says to the Gentile Christians, "but the root thee." There is but one Israel of God, one olive tree of God's planting, "a green olive tree, fair with goodly fruit" (Jer. xi. 16). Gentile Christians are wild slips grafted into it, and unbelieving Jews are branches broken off. The very absurdity of the metaphor from a horticultural point of view,[1] while it doubtless indicates a regrettable absence in the Apostle of that rural bias so necessary to a missionary, is surely of primary significance in reminding us of the immense importance which he attached to this theological truth, even in the midst of his polemic against the Judaisers.

But what is the manner of ingrafting? To many it seemed obvious that it must be what it had always been, the acceptance of the covenants and of the outward seal of circumcision. "It is needful to circumcise them and to charge them to keep the law of Moses" (Acts xv. 5). If these things, which surely belong to the fundamental constitution of Israel, are omitted, what is left of the claim to be in truth the Israel of God? This was a cogent argument and it was pressed upon the young Church with power and persistence. Why was it finally rejected?

It is important to notice firstly that it was, if one may put it so, the mission field which drove the home Church to re-think its position. It was as the result of responsible adventures in evangelism, of obedience to the fundamental apostolic commission, that the Church was led into new truth about its own nature. The first landmark in the story is Peter's preaching in the house of Cornelius. He had gone there in obedience to God's guidance, though clearly filled with doubts about the propriety of what he was being called to do. He obeyed, and went, and spoke the word. And as the fruit of his obedience a family believed the Gospel and received the Holy Spirit. It was something so plain that no man could gainsay it. "They of the circumcision which believed were amazed." But—and this is the important fact—amazing and irregular as this uncovenanted spiritual experience was, Peter knew at once that he was in the presence of something which required not argument but recognition and obedience. Here was an act of God, and man had but to recognize and follow. "Who was I, that I could withstand God?"

[1] C. H. Dodd, Moffatt New Testament Commentary, *ad loc.*

One can picture many later holders of the apostolic office dealing with this situation in a very different way. The phrase "*Deus non alligatur sacramentis, sed nos*" would have been called into service, and a thankful acknowledgment of God's irregular operations would have been followed by a reverent regularizing of them. In other words Cornelius and his family would have been circumcised first and then baptized.[1] We do not know precisely the ground taken up by Paul's Judaising opponents, but it may be supposed that they did not deny the reality of the spiritual fruits of the Gentile mission, but insisted that the outward act of incorporation in the people of God could not be dispensed with. What one notices in the records both of the controversy which followed the conversion of Cornelius, and also of that which followed the success of the mission of Paul and Barnabas, is the readiness of the Church to reckon with the new acts of the living God, and to believe that they have to follow where the Lord leads them.

The book of Acts records in bare outline the fact that those who sought to insist on circumcision were defeated, but it does not give us a full picture of the issues involved as they appeared to those concerned in the struggle at the time. For this we turn to St. Paul. The epistles in which this issue is dealt with most directly are Galatians and Romans. In Galatians he is dealing with a Church which threatens to succumb to the teaching of the Judaisers. He tells them that if they receive circumcision Christ will profit them nothing, that they will be severed from Christ, fallen away from grace. And he goes on, "For we through the Spirit by faith wait for the hope of righteousness. For in Christ Jesus neither circumcision availeth anything nor uncircumcision but faith working through love" (Gal. v. 1-6). A large part of the argument is devoted to proving that this is no new thing, but that faith has always been in fact—from the human side—the constitutive fact of Israel's existence as the people of God. Abraham's believing response to God's promises antedates circumcision and law, and it is the faithful, not the circumcised, who are sons of Abraham (iii. 7). The argument is strengthened by reference to the story of Ishmael and Isaac, the son born after the flesh and the son born through promise. These are regarded as types, the former of the " Jerusalem that now is "—" Israel after the flesh "

---

[1] See *Jewish Antecedents of the Christian Sacraments*, F. Gavin, pp. 31-5.

(1 Cor. x. 18), and the latter of the true Israel, the children of the Jerusalem that is above (Gal. iv. 26), who through the Spirit by faith wait for the hope of righteousness. The true Israel is and has always been, not Israel after the flesh but the children of the promise. To accept circumcision after having heard and believed the Gospel is to be severed from Christ, the one true seed of Abraham (iii. 16). It is to compromise with those who desire only "to make a fair show in the flesh" (vi. 12).

In Romans the same argument is developed with greater fulness, though without the pointed personal reference that it has in Galatians. He begins by depicting the total alienation of the Gentile world from God. He goes on to remind the Jew that his place in the visible commonwealth of Israel does not secure his relation with God. "For he is not a Jew which is one outwardly, neither is that circumcision which is outward in the flesh: but he is a Jew which is one inwardly, and circumcision is that of the heart, in the spirit, not in the letter; whose praise is not of men but of God" (ii. 28-9). Having convicted Jew and Gentile alike of being "under sin," he turns to speak of the thing now revealed "the righteousness of God through faith in Jesus Christ," "the redemption that is in Christ Jesus whom God set forth to be a propitiation through faith by his blood . . . that he might himself be just and the justifier of him that hath faith in Jesus" (iii. 22, 24-5, 26). Immediately he turns to face the question of the relation of this righteousness of God by faith to the ancient people of Israel. He affirms that Abraham was justified not by works, but by faith while he was still uncircumcised (iv. 1-10), and that circumcision was "a seal of the righteousness of the faith which he had while he was in uncircumcision, that he might be the father of all them that believe, though they be in uncircumcision, that righteousness might be reckoned unto them, and the father of circumcision to them who not only are of the circumcision but who also walk in the steps of that faith of our father Abraham which he had in uncircumcision" (iv. 11-12). Not circumcision, but faith, is the human condition of membership in the Israel of God. In chapters ix-xi the Apostle returns to a very thorough discussion of the relation between Israel after the flesh and Israel after the Spirit, to part of which I have already referred. He begins from the point asserted in the earlier chapters: "For they are not all Israel which are of Israel: neither because they are Abraham's seed are they all children: but, 'In Isaac shall thy seed be called.' That is, it is not the children of the flesh that are children of God, but the children of the promise are reckoned for a seed" (ix. 6-8). He points out the absolute freedom which God as creator has over against his creatures, a freedom which was asserted even under the old covenant; " As he saith also in Hosea, I will call that my people which was not my people and her beloved which was not beloved. And it shall be that in the place where it was said unto them, 'Ye are not my people,' there shall they be called sons of the living God " (ix. 25-6). Again the difference between the righteousness of God by faith and the righteousness of works is expounded. The former, the true righteousness, comes of hearing and believing and confessing. It is equally available to all, Jew and Gentile, "for the same Lord is Lord of all and is rich unto all that call upon him " (x. 1-12). But Israel would not hear; it is the people outside the covenant who hear. "I was found of them that sought me not; I became manifest to them that asked not of me. But as to Israel, he saith, all the day long did I spread out my hands to a disobedient and gainsaying people " (x. 20-1). Yet this is not the whole truth, for in Israel there was and is a remnant " according to the election of grace," while the rest have been hardened. Yet the purpose of it all is the salvation of all (xi. 1-12). In the allegory of the olive tree the Gentile Christians are reminded that they are but grafts of wild olive into the ancient tree: they have no ground whatever for pride. God can break them off again and graft the Jews in again (xi. 13, 24). In truth there is no doubt or vacillation in God's purpose. The truth is that he " hath shut up all unto disobedience, that he might have mercy upon all " (xi. 32). And the whole great argument rises to a burst of praise, " O the depth of the riches both of the wisdom and the knowledge of God! how unsearchable are his judgments and his ways past tracing out! . . . For of him and through him and unto him are all things. To him be the glory for ever. Amen." This doxology perhaps gives the essential clue to the whole argument, for it is the sense of the living God, free and sovereign, all wise and all holy, which dominates it from beginning to end. The Apostle's thought about the Church, its unity and its continuity, never strays far from this. It never, as later thought has so often done, proceeds as though this vertical dimension of the Church's existence could, for the temporary purposes of argument, be left out of account, as though the Church could for purposes of argument be defined in terms of its historically continuous structure. The Church, the Israel of God, depends from moment to moment of its existence upon the sovereign grace of the living God whose mercies are, in sober truth, new every morning.[1]

Other epistles contain echoes of the controversy, but do not add much to the picture of St. Paul's position on this point which we derive from Galatians and Romans. To the Corinthians he says again, "Circumcision is nothing, and uncircumcision is nothing; but the keeping of the commandments of God" (1 Cor. vii. 19). He warns the Philippians against "the concision" and goes on, "For we are the circumcision who worship by the Spirit of God and glory in Christ Jesus and have no confidence in the flesh." He elaborates this by speaking in detail of his own privileges as a member of "Israel after the flesh," and adding that he counted them all refuse that he might gain Christ and have that righteousness which is through faith in Christ, "the righteousness which is of God by faith" (Phil. iii. 1-9). To the Colossians he speaks of Christ, the head of all principality and power, "in whom ye were also circumcised with a circumcision not made with hands, in the putting off of the body of the flesh, in the circumcision of Christ" (ii. 10-11). This may be compared with the reference in Ephesians to the Jews as "that which is called circumcision in the flesh, made with hands" (Eph. ii. 11). There is an echo in these phrases of the words attributed to our Lord by His accusers, "Destroy this temple that is made with hands, and in three days I will build another made without hands" (Mark xiv. 58).

These, then, were the arguments with which the Apostle met and overcame the demand that Gentile Christians should be circumcised. At the risk of distortion we must attempt to summarize in a few sentences the evidence we have reviewed. What was common to both parties in the dispute was that the Church is the Israel of God, the ancient olive and not a new plant. What was at issue was the manner of incorporation into it of those who had been (to change the metaphor) strangers to the commonwealth of Israel. The question concerned, as questions of reunion do to-day, the fundamental character of the Church, the nature of its unity and continuity. The question had arisen simply because Gentiles had heard and believed the Gospel and God had sealed them with

[1] Cf. George Johnston: *The New Testament Doctrine of the Church*, p. 78.

the gift of the Spirit in a manner that none could gainsay. The first response, after the natural amazement at this new fact, had been simply to recognize it as a fact and conclude, "Then to the Gentiles also hath God granted repentance unto life" (Acts xi. 18). The second reaction was, as might be expected, a conservative one. Circumcision had always been the mark of membership in Israel. It had not been superseded. Nothing had happened to justify the Church in dispensing with something which had belonged from the beginning to the constitution of God's people. Therefore the Gentile Christian must be circumcised and his position validated and regularized. Only so could he be regarded as a member incorporate in Israel.

If it is permissible to dissect and summarize the passionate pleading with which the Apostle flings his whole soul against this claim, we may express it in these three bare statements:

(1) The only standing ground that a Christian has before God—whether he be Jew or Gentile—is that which has been provided by Christ Jesus "whom God set forth to be a propitiation through faith." Reliance upon any other security is incompatible with acceptance of this.

(2) In fact the emphasis upon faith is not a new departure. It has been the true essence of Israel from the beginning. From Abraham onwards it has been faith, not circumcision, which has been acceptable to God.

(3) Therefore to insist on circumcision for the Gentile Christians is to violate the fundamental nature of the Church. It is to turn from reliance on the Spirit to reliance on the flesh, from the things not made with hands to the things made with hands. It is to make Christ unnecessary. It is to fall away from His grace, to turn back again to the things which before enslaved the soul, to be entangled again in a yoke of bondage.

Dominating all the writings we have reviewed, as also the actions of the Apostles and brethren as we see them depicted in Acts, is the faith that God is the living God, free and sovereign, and that His purpose is the salvation of mankind.

From a later and more irenic epistle, dating from the time when the incorporation of the Gentiles in the Church was an accomplished fact and when the issue of circumcision had been decided once and for all, we may quote the following very rich and full picture of this momentous chapter in the history of the People of

God. "Wherefore remember, that aforetime ye, the Gentiles in the flesh, who are called Uncircumcision by that which is called Circumcision, in the flesh, made by hands; that ye were at that time separate from Christ, alienated from the commonwealth of Israel, and strangers from the covenants of the promise, having no hope and without God in the world. But now in Christ Jesus ye that once were far off are made nigh in the blood of Christ. For he is our peace, who made both one, and brake down the middle wall of partition, having abolished in his flesh the enmity, even the law of commandments contained in ordinances; that he might create in himself of the twain one new man, so making peace; and might reconcile them both in one body unto God through the cross, having slain the enmity thereby: and he came and preached peace to you that were far off, and peace to them that were nigh: for through him we both have our access in one Spirit unto the Father. So then ye are no more strangers and sojourners, but ye are fellow-citizens with the saints, and of the household of God, being built upon the foundation of the apostles and prophets, Christ Jesus himself being the chief corner stone; in whom each several building, fitly framed together, groweth into a holy temple in the Lord; in whom ye also are builded together for a habitation of God in the Spirit" (Eph. ii. 11-22). Here the thought of unity and continuity is in the foreground. The fruit of God's act in Christ is the breaking down of the partition, the reconciling of Jew and Gentile in one body, the incorporation of aliens in the commonwealth of Israel, the adoption of strangers into the household of God, the growth of a holy temple in the Lord, the building together of many stones for a habitation of God in the Spirit. This miracle of unity visibly wrought before men's eyes "to the intent that even now unto the principalities and powers in the heavenly places might be known through the Church the manifold wisdom of God" is the central theme of the early chapters of the Epistle. But the thought of God's fresh and sovereign activity is not far in the background. It is the new act of God in Christ that has wrought this unity. There is a passing reference to "circumcision in the flesh, made with hands"—an echo of old controversies—and it is in one Spirit that we both have our access to the Father. This new unity has been accomplished "in the blood of Christ": it is His victory on the Cross (cf. v. 15 with Col. ii. 14-15), destroying the power of the Law, which has made the reconciliation possible. And the possibility is actualized because "He came with a gospel of peace for those far away (that is, for you) and for those who were near" (Moffatt), for "How shall they believe in him whom they have not heard, and how shall they hear without a preacher" (Rom. x. 14). It is by "the hearing of faith" that the Spirit is received (Gal. iii. 2). The believing Gentile has access in the Spirit to the Father equally with the Jew, and both are built together, upon the foundation of apostles and prophets, Christ Jesus Himself being the chief cornerstone, Jesus the author of that gospel of peace, and the apostles whom He sent to be His messengers (Matt. x. 1-8; John xx. 21; 1 Cor. i. 17).

The studies we have made do not provide a simple answer to the question with which we started. It is necessary to accept the fact that the relation between the Church's visible continuity and unity as a historical institution and its spiritual unity in Christ is not simple. We are trying to view together two things which Catholicism and Protestantism have viewed separately, and thereby distorted. We have seen how the record of God's saving revelation is the record of the story of His people, and how it is through this one Israel of God that He wills to redeem all men and draw them into one. We have considered especially that decisive conflict which was fought on the issue of the manner of incorporation of the Gentiles into the Church. We have surveyed all the passages dealing explicitly with this issue. We have seen that while St. Paul shared to the full the common conviction that the Church is the Israel of God, he resisted as a denial of the Church's true nature the demand that Gentile Christians should be circumcised. The human condition of membership in Israel is not circumcision but faith. To insist on outward and institutional continuity with "Israel after the flesh" is to contradict the Church's nature. It is to misunderstand both the old and the new covenants. It is to dishonour Christ. Though an angel from heaven should propose this addition to the Gospel, he is to be anathema (Gal. i. 8). But once this threat has been removed we see the thought of the unity and continuity of God's people moving again into the centre of the Apostle's concern. He glories in the fact that the Gentile stranger has been incorporated into the commonwealth of Israel; he dares to hope for the day when unbelieving Jews shall be grafted back again into the stock whence they were broken off;

and with a wealth of metaphor he celebrates the growth of the new habitation of God in the Spirit which is the universal Church. Yet over all these hovers, as it were, the ever-present sense of the sovereign freedom of God, His power to break off and to graft in, to build and to plant, His grace by which the Church lives and grows from day to day.

Thus beginning from the thought of the Church as God's Israel we have seen how fundamental it is to the teaching of the New Testament that the Church is not Israel after the flesh but Israel after the Spirit, and that the authentic mark of membership in Israel is not circumcision but faith. We now turn to look at the question, as it were, from the other side. Beginning from the thought of life " after the Spirit " we shall see how this is related in the teaching of St. Paul to the unity and continuity of the Church.

Detached note: Faith, Circumcision, Baptism and Confirmation

The above argument has not touched on the relation between circumcision and the Christian rites of initiation. The point of the argument is the bearing of the circumcision controversy on the question of the nature of the unity and continuity of Israel—a unity and continuity which both parties in the controversy take for granted. We nowhere find as a parallel to St. Paul's insistence that Gentile converts must not be circumcised a corresponding insistence that they must be baptized; but he appears to assume that all the Churches to which he writes consist of baptized persons. There is apparently no controversy about this. (E.g., 1 Cor. xii, 13; Eph. iv. 5, v. 26; Titus iii. 5.) In none of the controversial passages regarding the circumcision question does baptism appear as a factor in the controversy. It is not the Christian equivalent of circumcision. As already indicated, circumcision is contrasted with faith, as the false with the true mark of the people of God (Gal. v. 6; Rom. iv. 10-12). It is spoken of as something belonging to the flesh, as opposed to that which is of the Spirit (Gal. vi. 13; Eph. ii. 11; Phil. iii. 3; Col. ii. 11), as something outward as contrasted with that which is inward (Rom. ii. 28-9). It is *never* contrasted with baptism, as the old with the new, the Jewish with the Christian.

Baptism appears in the course of the apostles' arguments in a different way. In Galatians (iii. 23-9) it appears incidentally in the course of an exposition of the fact that our justification (iii. 24) and adoption (iii. 26) are through faith. This is in continuation of the earlier argument of the chapter that it is "they which be of faith" who are sons of Abraham. Baptism finds its place in an exposition of the meaning of faith because baptism always follows the hearing and believing of the Word.[1] To be baptized into Christ, therefore, is to become part of Abraham's seed. In Romans vi baptism appears not in the course of argument about circumcision, but when the Apostle is dealing with those who assert that the doctrine of justification by faith, which he is expounding, will lead men into moral laxity. He reminds his readers of what happened when they believed and were baptized. They were united with Christ in His death and resurrection. Their life now is a sharing in His risen life. Having been baptized they are to reckon themselves dead to sin and alive to God in Christ. The same thought is expressed in the passage in Colossians where a reminder of that true and inward circumcision which Christians have received is followed by the same exposition of baptism as the event in which the believer was made one with Christ's death and with His risen life. This is the only place in the New Testament where circumcision and baptism are placed side by side. But it comes from a time when the circumcision issue has been settled. It is not baptism, but the "circumcision not made with hands," which is here implicitly (and as it were in parenthesis) contrasted with the Jewish rite.

Father Lionel Thornton,[2] however, identifies this "circumcision not made with hands" with the rite of confirmation or chrismation. Starting from the Jewish customs for the initiation of proselytes, in which circumcision preceded baptism, he argues that the story of Joshua circumcising the children of Israel after the crossing of the Jordan provided the basis for the Christian reversal of the order of the rites of initiation, so that baptism was followed by the rite of chrismation, the sealing of the forehead of the neophyte by the bishop (or apostle). The gift of the Spirit was connected primarily with this rite. "All the graces of baptism are referred by St. Paul to that writing of the Spirit upon the heart

[1] The examples in Acts are, Acts ii. 38-41; viii. 12ff.; viii. 38; x. 47; xvi. 15; xvi. 33; xviii. 8; xix. 4-6. The exception is the baptism of Saul at Damascus (ix. 18; xxii. 16) where it is the appearance of the Risen Lord Himself which is the precondition of his baptism.
[2] *The Unity of Baptism and Confirmation in Scripture.*

which takes effect through the seal of confirmation." At first sight this appears to diminish the importance of baptism, but in truth both rites are really one, as Christ's death and resurrection are really one.

It is impossible in a short note either to reproduce or to examine the feats of exegesis by which this view is supported.[1] But with regard to Father Thornton's contention in this pamphlet it is sufficient to say two things:

(1) The idea of a circumcision not made with hands, a circumcision of the heart, one which is inward and not outward, is not a new idea in the New Testament. It occurs in Deuteronomy (x. 16; xxx. 6) and in Jeremiah (iv. 4). And St. Paul claims that in fact it was always this inward circumcision which was the mark of the true Jew. But in these contexts what is referred to is, of course, not another rite distinct from the rite of circumcision, but precisely something which is not a rite—namely faith. It is not possible to believe that St. Paul used this striking and important phrase at some points to describe the distinctive Christian rite of initiation in contrast to the Jewish rite, and at others to describe something of which the essence was that it was not a rite at all; and this without any explanation at all of the difference in usage.

(2) In the crucial passage (Rom. iv) in which circumcision and faith are brought together, circumcision is referred to as "a seal of the righteousness of that faith which he had while he was in uncircumcision." There is no mention of an analogous seal for Christians. Father Thornton says "An unsealed document may have its validity challenged; and the owner's seal attached to an object of value will enhance its security," and he finds that " there is clearly an analogy between the seal of the Spirit and the seal of circumcision." There is, but the evidence is emphatically against the idea that the seal of the Spirit was—in the Apostle's mind—a rite analogous to the rite of circumcision. His argument is:

---

[1] With all respect one must enter a protest against the kind of use of the Scriptures of which this pamphlet is an illustration.

St. Paul's epistles are the writings of an evangelist and a pastor passionately concerned that his spiritual children should know the truth and be guarded against falsehood. They are written to be understood. It is not fitting that an expositor should use them as though they were a collection of detached clues in a crossword puzzle. There is an abundant literature on such subjects as the millennium and the Great Pyramid to remind us that with these methods anything may be proved from Scripture, but nothing will be learned.

THE ISRAEL OF GOD

"Abraham was justified not by circumcision but by faith (that is as regards the *human* condition of justification). Circumcision was added as a seal of the righteousness he already had. You are justified by faith. And you have received God's seal—the gift of the Spirit. And it is by the hearing of faith that the Spirit is received." The Galatians were precisely in the position of having the validity of their inheritance challenged, of having an enhanced security offered to them in the seal of circumcision. Paul answered that if they accepted that seal they would be severed from Christ. They were baptized Christians and had presumably also received the full rites of initiation upon the history of which Father Thornton and others are throwing valuable light. But St. Paul does not appeal to these as being a sufficient seal for the document. It is not in any rite of initiation that he asks them to put their trust. He begins his appeal to the Galatians with these words, reminding them of a Word heard and believed, not of a rite administered: "O foolish Galatians, who did bewitch you, before whose eyes Jesus Christ was openly set forth crucified? This only would I learn from you, Received ye the Spirit by the works of the law or by the hearing of faith? Are ye so foolish? having begun in the Spirit, are ye now perfected in the flesh?" And he ends with these words, a postscript in his own hand to his beloved children, of whom he is again in travail till Christ be formed in them—baptized Christians though they were: "They desire to have you circumcised that they may glory in your flesh. But far be it from me to glory save in the Cross of our Lord Jesus Christ, through which the world hath been crucified unto me and I unto the world." The confidence, the glory, of the man in Christ is in this alone—in the Cross of the Lord Jesus Christ. Israel lives by faith.

CHAPTER FOUR

THE SPIRIT, THE BODY AND THE FLESH

WE turn now to consider the relations between these two aspects of the Church's life from the other side. And, as in the previous chapter, we shall seek to understand the truth of the matter by looking at St. Paul's polemic against a perversion of the truth. The Epistle to the Galatians was addressed to people who were seeking in the outward rite of incorporation into the Israel of God an additional assurance of their salvation. The First Epistle to the Corinthians was written to people whose confidence in their own possession of the Spirit was destroying the unity of the Body. They were thus threatened with what might be described as the opposite perversion of the truth to that which threatened the Galatians. Their confidence that they were the possessors of the gifts which the Holy Spirit bestows upon believers was leading them into factions and jealousy, into extreme laxity on moral questions, into abuse of the Lord's Supper, and into the perversion of Christian liberty into a self-destructive anarchy. Factions had developed, each boasting the name of some revered leader and each—apparently—glorying in the possession of particular spiritual gifts. They were destroying the temple of God, the Church. They were denying the unity of the Body of Christ. They were misusing the Spirit's greatest gift, which is a love that never boasts, never envies, never seeks its own. The apostle uses of them a word that must have surprised and shocked them. He calls them " carnal," and his use of that word throws a flood of light upon what the words " flesh " and " Spirit " mean in his writings.

After the introductory salutations (i. 1-3) he thanks God for the spiritual gifts which He has bestowed on them (i. 4-9). Then he goes on immediately to speak about their factions—not forgetting to specify the source of his information. " Is Christ divided? " he asks. The Church does not consist in adherence to any man: it exists in Christ. Baptism is baptism into Christ, not into a society of followers of some man. He even thanks God that he did not baptize any of them, lest such an appalling confusion between the apostle and the Lord should be created in anyone's mind. It was not to baptize but to preach the Gospel that he received the apostolate from Christ. The preacher's work is to preach Christ, not himself, to point away from himself to Christ. He has especially to avoid that subtle and deadly betrayal of his task which consists in preaching "in wisdom of words" and so making void the Cross of Christ—preaching, in other words, in such wise that men gather round him and find their "glorying" in being able to say, "I am of Paul," instead of having to confess, "God forbid that I should glory save in the Cross of our Lord Jesus Christ" (i. 10-17). It is "the word of the Cross" that the apostle has to bring, and before this all human confidence, whether of the religious man or of the philosopher is shattered (i. 18-25). Even the character of the Christian Church itself is a reminder of this, for it is the "scum of the earth" that God has chosen (i. 26-8). The purpose is that every basis of confidence should be destroyed and men should have confidence in God alone (i. 29-31). The apostle's own preaching in Corinth was not designed to attract men to himself as a great preacher. There was nothing in it but Jesus Christ and Him crucified, and the power wrought through it was the power of God's Spirit given to those who believe the Gospel, not the power of human persuasiveness (ii. 1-5). There *is* a wisdom that belongs to those who live in the Spirit, but it is totally different from the wisdom of the world and is unintelligible to the natural man (ii. 6-16). But the Corinthians are not ready to receive that wisdom yet. As long as they are divided up into parties, boasting of the fact that they belong to this or that Christian leader, they are not living the life in the Spirit at all. They are carnal. They are building on human foundations and not on the only foundation-stone which God has laid, Christ Himself. Who are these Christian leaders? They are God's servants. "It is not for you to judge among them and set this one up against that," he says; "God will judge them—according to their work. You don't belong to them, they belong to you. But you belong to Christ for He has bought you. It is in Him you should therefore put your trust, not in men however great. You are God's temple. That temple is holy—it is His alone."

The Apostle writes elsewhere of the gifts of the Holy Spirit as the "seal" which God has given to believers (Eph. i. 13; iv. 30; 2 Cor. i. 22). Here he is dealing with people who have turned this truth into a means of falsehood, who have substituted confidence in their possession of these gifts for confidence in the one rock that is given to sinful man to trust in—Jesus Christ and Him crucified. He tells them that they are not spiritual but carnal. It is important to see clearly why he uses this word. There is an absolute distinction between a society founded upon common loyalty to some teacher, common adherence to some programme, or common assent to some body of doctrine, and the society which is founded upon the Gospel of Christ's atoning death. The former is a human society in the ordinary sense of the word. It shares the common characteristics of human groups. It exists by virtue of what is distinctive in it, what divides it from other groups, and therefore its corporate interest is in the direction of emphasizing this distinction. It offers to its members a larger self in which the individual's sense of insecurity can find compensation, whether it be his physical insecurity, or the insecurity that belongs to all his attempts to understand the world he lives in. Because of the nature of the psychological forces which hold it together it tends to be more self-assertive and aggressive in its relations with other groups than the individuals composing it are in their private dealings. Such groupings form the normal units of man's natural life and the relations between them constitute a large part of his history.

In contrast to all such groups the Church is, in its real nature, founded upon the shattering of all human egotism, upon the reconstitution of human nature in that relation of loving dependence upon God for which man was created. When a man hears and believes the Gospel; when he understands and believes, in their personal application to himself, the facts that Christ died for our sins according to the Scriptures and rose again, there takes place in him a process of breaking down and building up, of death and rebirth. In the face of the Cross, and of the Lord of Glory crucified thereon for his sins, no man can build even the smallest hope upon his own virtue or wisdom. In common with the whole race he stands there convicted and under the sentence of death. But at the same place he receives the gift of a new life, not a reprieve for the old one, but the gift of a new one which is the creation of the Redeemer's love. He becomes Christ's. At the same moment that every foothold of virtue to which he has ever clung slips from under him and he knows himself a lost soul fit only for perdition, he finds himself gripped by the Hand which he has wounded, held fast in the love of Christ. For the first time he becomes what he was created to be, a creature knowing that he owes everything to God's grace. In that moment the "natural" man, that most unnatural self-contradiction, a creature made for God yet resisting God, is done away. The barriers that he erects against God and his fellow-men are broken down. The anxieties and fears, the unfulfillable desires and ambitions, which are the inevitable consequence of his desire to be his own god, are banished. Across all that constitutes the natural man is written "Murderer of the Son of God." But a new man is born, begotten of His love alone, the product of no natural vitality, but called into being as it were out of nothing by the might of His creative love, "born not of the will of the flesh nor of the will of man, but of God."

We are here speaking of something so simple that the simplest Christian understands it and yet so fundamental that it raises almost every issue in theology. In particular what has here been spoken of as though it were the experience of an individual at a point in time is, of course, something much more than this. The life in Christ rests upon God's justifying act, but is a lifelong process of growth in holiness. Yet there is no simple chronological relation between these two things. Again the individual and solitary element in the life in Christ cannot without falsehood be separated from its beginning and its end in fellowship. Something will be said on these two issues later. But I must beg forbearance if for the moment I leave this over-simplified picture of the soul before the Cross of Christ in order to bring out the meaning of the Apostle's charge of "carnality" in the Corinthian Church.

That event of death and rebirth is the beginning of, and the condition of, the life in Christ and in the Holy Spirit. The breaking down of the fortifications that we erect against God is the condition of His entering into that lordship of our souls through the Holy Spirit which is the life in Christ. The soul that stands believing before the Cross of Christ is open to the Spirit of God. Here the fears and pride and egotism that divide me from my neighbour are done away and I am set free from myself to be at the service of my neighbour. Here, therefore, there is born a new life in fellowship; each is the servant of all for Christ's sake, and all share in common those new gifts of creative energy which flow through the soul that has been laid open to its Creator. This common life of sharing in the creative power and love of God is the life in the Spirit. It is a sharing in the life of the Blessed Trinity itself. It is the receiving of a citizenship in heaven, of a translation into the kingdom of the Son of God's love. It is a sharing in the life of the Body of Christ, visibly present in the common life of the Church on earth, invisibly sustained by a life hid with Christ in God (Col. iii. 3); a life lived in the flesh yet lived by the faith which is in the Son of God who loved me and gave Himself up for me (Gal. ii. 20).

"In the flesh, yet by faith." That is the crux of the problem of the Church. Christ is even now our life, yet we still await and long for the day when He shall be manifested, that we also may be manifested with Him in glory (Col. iii. 4). In the meantime we still have to be warned to stand fast against evil and fight the good fight of faith. Sin still works in the Church. The very greatness and glory of the Christian's inheritance tempts him once again to seek sufficiency in himself. The gifts of the Holy Spirit are turned into matter for boasting. Christians begin to speak of "my gifts" and "your gifts." Instead of rejoicing in one another's gifts Christians begin to make the gifts subjects for envying and rivalry. The old story repeats itself on a new level. Individual egotisms merge themselves into group egotisms. "I am of Paul," says one, "I of Apollos," says another, each seeking to buttress his own sense of weakness by identifying himself with a larger group. The Church ceases to be simply humanity re-made in Christ and becomes a series of human societies each standing for some point of view, some type of practice, some tradition of piety. The good gifts that each "Church" has received become grounds for glorying. Each "Church" lives largely by the things in which it is distinct from others, and is therefore quite incapable of taking seriously the idea that the Church exists to draw *all men* into one. From being the centre in which all the strife of sinful men finds its reconciliation the Church becomes itself a centre of human strife and faction.

The moment the Church ceases to put "the word of the Cross" in the centre of its life and begins to rely upon some possession of its own, it becomes a carnal association. Its life becomes part of the complex interplay of forces which make up the history of unredeemed humanity. Life in the Spirit is life in faith—"the faith which is in the Son of God who loved me and gave Himself up for me." It is life built on this confidence alone, that Christ died for our sins and rose again. It has no ground of glorying save in the Cross of Jesus Christ. In so far as the Church permits any other ground of confidence to displace this, whether it be confidence in a great leader, in a great preacher, in some tradition of spirituality, of learning, or of order, it becomes simply a human association, not spiritual but carnal, not the nucleus of regenerate humanity, but an ordinary human society. There is a life hid with Christ in God which is the secret of the Church's existence. The Church lives by virtue of that creative act of God which I have tried to describe partially in terms of individual experience. That which gives life to the Church is the power that raised Christ from the dead and that perpetually raises to new life the soul that dies with Christ. Apart from that death and rebirth perpetually operative in its members, there is no Church. The Church lives by the Word of the Cross made powerful by the Holy Spirit in the soul that receives and believes.

This brief review of St. Paul's use of the word "carnal" in regard to the Corinthian Church should remind us how far removed is his use of the phrases "spiritual" and "carnal," from the current popular use of the words "spiritual" and "material." Our use of these words is heavily infected by the idea—totally foreign to the Bible—that the spiritual is in itself good and the material in itself bad. This idea often consciously or unconsciously reinforces in popular discussion a tendency to regard the visible institutional unity of the Church as a matter of secondary importance. The Biblical doctrine of the creation of the world by God is entirely incompatible with such a view of the material world, and in the New Testament it is the spiritual sins of pride and hypocrisy rather than the so-called "sins of the flesh" which are regarded as the most deadly manifestations of man's rebellion against God. "The Flesh" in the New Testament normally means simply humanity, or human nature, and especially human nature in its state of separation from God. When St. Paul calls the Corinthians carnal his meaning is that they have fallen away from dependence solely on God and His grace and have begun to depend on possessions of their own, upon human leaders and the particular spiritual gifts which each has. Dependence upon the one Holy Spirit would have produced the visible unity of the one Body. Their divisions are the outward sign of their carnality, of the fact that they have fallen back on man. "After the flesh" and "after the Spirit" are contraries for St. Paul, but the Spirit and the

Body are correlates. "In one Spirit were we all baptized into one body," he says, and when he urges the Ephesians to guard the unity which they have in the Spirit (Eph. iv. 3) he is not (as the following verse so clearly shows) speaking of a spiritual unity which is distinct from a bodily unity, but precisely of their unity in one visible fellowship which is the gift to them of the one Spirit.

The common use of the phrase "spiritual unity" to refer to something which is understood to be preferable to corporeal unity, something indeed which makes corporeal unity unnecessary, is totally irreconcilable with the teaching of the New Testament. Indeed it is a phrase to which it is often very difficult to give any serious meaning at all. The only purely spiritual thing in our experience is an intention: the moment we begin to put our intentions into effect, they become mixed up inextricably with the world of things, acts, organizations and the like. And, in particular, that holiest of intentions which we call love, the intention to seek in all things the highest good of the beloved, leads into a whole world of acts of service and co-operation, and into all kinds of associations. In the centre of human life God has set the love of man and woman, parents and children, and has bound it up inextricably with the physical and economic facts of family life. And when men and women take the vows of marriage, and bind themselves, for better, for worse, to live together in one home and to support one another all the days of their life, we do not think that this is a declension from the highest kind of love because it ceases to be purely spiritual and binds itself to a certain kind of association. On the contrary, we recognize in such a taking of vows the true fulfilment of love—love ceasing to be a fluctuating emotion and revealing itself as a dedication of the whole personality. It is the same with other kinds of human association: just in proportion as men are fully determined to seek one another's good, they will pledge themselves up to the hilt to one another in vows that embrace not merely casual co-operation but permanent association in obedience to the common purpose. Such visible outward organizational unity is the normal and proper expression of love—as we know perfectly well in our experience of all kinds of associations. Where love is lacking, the organization becomes a mere brittle skeleton that breaks at the first strain. But where love is real and deep and steady, organization is the strong, living, bony system that gives the body power to act with determination and unity. A purely spiritual unity would be a unity of mere intention which had failed to lead on to action. This failure may be due to valid causes, or it may merely show that the intention is not really strong and serious enough for the task. But where people are *content* with a merely spiritual unity, not seeking to express their unity by actual deeds and vows of association, then we must bluntly say that they delude themselves. An intention which does not seek expression in deeds is no intention at all.

In First Corinthians St. Paul, after dealing with the various issues which called for action, returns to deal in great fulness with the whole question of the relation between the Spirit and the Body (chaps. xii-xiv). He begins with the criterion by which what claims to be of the Spirit is to be tested—the confession of the Lordship of Christ. There are many so-called spiritual powers. There is but one Holy Spirit of God. He who is possessed by the Holy Spirit will acknowledge Jesus and none other as Lord. We know something of the kind of pagan spirituality which is but a form of the hydra-headed egotism of unregenerate man and which speaks all the languages of Babel. The presence of the Holy Spirit of God will be attested by the confession that Jesus is Lord (xii. 1-3).

This one Spirit is the Giver of diverse gifts (xii. 4-11). They are diverse in order that each may be used for the service of all. They are not to be made the ground of boasting, but the ground of a sense of responsibility to use them for the whole Body. The one Body is thus the counterpart of the one Spirit. Where the differences in spiritual endowment are made the ground of separation the Body is disrupted and the gift itself becomes profitless (xii. 12-31). For this reason the greatest of all the gifts of the Spirit is love —that which builds up the Body, that which seeks not its own but rejoices equally in the gifts of others (chap. xiii). And all this bears directly on the ordinary day-to-day difficulties which are vexing the Church in Corinth. It does not refer to some ideal or abstract entity, but to the very particular and, indeed, troublesome group of brothers in Corinth, and it dictates the sort of arrangements which have to be made for the ordering of their worship (chap. xiv). " *Ye* are the body of Christ."

We may sum up the teaching which we have reviewed in three sentences: The unity of the Church is of its essence. That unity is a spiritual unity. It is also a corporeal unity.

THE REUNION OF THE CHURCH

1. *The Unity of the Church is of its Essence*: To be in the Church is to be in Christ, and as there is but one Lord Jesus Christ so there can be only one Church. Christ cannot be divided. Christ was lifted up to draw all men to Himself. We cannot draw near to Him except as we draw near to all others whom He draws. The things which divide us from one another and make it impossible for us to live as members of one family are precisely the marks of the old man, the rebel against God who is to be crucified with Christ. In the new man, reborn and raised up with Him, there can be no place for such divisions. The Church is the one temple of the one Holy Spirit. Factions and divisions are the signs of a relapse into carnality, into life after the flesh.

2. *The Unity of the Church is a Spiritual Unity*: It is " a unity in Christ and in the Father through the Holy Spirit, and is therefore fundamentally a reality of the spiritual realm."[1] It is that common sharing in a life of personal communion and trust, which is the inner life of the Blessed Trinity, and into which we are permitted to enter through that sharing in the Holy Spirit given to us through faith in Christ. Our unity with one another in Christ does not consist in our agreement regarding certain doctrines, nor in our sharing in common practices of worship, nor in our common assent to certain moral principles, nor even in our common loyalty to Christ as leader—vital though these are to our life in Him. It consists in our sharing in a life of mutual love and trust which is made possible by our rebirth in Christ. We receive this rebirth through faith in Christ and in His atoning death. When we believe that He died and rose again for us, and accept for ourselves the standing-ground before God which He has given, we are at the same time committed to accepting for His sake those who share with us this common standing-ground. We cannot accept Christ's gift of redemption at the Cross and at the same time retain those barriers which we erect against our brothers. We cannot receive His pardon and refuse it to the man who stands there beside us. The breaking of the shell of pride that opens our hearts to God opens them equally to our neighbours.

This means that there is an indestructible element of solitariness at the heart of the Christian life of fellowship. It is in the personal decision of faith that we accept Christ's gift of redemption. No one can make that decision for us; it is our own. And the out-

---

[1] *Scheme of Church Union in South India*. Basis of Union, I, 1.

going act of self-giving and trust towards our brother which is the necessary corollary of this is likewise a personal act. The basis of fellowship is trust, and trust is possible only between those who can accept personal responsibility. The enemy of fellowship is faction, and faction is what happens when we seek to evade the responsibilities involved in personal encounter by sheltering in the anonymity of the group. It is what happens when we evade the direct encounter of " I " and " Thou," and seek solace in the place where we can talk undisturbed about " Us " and " Them." The unity of the Church is a unity in love, and love means the accepting of responsibility for one another. The solitude of the soul before God is not its opposite but its necessary counterpart, for we only learn to love one another at that place where we learn, in the solitude of penitence, how much Christ has loved us. The Church's unity exists not in that place where a group of people agree that " we " hold such and such views as opposed to " them " who hold others; it exists where men bring their whole common life consciously and steadily into the presence of Christ, and under the judgment and mercy of the word of the Cross, and then as reborn men learn to deal with one another in love, forgiving one another as Christ forgave them, facing without evasion the tensions of differing views and rival interests, content to live for the task of building one another up in love.

3. *The Unity of the Church is a Corporeal Unity*: As has already been said, the words spirit and body are—in the New Testament—not contraries but correlates. Nothing could more completely reverse the meaning of the New Testament insistence on the spiritual nature of the Church's unity than to say that it meant that visible, corporeal unity was of secondary importance. It is a unity in love, and love deals with the beloved as a person and not simply as a " soul." Perhaps the Church has never taken the Biblical doctrine of creation with sufficient seriousness to enable it to resist the pagan idea of " the spiritual " as that which is to be set over against " the material." Certainly in an Indian setting the Church has an even harder task than in the West to assert the true nature of spirituality, to insist, for instance, that to visit the sick or keep honest accounts is as much a work of the Holy Spirit as to speak with tongues. At any rate, nothing could be clearer than the teaching of St. Paul on this point. It is that which builds up the visible fellowship of the Church which is to

be adjudged the greatest gift of the Spirit. The most sublime theological arguments are used to reinforce the simplest and most homely lessons about living together as one brotherhood. Even perfectly sound convictions regarding such matters as the eating of meat sacrificed to idols are not to be so used as to break fellowship with those who do not share them, for it is the responsibility of each for all which is the controlling principle. And when the exuberant "spirituality" of the Corinthian Church blossoms into an imposing series of "schools of thought," Paul bluntly tells them, "Ye are yet carnal." There is one Spirit, and it follows that there is one Body. If the Body is divided it is because Christians are not spiritual but carnal, not walking after the Spirit, but after the flesh.

If this is the teaching of the New Testament what are we to say of our present divisions? We are precluded by the plain teaching of Scripture from taking comfort in the existence of a "spiritual unity" underlying our visible separations. These visible separations are the evidence of the precise opposite of unity in the Spirit. They are the proof of our carnality. Are we to fall back, then, on the other possible explanation? Are we to say that, since there is one Body, if the Church still exists, that one Body must be recognizably present in the world to-day? Shall we reconsider the provisional conclusions of our study of the circumcision issue, and ask whether we may not recognize the one Body now in the twentieth century by its outward marks, by its continuity as a visible institution, from the time of the Apostles? If we can certainly identify the one Body, may we not then be sure that, whatever be His other operations, the one Spirit is assuredly present here, and that we may thus find our way back to unity in Him by accepting incorporation into the one Church which is here present, one among the medley of "Churches"? To a brief consideration of this possibility we now turn.

CHAPTER FIVE

THE EXTENSION OF THE INCARNATION?

THE Church is portrayed in the New Testament as a spiritual and corporeal unity. It is both one in the sense that it is not divided, and one in the sense that it is unique. There is but one Christ and there is therefore but one Church. Outward division of the Church can only mean that Christ is divided, which is absurd. As there is one Lord Jesus Christ, made flesh in order that we might see and hear and touch, that having seen Him we might see the Father, so there is one Church, the temple of the Spirit, whereto all men may come and find Him.

No one can deny, I think, that this is the teaching of St. Paul. Does it enable us to answer the question, How can I know to-day which among "the churches" is the Church, and which not? Let us follow what seems to be one obvious line of reasoning from the facts just summarized. The Church is a visible institution. One is either a member of it, or not, and membership is attested by visible and universally recognizable signs. There may be many who are members of the Church but who are inwardly resisting the work of the Holy Spirit, and there may be many outside the Church in whom the Holy Spirit is at work in the sovereign freedom of grace. This does not affect the point. The Church, i.e., the visible institution, is the temple of the Holy Spirit. It is the means which Christ has appointed to draw all men to Himself. If a body of people leaves this institution and founds another distinct and separate institution, calling itself a Church, that is not a Church. There is only one Church, as Christ is one, and this institution founded by Christ and His Apostles is the Church. Though the second "church" should exist for a thousand years, maintaining its identity across the centuries by the regular and orderly appointment of authorized officers, that does not make it the Church. And though it should manifest every token of the gracious activity of the Holy Spirit in the lives of its members (for God is not bound to His sacraments), and though it should perform correctly all the rites and teach correctly all the doctrines of the Church, that does not make it the Church. There is only one Church, and though a hundred other bodies should call themselves Churches, they are not Churches. The Church is a visible society founded by Christ and His apostles. Where their accredited and authorized successors are, there and there alone is the Church.

It is easier to reject this reasoning than to answer it, if one is to remain faithful to the evidence of the New Testament. There corporeal and spiritual unity are indissolubly linked, and corporeal unity necessarily carries with it historically continuous succession. Continuous succession is but the effect of corporeal unity extended over time. A corporation does not retain its identity over many centuries by retaining identical customs, habits, functions, etc. These may all change. It retains it through the uninterrupted transmission of authority. Its officers in this century may be called by different names and do different things from those of previous centuries. This does not destroy its identity. What is essential is that these officers should have been lawfully appointed by those who authoritatively represented the corporation. Where the body continues with no break in its unity, its officers will always be those who have received this authoritative appointment. Continuous succession in this sense is but unity expressed in the dimension of time. Where there has been at some point a break in unity then officers will have been appointed without the authority of the whole body. The breach in succession is the outward mark of a breach in unity.[1] From this point of view, therefore, the Church only retains its identity through this continuous transmission of office. The one Church of which the New Testament speaks is that body which has in this sense retained its identity from the time of the apostles, and which has at no time departed from the visible standard of unity accepted by the whole Church. Of this Church we have to say both *ubi Christus, ibi Ecclesia* and *ubi Petrus ibi Ecclesia*, " because the inward fellowship is realized by human means, an apostolic ministry which has in Peter its visible standard of unity."[2]

The argument here very crudely summarized is familiar in both its Anglican and its Roman forms. I venture to suggest that the Anglo-Catholic development of this line of thought is faced with logical difficulties (not to say incoherences) from which the Roman Catholic is free, and I shall therefore take a Roman Catholic

---

[1] See Burn-Murdoch: *Church, Continuity and Unity*, pp. 38-43.
[2] Congar: *Divided Christendom*, p. 88.

THE EXTENSION OF THE INCARNATION?

statement of it for purposes of examination. I refer to the chapter on "The Oneness of the Church" in Father Congar's book, *Divided Christendom*, which has the advantage of being written with the non-Roman ecumenical movement in view.

Fr. Congar's chapter is in three parts. The first, entitled "*Ecclesia de Trinitate,*" deals with the fundamental nature of the Church as the extension to creatures of the oneness of God, by the imparting to them of the very life of God Himself. The Holy Spirit is the Soul of the Church—not that He is the interior form of the Church as our soul is of our body, but that He is the cause of her immanent form. That immanent form is faith (understood rather as in Heb. xi. 6 than as in Gal. ii. 20) and charity. Faith enables us to see things as God sees them and so to love as God loves. The Church is the community of souls living the very life of the Trinity because the object of their lives is the same as that of the life of God Himself. There is a distinction, but also an indissoluble link, between the union of God with man in Christ (two natures in one person) and that in the Church (many persons in one life).

The second section, linking the first and the third, deals with "*Ecclesia in Christo.*" *Ecclesia de Trinitate* only becomes *Ecclesia ex hominibus* because God was made Man in Christ. We become sharers in the divine life only through Christ, and our contact with Him is "in the sacramental order." "It is because of baptism and the Eucharist that we are one Body, which is the Body of Christ."

The third and longest section deals therefore with the Church in its human mode. For the divine life can only be given to us here on earth in sensible forms and institutions, in conflict and in authoritative government. The Church on earth follows "the law of incarnation"; it is both human through and through and divine through and through. As a human society it has to have organization and "magisterium." Yet this same human institution *is* at the same time the Mystical Body of Christ. The two coincide. Thus the Church is to be regarded in every part of its life under two aspects. We have to predicate different things of it according as we look at it from its divine side or from its human side. Yet it is *one* thing. Of this the unity of body and soul is an analogy. The unity of Christ's person is a still better one: we have to avoid both monophysitism and Nestorianism in our doctrine of the

Church. But the analogy of the unity of body and soul is instructive, for (1) the soul is that by which the body lives, (2) the soul is perceptible only by means of the body, and (3) the body is the instrument of the soul. The meeting-place of the two planes of the Church's existence is in the sacraments. The whole life and teaching of the Church is, in a broad sense, sacramental. The mystical Christ and the institutional Church are "one flesh."

This true doctrine of the Church stands midway between two opposite errors, that of the Orthodox who so emphasize the heavenly aspect of the Church's existence that they underestimate the importance of the human and institutional aspect, and that of Protestants who believe that the divine life is not given but only promised, and who forget that "since John the Baptist God is Incarnate."

This chapter brings out with remarkable clarity and completeness the distinction between these two aspects of the Church's unity—its spiritual unity in and with the life of the Blessed Trinity, the love of God shed abroad in our hearts through the Holy Spirit, and its corporeal unity as a human institution. What we have here to examine is the teaching of the chapter regarding the relation of these two aspects to one another. It will be noted that this teaching is along three distinct lines:

- (a) that there is an analogy between the unity of the mystical body with the outward institution and the unity in Christ of the divine and human natures;
- (b) that there is an analogy between this unity and the unity of soul and body in human nature;
- (c) that "the meeting-place of the two planes and the two laws of which we have spoken is found in the sacraments." Here there is no mention of analogy. The whole life of the Church *is* sacramental.

Before we examine these three lines of thought separately it will be noticed that their combination in one coherent whole raises some difficulties. For instance, the unity of two natures in the Person of Christ is certainly not analogous to the unity of soul and body in man. Nor is the unity of body and soul in itself a sacramental unity. The three lines of thought seem rather to diverge than to converge. Our task, however, is to ask how much light each of them throws on the nature of the Church.

THE EXTENSION OF THE INCARNATION?

(a) *The Church as the Extension of the Incarnation*

Here one meets a preliminary difficulty in that the use of this " analogy " is not quite consistent. Where he first introduces it, Fr. Congar is dealing purely with the Church as the mystical body, and he points out both the connection and also the distinction between the union of God with man in the Person of Christ and the union of man with God in the Church (p. 58). Later, without any such qualification, he speaks of the unity of the two " aspects " of the Church in Christological terms. Here the unity referred to is not the unity of men with God, but the unity (in the sense of identity) of the mystical body and the visible society, i.e. the unity of the two " aspects " of the Church. Of this the union of natures in Christ is spoken of only as an analogy and an " archetype " (p. 80). In the concluding section, however, in his reference to Protestantism, he says that " since John the Baptist God is Incarnate," a phrase which seems to pass beyond analogy to a predication of the unity of two natures in the Church in the same manner as in Christ Jesus (p. 91). The same impression is given by the use of the phrase " the law of incarnation " to subsume the whole history of the People of God (p. 68f.). Fr. Congar is here, however, only stressing the truth that God deals with men where they are, within history, and the phrase " the law of incarnation " is perhaps intended only in an analogical sense. But one has to ask the question, How far, and in what sense, is the unity of divine and human in the Church analogous to the divine and human in Christ? In what sense, if at all, is the Church " the extension of the Incarnation "?

Let us for a moment try to focus the question even more sharply. We are not for the moment speaking of the unity of men with God in the Holy Spirit which is the constitutive fact of the Church. This is that unity of those who believe in Christ through the word of His apostles, for whom He prayed " that they all may be one; even as thou, Father, art in me and I in thee, that they also may be in us." We are speaking of the unity between two " aspects " in which the Church can be regarded: its aspect, namely, as such a spiritual unity with God as we have just referred to, and its aspect as a single, unique and undivided human society. We believe that Christ Jesus was in such wise both Man and God (two natures in one person), that among all the men who lived in Nazareth in a certain year this man was God Incarnate, and the rest were not.

THE REUNION OF THE CHURCH

Do we believe that among all the existing societies calling themselves "The Church," one is God Incarnate, and the others are not? That is but to put sharply what seems to be involved in the phrase "Since John the Baptist God is Incarnate."

In this full and precise sense, the idea that the Church is the extension of the Incarnation is quite irreconcilable with the New Testament evidence. What is absolutely clear from this evidence is that Christ's presence with His Church since Pentecost is in a different manner from His presence on earth "in the days of His flesh." There is absolutely nothing to support the idea that "the days of His flesh" continue through His death, resurrection and ascension and through the day of Pentecost into the present life of the Church. There is, on the contrary, everything to refute it. The same evangelist who alone uses the phrase "the word became flesh" is he who reports the Lord as saying to those who murmured at His references to "eating my flesh"—"What then if ye should behold the Son of Man ascending where He was before? It is the Spirit that quickeneth; the flesh profiteth nothing"; to the disciples at the Last Supper, "It is expedient for you that I go away: for if I go not away, the Comforter will not come unto you; but if I go, I will send him unto you"; to Mary, anxious—it would seem—to have Him still in the flesh, "Touch me not; for I am not yet ascended to the Father." It is not necessary to multiply reminders of the fact that the whole stress of the New Testament ecclesiology is upon the crucified, risen and ascended Lord; that it is most clearly taught that the gift to the Church of the Holy Spirit is given precisely because Christ has ascended to the right hand of the Father; that the mode of Christ's presence with His disciples after Pentecost is decisively different from the mode of His presence in the days of which it was said that "the Spirit was not yet given; because Jesus was not yet glorified." While, as I have repeatedly urged, the whole Bible is the story of the People of God, of God dealing with men on the plane of history through a particular people and a particular society, yet it is a confusion of terms to subsume this under "the law of incarnation," for the Incarnation was an event, the crucial event, *within* this whole history. It had a beginning and an end. It was something done "once" (1 Peter iii. 18; Heb. ix. 26-8), in the sense of "once and for all."

It is thus inevitable that when the idea of the Church as the

THE EXTENSION OF THE INCARNATION?

extension of the Incarnation is taken seriously, the proclamation of these events upon which the New Testament lays all its stress (the death, resurrection and ascension of our Lord) drops into the background. I remember being present at a meeting at which a Protestant and a Roman Catholic read papers on the Christian doctrine of forgiveness. The Protestant paper dealt mainly with the meaning of the Atonement. The Roman Catholic, in a forty-minute paper, did not once mention the death of Christ. Beginning from the word of Christ to Peter he explained that the authority to forgive sins which had then been conferred had been transmitted in uninterrupted succession through the centuries and was now possessed by the Church to be dispensed to men. The Church thus meets men in this respect not as Christ's representative, but as Christ, possessing *in itself* without reference[1] to any higher source, the power to forgive sins. The Church replaces Christ, and it becomes no longer necessary to refer to the events by which the Church was initially called into being. The idea of "the Word" practically disappears. There is still teaching (*didache*) as to what the Church believes and does. But there is no preaching (*kerygma*) of that Word by which the Church, not only initially but always, lives. If the Church is in itself, as an institution, the incarnation of God, then there is no need for it to point beyond itself to Christ—as true preaching must do. But if it be once admitted that the Church must look beyond itself to Him, and especially must look to His Cross and Resurrection, must not only transmit His authority but also submit afresh in every age to His authority; if it be admitted that its sacraments are sacraments *of the Gospel,* always to be administered with the Word that points men back to their source, then it cannot be agreed that the Church is an extension of the Incarnation. The Church is the Body called into being by the work of the Holy Spirit, that Spirit who could only be given when Jesus was glorified, and who is given to those who hear and believe the Gospel. And the Gospel is, basically, this: "That Christ died for our sins according to the Scriptures; and that he was buried; and that he hath been raised on the third day according to the Scriptures" (1 Cor. xv. 3, 4). Of this Gospel the Apostles are heralds because they are witnesses. The Church is related to the Gospel not merely

---

[1] That is, without *explicit* reference. I do not forget that Roman Catholic theologians teach that Christ is the *Minister Principalis* of the sacraments.

by the fact that its historical origins are to be found in these facts. The Church now and always lives by the Gospel.

I have already tried to suggest what is meant by the statement that the Church lives by the Gospel. We shall have to consider further the nature of this faith in the Gospel by which the Church is constituted. But at least this is clear and relevant at this point, that the Church as a society within history is made up of a multitude of human and sinful wills, and that the fact of incorporation in the Church does not here—*in via*—remove this sinful element. Even the man in Christ is a sinner. That fact alone makes the analogy of the Incarnation an extremely misleading one. What is characteristic of the Church as a human society is not merely that it is visible and tangible as Christ was in His flesh, but that it is sinful, which He was not. Fr. Congar, of course, recognizes this fact and explains that because the Church on earth is "imperfect" she needs to be guided towards her proper end, and has to have rulers. But rulers are also "imperfect," and while government can restrain some forms of sin it can also mightily increase and multiply sin in other forms. Few forms of power can corrupt men so radically as spiritual and ecclesiastical power. Not only in Christians as individuals but also in the Church as an institution there are to be found the marks of man's sinful will, not least in the fact that we are more conscious of the truth of this statement as it applies to other Churches than as it applies to our own. The relation between the human and the divine in the Church is thus not clarified but profoundly obscured by calling the Church the extension of the Incarnation.

The force of this criticism is often missed because the phrases "the law of incarnation," and "the incarnational principle," are used in a loose way which does not rest upon a clear understanding of the nature of the Incarnation of the Son of God. They are used in a way which suggests that by the Incarnation a new relationship was set up between spirit and matter, and that consequently the outward and visible structure and activity of the Church bears a different kind of relation to the corresponding inward and spiritual realities from the kind of relation between outward and inward which prevails elsewhere. But this is not the case. The Incarnation was not an event in which spirit entered into matter. To treat it so is to forsake the whole Biblical doctrine that man in his totality as an "ensouled body" is the creation of God; that

THE EXTENSION OF THE INCARNATION?

"matter" and "spirit" are equally His creation and are indissolubly bound together by that fact. It was not that spirit entered into matter, but that the Creator entered into humanity, that the Word became flesh, that God lived a human life and died a human death. And the reality of that Incarnation, the proof of the fulness of His humanity, is shown in the fact that in the days of His flesh He had to face just that spiritual warfare by which alone inwardly perceived truth can be embodied in visible, historical act. He was tempted in all points like as we are, yet without sin.

The doctrine of the Incarnation is sometimes stated in such a way that it would seem as though even had our Lord died at birth or in infancy the essential event by which man's relationship to God is changed would have been accomplished, as though the fact of His birth in human flesh were by itself the atoning fact. Upon such a belief as this it is easy to build a doctrine of the Church as, in itself, the extension of the Incarnation. But we know that when St. John wrote "The Word became flesh and dwelt among us (and we beheld his glory, glory as of the only begotten from the Father) full of grace and truth," he was thinking not only of the birth of Jesus, but of His whole human life and death. What the Gospels record is the fully human life of the sinless Son of God, and it was a human life in this also, that He accepted and became subject to the conditions of our human existence at the point of intersection of the spiritual and the material, as body-soul unities. The words "spiritual" and "material" are words which hardly two people use in the same sense, and it is impossible to speak here other than loosely unless one were to embark upon a long definition of terms. Perhaps the simplest thing to say is that Jesus dealt with men as persons, seeking all the time their faith, trust and love. What He did was not to accomplish a rearrangement between two elements in the created world—the material and the spiritual. It was to accomplish on behalf of all men an atonement with God their Creator which was to be appropriated by faith. The Church is the body of those who believe in and live by that atonement. The basis of its unity is a personal trust and love which are the work of the Holy Spirit in hearts made open to His presence by the Gospel of Christ's redeeming death. It belongs to the nature of the Church that here—in human history—this unity must express itself in a visible institutional form. But because sin also works even in those who believe, the consequences of sin will be apparent not only in individual lives but, perhaps even more impressively, in the life of the institution. Its corporate acts may be marked by pride, greed and sloth. Because this is so it is an obscuring of the truth to call the Church the extension of the Incarnation. The Church, like Jesus in His flesh, is visible. She is, and ought to be, institutional. But unlike Jesus she is, and ought not to be, sinful. But because the Church is an institution, historic continuity belongs to her proper nature as the visible expression of unity in love. Because she is sinful it is wrong to define the Church solely in terms of historic continuity apart from reference to that Gospel by faith in which the Church at all times lives. When once reference is made to that Gospel another principle of identification has been introduced besides that of historic continuity. The conflict between these two is the essence of our problem. The idea of "law of incarnation," so far from settling the dispute, is itself an entirely misleading explanation of the nature of the Church's existence.

(b) The Body and the Soul of the Church

The very fact that we have constantly spoken of the spiritual and corporeal unity of the Church is a reminder of the fact that the human body and soul provide a natural analogy for the two aspects of the Church's existence which we are trying to describe. Nevertheless the analogy is only a very partial one, and is liable to a confusing ambiguity in use. In the early part of the chapter under review Fr. Congar is careful to say that Christ is not the soul of the Church in the sense that our souls are the souls of our bodies. But in fact his later elaboration of the analogy does not succeed in keeping the distinction clear. We have again to remind ourselves of the distinction to be drawn between two different distinctions which are apt to be confused with one another. There is the distinction between the holy and righteous will of God, and the wills of souls united to Christ by faith and through His atonement made sharers in the communion of the Holy Spirit, yet still also sinful and sinning. There is, on the other hand, the distinction between the spiritual communion of souls thus united with Christ, and the corporate unification of Christians by baptism in the historical and visible institution of the Church. There is, in other words, the distinction between the Church as God wills it to be and the Church as it is—a distinction caused by sin; and the distinction between the Church viewed as a unity in the Spirit constituted by the union of its members with Christ through faith, and the Church viewed as a corporeal unity constituted by the common acceptance of an institutional order and authority—a distinction which would remain even if we could imagine human life without sin. It is important to distinguish these two distinctions just because we tend to confuse corporeality with sin. Just as the seat of sin does not lie in the human body as distinct from the soul, so it does not lie in the institutional life of the Church as distinct from its spiritual life.

The Church as a visible institution is not related to Christ as the human body is to the soul. Here we are in agreement with Fr. Congar. Christ is described as the Head of the Body, not as its soul. St. Paul's metaphor of the Church as the Body of Christ has to be held in its proper relation to the other metaphors used to describe the relation between Christ and His Church. Nevertheless the analogy of body and soul is, as Fr. Congar says, instructive. It is through the visible works and words of the Church that Christ is manifested to the world, that He meets with men and does His will in them. In this sense the relation between the Church's existence as a spiritual unity in Christ and its existence as a visible society is analogous to the relation between soul and body. If we could conceive a situation in which the Church consisted entirely of persons wholly surrendered to Christ and wholly delivered from sin, the analogy would be complete. The Church would be both an organism and an organization perfectly expressing the will of Christ. It would be quite unnecessary indeed for the Church to preach. It would itself be, by its own life, the adequate revelation and instrument of God's redeeming love. In that case the Church would be one undivided and continuous institution, of which one could say *ubi ecclesia ibi Christus*. But these are not the terms on which the Church lives. Sin creates a situation in which the Church as an institution is filled with spirits which are not the Spirit of God, by the collective and separate prides and egotisms of men. There is within the life of the Church conflict between the will of God and the unruly wills and affections of sinful men. It would be absurdly naïve to suggest that in this conflict the *magisterium* of the Church as embodied in its hierarchy of ministers or courts is simply the assertion of God's will. It is often the most flagrant violation of it. The Church has to listen to the Gospel and believe the Gospel if it is to be in truth the Church. It cannot, in other words, treat the fact of its own continuous institutional existence as the test of its title to be the Church. If it were not for the fact of sin, it could do so. But because sin is still present in the Church there is always the possibility that the continuous institutional Church may in fact be fallen away from grace. The man justified before God is the man who can only say "God be merciful to me, a sinner." The Church, likewise, exists and is constituted by just such a relation of continual dependence upon God, the sinner upon the saviour. It lives by dying with Christ and being raised again. When it seeks to find the criterion of its status as a Church in the fact of its continuous institutional existence it has abandoned the one standing-ground that sinners have before God.

Christ's redeeming will is made known and done through the Church. And in so far as it is done the Church remains one united and continuing institution. This is the proper corporeal form of a spiritual unity. But in so far as God's will is not done the Church becomes an institution, or series of institutions, embodying another spirit. When that has happened, we cannot treat institutional continuity as the sole determining mark of the Church. To do so would be analogous to the treating of men not as persons but purely as units in the complex interplay of physical events. We know no man except through his body, yet no man can be fully a person who is not willing when the time and need come to face the end of his physical existence. Man is a body-soul, but to treat his physical nature as the constitutive fact of his existence is to do him deep wrong. So the Church also is in its proper nature a spiritual and corporeal unity. The fact that it is visibly divided is the evidence that it is also spiritually divided. The fact that this is so is part of the mystery of sin. To forget that fact and claim that where corporeal unity and continuity have been maintained there alone is the Church is to do the same deep wrong to the Church. For to treat institutional continuity as the constitutive fact of the Church's existence is to rob it of that life of continual dependence upon the living Christ by which alone it really lives.

(c) *The Church as a Sacrament*

Fr. Congar writes: "Incorporation in Christ is begun and effected—and this is all-important—by contact with Christ in the sacramental order." Consequently it follows that "On its earthly side the Church is, so to say, a vast sacrament in which everything is a sign and a means of an inward unity and grace." The thought has almost passed beyond analogy but for the saving clause "so to say." The point is that the essential part which the sacraments play in our incorporation in Christ provides the clue to the explanation of the relation of the Church's inward life of faith and charity to its outward life as an institution.

I do not propose here to embark on a discussion of sacraments in general, nor of the relation to each other of the two words which Fr. Congar uses—"sign" and "means." My purpose is simply to ask: What is involved in using the idea that the Church is itself a sacrament to explain and justify a Church polity which can say *ubi Petrus ibi ecclesia* because it treats institutional continuity as the essential mark of the Church? What is in effect claimed is that among the various institutions called Churches one has maintained institutional continuity and another has not; and that consequently upon the basis of this fact alone, without considering the character of the doctrine and life of the two bodies, one must pronounce the former to be the Church and the latter not. Now this claim can only find support in the statement that the Church as a whole is a sacrament if these two propositions at least be true:

(1) that the relation between outward and inward in the sacraments is analogous to the relation between the institutional unity of the Church and the spiritual communion of Christians with the Lord;
(2) that the Church is constituted by the fact that its members have received baptism simply considered as an objectively recognizable event and without considering its inward meaning. For the moment the inward meaning is considered alongside the outward event as of an equal importance with it, it ceases to be possible to use the analogy of the sacraments as support for the claim that institutional continuity is *by itself* determinative of a body's claim to be the Church.

On the first proposition I do not propose to say anything except that the points already discussed regarding the significance of sin as a factor operating within the souls of the members of the Church, and therefore expressing itself in the corporate life of the

Church, seem to me very gravely to weaken the force of the analogy between the sacraments and the Church.

As for the second proposition, it seems to me that the New Testament provides no warrant at all for speaking of the sacraments *alone and in isolation from the Word*, as Fr. Congar does, and must do, as the means of incorporation in Christ. What is surely the truth is that incorporation in Christ is in the personal order, wherein the Word heard and believed and the sacrament received in that faith are the means of incorporation. In fact, of course, no Church except in a few periods of extreme degeneracy so separates the sacraments from the Word as to make them simply *per se*, as external events, the means of incorporation in Christ. The sacraments are always in association with the Word. But the point is that in order to use the sacramental analogy to support the doctrine of the Church which he is expounding Fr. Congar is obliged to make this separation and to say that our incorporation in Christ is begun and effected by contact in the sacramental order.

One can only say that this is not the teaching of the New Testament. It is not necessary to reproduce the evidence already surveyed. In Acts baptism is always given to those who believe and to their households. It follows the hearing which leads to faith; it is not by itself, apart from the Word, the means by which contact with Christ is " begun." The Pauline epistles assume baptism but lay no stress on it. Paul even says that he received his apostleship not to baptize but to preach—doubtless a characteristically Hebraic way of saying that preaching was a more fundamental part of his apostolic ministry than baptizing. This certainly accords with the whole tenor of his epistles, even including the Pastorals where no instructions are given regarding administration of the sacraments. In all his references to baptism his anxiety is that Christians should know what it means, and he never raises questions regarding the validity of any particular administration. I am aware of the fact that it is very easy to interpret this evidence wrongly, and to conclude that St. Paul valued the sacraments lightly. On the contrary, the very absence of controversy regarding them, the nature of St. Paul's references to them, and all the evidence of the later periods, show that the two sacraments were from the beginning firmly and inseparably embedded in the life of the Church. It is simply taken for granted that Christians are baptized into one body and that they share in the one breaking of

THE EXTENSION OF THE INCARNATION?

bread. But what we cannot do unless we are to reject the teaching of St. Paul is to take the sacraments by themselves and say that *by these* the Church is constituted; to say, as Fr. Congar says, but as St. Paul never says, "*because* we have been baptized into Christ we are one Body of Christ."[1] What the apostle says is "in one Spirit were we all baptized into one body" and the Spirit is given to those who believe. "'He that believeth in me,'" said the Lord, "'out of his belly shall flow rivers of living water.' But this spake He of the Spirit which they that believed on Him were to receive." "Belief comes of hearing and hearing by the word of Christ." These words and hundreds like them cannot be excised from the New Testament, as they must be if we are to say simply that our contact with Christ is effected by the sacraments. Our partaking in the Eucharist does not make us one Body in a manner that can by-pass altogether that inner apprehension of the Word by faith, in which we thus judge that One died for all, therefore all died; and that He died for all that they which live should no longer live unto themselves but unto Him who for their sakes died and rose again. That constraining love of Christ meets us in the order of personal meeting, and of this both word and sacrament are the media. We cannot without violating the Church's real nature make the sacramental order alone decisive and say that by this the Church is constituted.

It is of course true that the perspective of the New Testament, where adult baptism is the norm, is necessarily somewhat different from that of a Church in which baptism is normally given in infancy followed many years later by the rite which precedes admission to full communicant membership in the Church. The fact that the vast majority of Christians were made members incorporate in the Body of Christ at a time long before the awakening of their own conscious faith is a reminder of the fact that God's grace is the sole cause of the Church's existence and that our faith is only the response to that grace. Yet even in infant baptism the Church requires a profession of faith in the parents or sponsors, and infant baptism requires to be completed by an act of reception into full membership by profession of faith and confirmation (or its equivalent). For the purpose of the present argument the point is that the nature of infant baptism is to be explained in terms of the life of the Church to which it is

[1] p. 63, italics in original.

the entry, not the nature of the Church's life in terms of infant baptism.[1]

The sacraments belong to the very essence of the Church. Unity in the Spirit and unity in the Body are not separable—except through sin. It belongs to the nature of the Church that it exists in a visible and institutional form. Christ has given to it the two sacraments which He instituted to be both signs and means of His grace towards sinners. These are at the heart of its existence as a visible institution. The one Bread is the centre of the Church's visible unity—a centre given to it by Christ Himself. Baptism is the visible mark of incorporation in the life of the crucified and ascended Saviour. These things are taken for granted in the New Testament just as the unity of the one Body and the one Spirit is taken for granted. But, as we have seen, sin in the Church destroys that relation of perfect correspondence and congruity which ought to exist between the unity of the one Spirit and the unity of the visible Body. The Body becomes divided and has to be called not spiritual but carnal. In the conditions created by sin it is not possible to use the analogy of the sacraments to substantiate the claim that where visible institutional continuity has been preserved, there and there alone is the Church. The sacraments belong, along with the Word, to the total order of personal meeting in which Christ makes us one with Himself in love and trust. It is in terms of that order that we have to understand the nature of the Church's unity.

(d) *The Two Dimensions of the Church's Existence*

We are agreed that the Church is both a visible corporeal institution having a historical existence upon earth alongside of other human societies, and also a unity of created souls with the Father and the Son in the Holy Spirit, a spiritual communion. We are examining a view of the Church which so relates these two aspects of its existence that we can say "*Ubi Petrus ibi Ecclesia*," where the visible institutional continuity can be seen, there alone is the Church. We have examined three analogies by which this

---

[1] Cf. Dix, *The Theology of Confirmation in Relation to Baptism*, p. 31: "The Church can very well afford infant baptism, even as the practice in the vast majority of cases (which it never was in pre-Nicene times) *provided that it is never allowed to be thought of as normal*, that it is regarded always as an abnormality, wholly incomplete by itself and absolutely needing completion by the gift of the Spirit and the conscious response of faith for the full living of the Christian ' eternal ' life in time." (Italics original.)

THE EXTENSION OF THE INCARNATION?

view of the relation between the two aspects of the Church's existence is supported. We have now to consider the bearing of the fact that the Church exists both in eternity and in time upon this view of the Church's nature.

The Christian believer is, so to say, connected with Christ in two distinguishable ways. He is connected with Him by nineteen centuries of church history, as a member in the Society which Christ instituted and to which He entrusted His saving work. And he is connected with Him as the living and ascended Lord, present where two or three are gathered together in His Name, meeting the soul here and now in the Word and Sacraments of the Gospel. How are these two ways related? They are, on the one hand, not totally separable. Christ does not make Himself known to men apart altogether from any contact with the Church, its ministry of Word and Sacrament, its teaching and its fellowship. But, on the other hand, they must be distinguished. The Christ who makes Himself known is not merely the Founder who sent out His first Apostles nineteen centuries ago, but the living Lord, our contemporary, the same yesterday, to-day and for ever. And, as all would agree, the fact of membership in the Church simply regarded as an institution does not itself ensure that communion with the living Lord, nor—on the other hand—are those who are outside that single historically continuous institution which is, *ex hypothesi*, the Church, necessarily excluded from all communion with Him. How is the Church's existence in time, as a continuous institution, related to its existence in eternity, as " an extension to creatures of the life of the Trinity "?

When we turn to the New Testament record there is one striking fact upon which all are agreed. Dr. Burn-Murdoch opens his chapter on " Continuity, an Essential of the Church and its Unity " as follows: " The New Testament and the evidence of early documents show how the organic life of the Church inevitably produced an actual succession in ministerial office in progress almost from the first. On the other hand it is long before any indication appears of consciousness of the fact, or of its importance. While the Second Coming and the end of all things were still momentarily expected, the future endurance of the Church in the world naturally received no thought." The primitive Church expected the End and therefore gave no thought to the question of continuity. But can we simply pass over this regrettable failure of the New

Testament writers to understand something which is "an essential of the Church," and proceed to correct its deficiencies in the light of our maturer knowledge? This is surely more than a mistake in a minor matter of detail: it concerns the nature of the Church, and in particular it concerns the relation of the Church to these two dimensions of its existence, time and eternity. We know that the expectation that the second coming of Christ might occur in the lifetime of the first generation of Christians was as a matter of fact not fulfilled. But we must surely pause to ask just what that means. Does it mean that they were wrong in believing that the Church is a society that lives on earth in the expectation of Christ's return, in reminding one another that "our citizenship is in heaven, from whence also we wait for a Saviour, the Lord Jesus Christ"? They may have been wrong about the date, but were they wrong about the fact, and about the place they gave it in their thought of the Church? If they were, then surely we must candidly confess that on a very fundamental matter regarding the nature of the Church we have found ourselves obliged to part company with the New Testament.

All human existence is involved in the double relation of man to time and to eternity. He is a creature in time, subject to growth and to death, and his history is likewise the history of the rise and fall of institutions and movements. Yet he is more than his history. He has an existence that transcends his part in the movement of history. Every man has a significance greater than the significance of his contribution to the total social history of mankind. He has significance for God. We are familiar with the denial of this in contemporary political movements. For a Marxist the individual human life does not have a significance which transcends the social process. On the contrary, it is his contribution to the total social process that gives to an individual life what significance it has. This means that the final test of any course of action lies in its calculated effects upon the whole process. It is the result that alone matters. To ask "Is it honest?" or "Is it sincere?" is totally irrelevant except in so far as dishonesty might affect the result. There is no appeal beyond the judgment of history. Against this the Christian asserts that the final judgment is not the judgment of history but the judgment of God. He asserts that even though the sacrifice a man may offer of everything he has and even of life itself may be completely buried and forgotten in the onward movement of history, yet it is not in vain, for God does not forget it, and the last word is with Him; and that on the other hand the wicked man may flourish all his days like the green bay tree and die in the odour of sanctity, and yet he will have to answer in the end before the judgment-seat of God, where the last judgment will be both pronounced and executed.

This is not the place for a general discussion of the eschatological element in Christian belief. I must be content here to state the conviction that belief in a final and effective judgment by God upon all men is both integral to the Christian faith and also indispensable for any fully reflective moral life. In face of the manifest triumph of wrong in history, it is not possible permanently to sustain a devotion to the right, even to the point of surrendering life itself, except upon the basis of a belief that there is an appeal beyond history, and that whatever the "judgment of history" may be, the final judgment, the last word, will be the vindication of the right. Certainly this belief in a real *eschaton*, a day of the Lord in which the righteous will be justified and the wicked punished, is quite central in the thought of the Old Testament. Sometimes in a crudely nationalist form, sometimes in a much more universal and ethical form, the Hebrew prophetic and apocalyptic writers expounded this theme of the end of history, God's final judgment, and His eternal reign. History is in God's hands. He has power to declare its end. The last word is not with the visible forces of history: it is with Him.

No one now needs to be reminded that the whole New Testament message is set firmly in the framework of this eschatological faith and cannot be understood apart from it. The first preaching of Jesus as recorded in the Gospels and the first preaching of the Apostles as recorded in Acts are both in effect the announcement that the End has come near. " The Eschaton has entered into history." But I have the impression that the recent re-emphasis upon the eschatological character of the whole New Testament has been achieved at the cost of removing the whole group of ideas which we call eschatological from the realm of reality to that of symbol. History has gone on for another nineteen centuries since the Lord announced its End. Is the idea of the End of History, perhaps, only a symbol? Was the old Jewish eschatology just a crudely realist groping after a truth which is really to be understood as rather a truth about human life as it is always, and not a truth about an event which is going to happen at some time in the future? Is God's judgment really something going on all the time, and therefore not something which is going to happen on "that great and terrible day" at the end of history? Can we treat the eschatological language of the New Testament simply as part of the Hebraic shell of the Gospel, and discard it when we have extracted the kernel? Can we regard "*the eschaton*" as essentially a symbol, not a real end to human history which is going to happen some time, though we don't know when, but the symbol of a certain fact about our human life, about the relation of the eternal to the temporal in it? Shall we, in other words, talk about the eschatological element in the Gospel, but avoid preaching about the Day of Judgment?

I have already stated that I do not believe it to be possible to remove from the Christian faith a belief in the reality of God's final and effective judgment upon human history. The eschatological element in the Gospel is there because the eschaton is a future certainty. Belief in eschatology without belief in a real end is like belief in religion without belief in God. Belief in God's judgment upon history is only possible if it means belief that God is in the end going to pronounce and execute His judgment. That He has manifestly not yet done. But we believe that He will do it. The belief that He will do it enables us to stake our all upon the doing of His will now, even though death and total failure may be the immediate result. The eschaton only enters into our experience because it qualifies our present existence. But it can only qualify our present existence if it be a future certainty. It is no more possible to speak intelligibly about eschatology, apart from belief in a real eschaton, than to speak intelligibly about mortality as an attribute of all things human apart from the certainty that all men are one day going to die.

The idea of a real eschaton is offensive and the idea of a symbolic eschaton is attractive to those whose view of the relation of eternity to time is expressed by the idea that all time is simultaneous to God. Upon the basis of this belief it is apparent that there can be no literal end or day of judgment. All events are simultaneously judged by God, and our idea of a final judgment is simply the form in which, as creatures in time, we are compelled to state this truth. But it is also apparent that upon this basis

THE EXTENSION OF THE INCARNATION?

human history is itself robbed of any meaning, for it can evidently have nothing at its end which was not equally present (to God) at its beginning. Such a view must inevitably tend to slide in the direction of pantheism. Edwyn Bevan[1] has shown conclusively that time must have a relation to the being of God quite different from that of space. Any attempt to regard temporal language as symbolic when used in reference to God must both rob the moral life of meaning and must also destroy any possibility of intercessory prayer. In fact the idea of eternity as the total simultaneity of time to God is quite irreconcilable with the Biblical doctrine of God. The Bible does not deal with these abstract ideas at all. It knows a personal God, beyond and above whom there is nothing. It knows His eternal purpose, the constancy of one loving will unresting and unhasting, seeing the end from the beginning, and by His might and mercy overruling the tangled and confused history of sinful men to that end. It looks to the end, which now we hope for but do not see, when all sin will be conquered and God will reign with His saints in perfect rest. The attempt to fit this view of the world, which makes the personal category the ultimate one, into a system of ideas such as "eternity" and "temporality" must fail. At least the Christian view, it seems to me, takes the personal category as ultimate. "In the beginning God . . ." The whole time process is but the working out of His eternal purpose. Its end will come when His purpose is accomplished. Its fruition is fellowship in His eternal joy. The ideas "eternity" and "temporality" are possible for us because we are created in His image for fellowship with Him (and therefore can in a measure share in His transcendence of time) and because we are called to be sharers in the fulfilling of His purpose (and are therefore subject to temporality). The whole Christian view of man and of his history seems to me to fall to the ground if there be not in history a movement which is real *to God,* and if there be not also to history a real end, hoped for but not yet seen, when God's purpose in human history shall have been accomplished.

I venture to express the opinion, therefore, which it is impossible adequately to support in a few short paragraphs, that the message of the New Testament cannot be interpreted *exclusively* in terms of "realized eschatology." There is a real end to history, and that

[1] *Symbolism and Belief.*

end is not yet. We hope for it but do not yet see it nor know when it will be. But that it will be is the conviction of both the Old and New Testaments. The essential New Testament proclamation is this, that in Jesus God has Himself come among men as a man, and that by His death He has opened up the way by which men may even now have that life in God which is the life of the Kingdom, eternal life. In Jesus, and in His mighty works of love and power, the long-awaited rule of God is actually here present among men exercising its power. Through faith in Him men are actually made one with the Father and the Son in the Spirit. They have been translated into the Kingdom of the Son of His love. In Paul's most common phrase they are justified by faith. Justification is an eschatological idea. The Jew who longed for God's kingdom to come longed above all for justification. The righteous were to be justified, and the wicked punished when God came to end this evil age and reign. The apostles announced a still more wonderful event—that now, " while we were yet sinners," Christ had died for the ungodly, and that those who were His were justified *now* by faith. They were sharers through the Spirit in the very life of God Himself. They were become a colony of heaven. This thrilling knowledge that in Christ the very life of God Himself (" eternal life ") has come among men, and men have become sharers of it, is the stuff of every part of the New Testament writings. The coming of God's kingdom is now no longer a far-off event. The King Himself has come and made them already citizens in it, and they tasted already its power and its glory. Yet the end is not yet. The rulers of this world still have their power. They crucified the Lord of Glory Himself, and they are blind to His revelation. In the same way the heirs of the Kingdom have to suffer with their King. They groan, waiting for their adoption. They eagerly await the return of the Lord in power and glory to reign for ever. And since they know not the hour of His coming, they are like servants alert for their Master's return, reckoning the sufferings of the present time as nothing to the glory which shall be revealed.

I do not think one can help feeling, as one reads the New Testament, that this intense sense of being already members in a kingdom that is beyond history is part of the very stuff of its message. The very life of God Himself has been manifested among us, and we have been made sharers in it. He has revealed

THE EXTENSION OF THE INCARNATION?

to us the mystery of His will, hid from all ages but now revealed, to sum up all things in Christ. We already share by faith in that life of blessed fellowship with God which is the end of history. This world's history still goes on, but we have seen its end, and the world will see it soon. This, surely, is the language of the first Christians. It is neither that they have already so become sharers in the eternal life of God that there is nothing left to hope for: nor is it that they simply long for a far-off vindication, at the end of history, of faith's stubborn stand within history. It is the eager, alert and active hope of those who, just because they have seen the Lord Himself, witnessed His victory over every power of evil and over death itself, and received the gift of the Spirit, that "earnest" of the glory to be, long the more passionately for the fulness of that which they have now as a foretaste. That sense of belonging already to God's kingdom, and that eager hope for the manifestation of the Kingdom in glory, belong to the very essence of Christianity. If hope so foreshortened the future as to lead some to expect the end within their lifetime, we have to agree that they were mistaken in their expectation. But we cannot, without parting company decisively with the New Testament, agree that they were wrong in the place they gave to that hope. The New Testament, and all authentic Christianity, lives between the accomplished redemption on the Cross and the longed-for victory when Christ shall come in glory, between thankfulness and hope. The Church takes its bearings afresh, so to say, on these two landmarks of its faith, every time it meets to show forth the Lord's death till He come. And any presentation of the Church's nature which shifts its emphasis from these two points to the continuing historical process, in such wise as to make that determinative of the Church's existence, must be gravely suspect. For these two points are, if one may put it so, the points at which eternity meets time; or—to speak in more fitting language—the points where the eternal God makes Himself known in history as Redeemer and as Judge of all men. The Church lives with its eyes on these points because it lives in history the life of God who is beyond history. Because it is in history the Church has the character of a developing human institution. But because its life is hid with Christ in God, until the day when He shall be manifested in glory, the question "where and what is the Church?" cannot be answered by examining simply the history of the Church as an institution.

This, however, is what is done when it is maintained that the Church only exists where the institutional continuity has been maintained. A true account of the essential nature of the Church cannot be written without reference to this eschatological dimension of the Church's existence. Yet writers in defence of the position we are examining seem to consider that the two subjects can be kept in separate compartments, that the question "Who are the Church?" can be discussed in total isolation from the question of God's final judgment. Fr. Congar points with satisfaction to the popular mediæval conviction that many popes and bishops go to hell. There is indeed no reason why, upon the premises we are criticizing, the one undivided Church should not consist exclusively of the damned.

The issue becomes an acutely practical one when we consider it in relation to the possibility of reform in the Church. Fr. Congar, in rejecting the appeal to the "Vincentian Canon" as an instrument of reform in the Church, writes: "The magisterium always living in the Church by the twofold principle of the apostolic succession and the assistance of the Holy Spirit, simply declares what is the belief of the universal Church. The past may be known by the fact of the present; the present is not determined by a reference to the past. Here we touch upon a decisive issue between the Protestant Reformation and the Church, for the very idea of reformation is involved. Is the nature of the Apostolic Church such that, having fundamentally erred, she can be brought back to the truth and reformed by professors in the name of critical study? Protestantism only exists by virtue of an affirmative answer to this question, justified by the Vincentian canon."[1] And, further down, "The Church is an organism. It was not founded by our Lord merely as a human leader founds a party or a society by giving it a charter and laying down its line of action; rather was it founded in the same way that life is propagated, as a living entity containing the principle and the law of its own development, as it were, in germ."[2] The Church is here defined in exclusively historical terms. The analogy of the organism containing in itself the law of its own development seems to exclude altogether what we have called the eschatological dimension of the Church's existence. The reference to a "twofold principle of the apostolic succession and the assistance of the Holy Spirit" gives

[1] *Op. cit.*, p. 183.   [2] *Op. cit.*, p. 186.

no hint as to the manner in which these two are related to each other, nor any ground for the belief that they are necessarily connected. That is, of course, the crucial question, with which we are concerned throughout this chapter. The essential point is that, upon this view, the Church exists as a historical institution which cannot be judged and reformed in the light of any reality beyond itself. The very fact that Fr. Congar should regard the Protestant Reformation as an appeal to the past by professors in the name of critical study shows how completely the eschatological dimension is excluded from his thought. An appeal to the facts of the Incarnation is not merely an appeal from the present to the past in a historical series. It is an appeal to the one revelation in time of the ever-living God as He eternally is. The Reformation was an appeal beyond the Church as it was to the living God Himself, known in His redeeming work in Christ, and its central re-emphasis was upon that fundamentally eschatological idea, justification by faith.

We must agree that the Church is not simply a society founded by our Lord in such a way that its future is for ever determined for it by the pattern of its past. There is an archæological appeal to Scripture and the Fathers which is foreign to the proper character of the Church. The Church is a communion with the living God in the Holy Spirit. But the Church lives by reason of, and by reference to, what God did once for all in Christ. It shares in the Holy Spirit precisely because it believes in Christ and lives by faith in His atonement. It looks for the coming of the perfect kingdom when history shall be brought to its end. When a body of Christians claims to possess in itself the law of its own development and denies the possibility of any appeal beyond itself to its Lord, it has come perilously near to denying its right to be called the Church.

Christianity is challenged by views of man which deny to the individual any significance beyond his significance to the historical process. It asserts that the final judgment on all human life is not the judgment of history but the judgment of God. It looks to the time when the Lord comes, who will both bring to light the hidden things of darkness and make manifest the counsels of the heart. It reminds every man that he will have to stand at the last and accept responsibility both for the things done in the body and for the counsels of the heart. This responsibility no man can delegate. It is given him by God in the fact of his creation in His image, and he and no other must render an account of his discharge of it to God. The intersection of eternity and time is in the soul of the individual as he faces his responsibility before the eternal God to do his duty here in history. If the eternal dimension is wholly blotted out of his consciousness, if he loses altogether the conviction that he must in the end face the judgment seat of God, then he is finally at the mercy of the forces of history and ultimately of those whose view of what is expedient prevails. There is here the ultimate point of conflict between Christianity and the collectivist creeds of our day, and it concerns that responsibility which every man finally and inalienably has as an individual before God, the responsibility to obey Him.

The institutional life of the Church, so far from superseding this individual responsibility of every soul before God, rests upon it. The "living interior form" of the Church, as Fr. Congar says, is faith and charity. But faith and charity are activities of persons. The Christian believes, and loves because he believes. Faith is first. In faith he accepts the redemption accomplished for him by Christ and gives himself to his Redeemer to whom he belongs. Being delivered from the bondage of sin he is set free to serve God. And the service God asks is the serving of one's neighbour for Christ's sake. The content of charity is the acceptance of responsibility for one's neighbour. It looks back to God's revelation in Christ ("If God so loved us we ought also to love one another") and forward to his final appearing ("inasmuch as ye did it unto the least of these . . ."). It lives by reference to the eternal, but it serves in the temporal. It delights in all tasks, however menial, that serve to the building up of the fellowship in love: but it does so in the power of a salvation that looks beyond time to eternity. Here is the real point of intersection of time and eternity in the life of the Church, and the place where the relation of its two dimensions to one another may be understood.

There is thus at the heart of the Church's existence an ineradicable individualism. Every man has to stand at the last before God and render his own account. The opposite of this true individualism is not fellowship, but the crowd and the clique, the place to which we run when we want to avoid personal responsibility. True charity rests upon an acceptance of responsibility before God for the beloved. The deeper and truer the mutual love is, the more does it remain true that there is at the heart of it the unshared responsibility of each before God for the other. The Church is the society bound together in mutual love, the love of God shed abroad in the hearts of its members through the Holy Ghost which was given them through faith in Christ. It is both a unity in the Spirit and a corporeal institutional unity, and it is the second because it is the first, for he who says "I love God" and does not love his brother is a liar. The point of intersection of these two dimensions of its existence is in the soul of the believer facing his responsibility to God for his neighbour. It is because the Church knows and lives by the eternal life of God Himself, believing in His revelation once for all in Jesus Christ, hoping for His return to reign in glory, and ministering here on earth the love which is His life, that she can withstand the claims of those who know of no tribunal beyond historical success.

The view of the Church we are criticizing is in contradiction to the Christian faith at this decisive point. By denying *in principle* and as a matter of logical necessity all possibility of appeal beyond the actual historically developing society to the eternal God made known in Christ it removes in principle the eschatological dimension from the Church's existence, and reduces it to the level of a purely historical movement containing, as Fr. Congar says, the law of its own development in itself. It is of necessity that the Roman Church does not and will not renounce the use of those methods which are the characteristics of a totalitarian state, for —like them—it has removed the doctrine of God's final judgment from all practical bearing upon its institutional life here in history.

The foregoing criticism of a view of the Church which regards institutional continuity as of its essence has in fact led us at the end of each section to one fact—the fact of sin in the Church. If there were no sin in the Church there would be perfect congruity between the outward and the inward. It would be possible to say with complete reality *ubi Petrus ibi ecclesia*. If there were no sin in the Church there would be no question of an appeal beyond the Church to God's revelation. The Church would itself, in the whole range of its institutional life, reveal and mediate the divine life. The whole of our problem lies in this—the bearing of the fact of sin upon the nature of the Church as a visible historical institution. In the section just concluded we have found that the doctrine of justification by faith has met us as an expression of the fundamentally eschatological character of the Church's existence. Clearly these two matters are intimately related. Upon the meaning attached to the doctrine of justification by faith will depend our doctrine of the place of sin in the life of the Church. If it be true that the point of intersection of the temporal and the eternal dimensions in the life of the Church is in the experience of the Christian facing his responsibility to God for his neighbour, it is clear that the nature of this experience must be more closely studied. What, we have to ask, is the nature of that standing before God which the man in Christ has?

Detached Note: The above argument has dealt, for the reason stated, with the Roman rather than with Anglican conceptions of the continuity of the Church. A word may be added regarding the bearing of the argument upon the objections advanced by some Anglicans to the South India Scheme of Union on the ground that non-episcopal ministries are not in any sense ministries within the Catholic Church. Inasmuch as the Church of England at a certain point in its history repudiated the authority of the Pope which had hitherto been accepted, and detached itself from the sections of Western Christendom which remained under his authority, and inasmuch as it still stands by that repudiation, it is obviously impossible for Anglicans to claim that the historical and institutional continuity of the Church as one body is of its *esse*. Nor for the same reason can Anglicanism repudiate the possibility that even schism may be necessary in the interests of reformation where the Church has grievously erred. The denial that non-episcopal ministries are real ministries can only be made on the ground that not continuity in general but episcopacy in particular is of the *esse* of the Church, and that therefore the duty of reformation even at the cost of schism does not include the right of reformation at the cost of separation from the historically continuous episcopate. Arguments regarding the unity of the Church's spiritual and corporate existence obviously do not avail to prove this contention. What is required is proof that episcopacy is in such wise the essential constituent of the Church that where the necessary number of bishops repudiate the authority of the rest of the Church, those who consent with and follow them are still a part of the Church, whereas a similar secession which does not include the necessary

THE EXTENSION OF THE INCARNATION?

number of bishops puts those who follow it outside the Church. In other words, what is required is proof that the authority of bishops to ordain and consecrate is by itself, and apart from the unity and continuity of the whole body, the authority upon which the existence of the Church depends. This contention will fall to be examined in Chapter IX.

CHAPTER SIX

JUSTIFICATION BY FAITH

THE Church is both a union of created souls with the eternal God in the Holy Spirit and also a visible historical society among the various societies whose history goes to make up the story of mankind. We have already seen that there are involved in the relation between these two aspects of the Church's being two different distinctions. There is first the distinction between the spiritual unity and the corporeal unity of the Church; there is second the distinction between that perfect unity of will which exists in actuality within the being of the triune God, and which ought to be the nature of the Church's life, and the actual disunity and contrariety of wills within the Church caused by the presence within it of sin. There is, in other words, the problem of the corporeality of the Church, and there is the problem of sin in the Church. All our studies have combined to show that it is the problem of sin which is fundamental. But for sin the Church's outward institutional life would be as perfectly congruous with its life in the Spirit as were the words and works of the incarnate Lord with His Spirit. The dichotomy between body and spirit is, in fact, simply the product of that severance of man from God which is sin. Body and spirit are alike God's creation and are created to be the counterparts of one another. The conflict within man between body and spirit is the aftermath of his disobedience to God. The problem of the Church is the problem of sin in the Church. It can be stated, in fact, purely in terms of the Church's " spiritual " nature. The problem of the Church is that it is a communion of sinful souls with the Holy God. There is in the Church both union with Christ and also rebellion against Him— not that some are united and others rebellious, but that those who are truly " in Christ " are yet at the same time rebels against Christ. Or, to put the matter in the terms we used in the previous chapter, the Church consists of those who are already justified, and yet its members look still for a final judgment. The attempt to deny that the Church is really divided, whether the attempt be along the Roman Catholic line or along the Protestant, rests upon a denial of this fundamental paradox of the Church's being, that it is both holy and sinful.

What we have to do now is to examine this paradox. When dealing with the Biblical doctrine of the Israel of God we examined St. Paul's contention that it is faith and not circumcision which is the human condition of membership in God's people. In the course of the following section we looked briefly at the relation between faith and the gift of the Spirit, in whom believers are brought to share in the very life of God Himself. And in the last section we were led to consider the eschatological teaching of the Bible in its bearing upon the doctrine of justification by faith as the Pauline expression of the truth that in Christ " the eschaton has entered history." We have now to draw these ideas together in order to understand the nature of this faith which is the bond between sinful men and their holy God, which is the condition of their incorporation in His people, of their receiving His Spirit, and of their being justified. It is by understanding what is the nature of faith that we shall gain understanding of the fundamental paradox of the Church's existence as a communion of the sinful with the Holy.

It is first of all necessary to clear away two misconceptions which persistently befog the discussion of the doctrine of justification by faith. In the first place, the phrase does not mean that faith justifies, but that God justifies upon the condition of faith. The abstract noun " justification " is very rarely used in the New Testament. The verb " to justify " with God as subject is very constantly used. Justification is the act of God. Faith is the human condition. In the second place, the faith referred to is not faith in general but faith in Christ as Redeemer. In Dr. Vincent Taylor's summary statement, " by justification St. Paul means the gracious action of God in accepting men as righteous, in consequence of faith, resting upon His redemptive activity in Christ."[1] The sphere of justification is the Church. What constitutes the Church is from the Divine side this gracious action and from the human side this faith. The crucial question for us at the moment is in regard to the phrase " accepting men as righteous." In what sense can God accept men as righteous? Is it because they already are righteous, or are being made righteous, as Catholic theologians

---

[1] *Forgiveness and Reconciliation*, pp. 56-7. See the whole chapter for the evidence for this statement.

teach? Or is it because God "imputes" to them, in His mercy, a righteousness which they do not in fact possess, as some Protestant theologians teach? If, as we have urged, sin is a reality in the Church, no less in its corporate acts than in the individual lives of its members, what is the faith on condition of which God can, without fiction, accept it as righteous, as the Body of Christ on earth? The answer is that it is faith in Christ as Redeemer, faith which looks to God in His redemptive work in Christ. This faith places men in that relation with God for which men were created, and inasmuch as it becomes the settled direction of their wills it issues in the remoulding of their whole lives in conformity to the holy love of their Creator.

God's justifying activity rests upon His redemptive work in Christ and is conditional upon our acceptance in faith of what He has done for us in Christ. "God," says St. Paul, "set forth (Christ Jesus) to be a propitiation, through faith, by His blood . . . that He might Himself be just and the justifier of him that hath faith in Jesus" (Rom. iii. 25-6). Immediately beneath the surface of this language, of course, is the whole sacrificial system of the Old Covenant. The sacrifice is the objective condition of man's approach to God. Yet it is not man's effort to propitiate God, for the whole sacrificial system is provided by God Himself. What God has provided in Christ is something as objectively real. But it is not, as were the sacrifices of Israel after the flesh, merely symbolic. It, unlike them, has the power truly and actually to accomplish man's justification and reconciliation with God. Yet it has the power to effect this only "through faith." Christ's sacrificial death has expiatory value for us, and avails for our justification, only when it evokes in us the response of faith. And the purpose and effect of this is that God, who is Himself righteous (and who will manifest His righteousness in the Last Day), should so manifest His righteousness at this present season that He, the righteous One, might yet also accept as righteous all who (having sinned and fallen short of His glory) have faith in Jesus. God in His grace has, in Christ's death, provided a place where men, through faith, may share now in that relationship with Him which belongs properly to those who are declared righteous at the Last Day.

It is, of course, impossible to attempt here a full discussion of the doctrine of the work of Christ, but in brief outline four matters must be referred to:

JUSTIFICATION BY FAITH

(a) The nature of God's redemptive work in Christ.
(b) The nature of faith as our response to this work.
(c) The dependence of justification upon faith.
(d) The relation of justification to the life of the Church.

Naturally these four topics cannot be divided from one another by hard and fast lines, but by setting them out thus in order we may define the direction in which our thought must move.

(a) *God's Redemptive Work in Christ*

"I delivered unto you first of all that which I received, how that Christ died for our sins according to the scriptures; and that he was buried; and that he hath been raised on the third day according to the scriptures." This, says St. Paul, is "the gospel which I preached unto you, which also ye received, wherein also ye stand, by which also ye are saved" (1 Cor. xv. 1-4). Here is the solid rock upon which the Church stands, the work of Christ done and finished once for all. Christ has been, as the writer to Hebrews says, "once offered to bear the sins of many" (Heb. ix. 28). This one sacrificial offering is the condition of our approach to God.

The sacrificial system of the Old Testament, which provides the thought forms in which the New Testament generally describes the work of Christ, has running right through it the paradox that it is both something provided for man by God, and something offered by man to God. This element of paradox is necessarily involved in any true understanding of the expiation of sin. For, on the one hand, there is no way by which God can, as it were, wipe sin off the human face as a mother will wipe a tear from her child's eyes. Sin is possible only because God has given to men a measure of freedom and responsibility. Sin is man's abuse of that freedom to disown the lordship of God, and to refuse that loving self-surrender to God for which he was created. Sin is only removed when man freely offers that which God has given him the power to withhold. Nor, on the other hand, is there any way by which man, having sinned, can of himself return to God. There is no way by which man can expiate his sin. Even man's repentance and his resolve to amend cannot bring him back to that relation with God in which alone is his peace.[1] Having once

---

[1] I venture to refer to the elaboration of this point in my book, *Christian Freedom in the Modern World* (S.C.M. Press), Ch. IV.

sinned, his effort to return to his true relation with God becomes charged with the very egotism which is precisely the essence of his sin. Sinful man is not free to put away his sin and return to God, apart from the atonement which God has wrought for him. And this atonement, like the sacrificial system in which it was foreshadowed, is both a gift from God to men, and an offering of Man to God.

It is a gift from God, springing from the heart of God's love for the world (John iii. 16). In Christ's death for sinners God commends His own love to us (Rom. v. 8). But it is not merely a loving gesture from God's side of the gulf, an indication to us in our sinful isolation that He still loves us. It is an act which bridges the gulf, which effects reconciliation, which makes propitiation. The sinless Son of God Himself took our humanity upon Himself. He endured humiliating death at the hands of those who professed to be His servants, and who were living on His bounty. He of whose holy will it comes that the wages of sin is death, Himself endured death, the death of a degraded criminal. Emptying Himself of the power of His godhead, He so identified Himself with sinful men that at the last He cried out like a despairing sinner, "My God, my God, why hast thou forsaken me?" From His baptism at the hands of John to His agony upon the Cross, He, the sinless Son, the Word by whom all things were made, identified Himself with sinful men, rendering in their behalf and in full acceptance of their situation the obedience which they withhold from God, suffering in their behalf the penalties of their sin and accepting this cup of suffering from His Father's hand, offering in their behalf the perfect penitence which man's sin both requires him to make and precludes him from making.

The phrase "in their behalf" has a meaning which is neither simply representative nor simply substitutionary, but is in a unique sense both representative and substitutionary. Christ's death is not representative in the sense that he represents humanity as it is; it is representative in that in thus acting for man towards God He creates the possibility that all men may, through faith, thus act in and through Him towards God. He is the representative of *humanity re-created in Him.* His death is not substitutionary in the sense that what was due from man to God was rendered by Him in such wise that we no longer need to render it; it is substitutionary in the sense that He did for us something which it is in the nature of the case for ever impossible for us to do for ourselves, but which, because He has done it, we can do in and through Him.

In the words of the apostle, "while we were yet sinners, Christ died for us" (Rom. v. 8). That irremovable fact, preceding our understanding of it, our faith in it, our living by it in the sacramental fellowship of His Body, is the rock on which the Church stands.

(b) *Faith as the Response to Christ's Work*

St. Paul speaks of Christ's death as "a propitiation through faith" (Rom. iii. 25). What is the faith by which the death of Christ has this atoning power? It is a death and a rebirth. "I have been crucified with Christ; yet I live; and yet no longer I but Christ liveth in me: and that life which I now live in the flesh I live in faith, the faith which is in the Son of God who loved me and gave Himself up for me" (Gal. ii. 20). "We were buried therefore with him through baptism unto death: that like as Christ was raised from the dead through the glory of the Father, so we also might walk in newness of life" (Rom. vi. 4). "One died for all, therefore all died; and he died for all that they which live should no longer live unto themselves but unto him who for their sakes died and rose again" (2 Cor. v. 14-15). Faith is a dying and a rebirth to life "in faith," "in Christ," "in newness of life," "unto him." Yet it is so solely as a response to His dying love and in a manner which leaves no possibility of regarding faith as a meritorious achievement. When a man stands before the Cross as it is set before men in the Word and Sacraments of the Gospel, and understands that Christ died for his sins, there must be in him a double response of shattering and up-building, of self-loathing as he understands what his sin means to Christ, of wondering gratitude and new-found hope as he looks up to the Son of God who loved him and gave Himself up for him.

Before the Cross every ground of human confidence is destroyed. Every vestige of the pride with which man in his self-chosen independence from God surveys his own achievements in culture or in piety and godliness is utterly shamed and put to confusion. The message of the Cross breaks upon the busy world of human life, its culture, its morality, its religion, like the sudden threat of destruction by a mine upon the bustling life of a great ocean liner.

All its busy round of social activities, all its fears and ambitions, all its cliques and coteries, are suddenly dissolved at the opening out of a forgotten dimension of existence, and there is only one question for all—life or death. So across the world of human life, the less and more of human ethical standards, the competing prides of cultural and religious groups, the secret or open quest for human recognition and social security that every man pursues, the message of the Cross comes as the opening up of a forgotten dimension of existence. Every man is seen to stand in this one awful situation—a sinner before his God, a rebel before his Creator, a traitor before his King. Every man hears in his own ears the terrible sentence pronounced against him, " Murderer of the Son of God." A man must either blot the Word of the Cross out of vision and memory or else confess that his life is forfeit. If this were all, the recognition of it would be impossible because intolerable. It could only end where it ended for Judas, who, when he saw what he had done, went out and hanged himself. But it is not all, for the Word of the Cross is at the same moment the creative word of divine love itself. " Christ died for our sins." That is the measure of His love for us, as well as the measure of our sin against Him. Of His free will and choice He laid down His life for us. And the manner of His laying it down was that in His love for us He made Himself one with us, felt upon Himself the whole weight of our sin which we could not feel because of our sin, offered the perfect penitence which only the sinless can offer, and endured to the very end the penalties of our sin. The man who understands that hears at the same time and along with the word of judgment, the word of mercy: " Ye are not your own, ye were bought with a price. The Son of Man came to give His life a ransom for many." " Murderer of God: beloved of God." This double confession wrung from the heart of a man who understands what was done for him on the Cross is itself the echo in his heart of Christ's perfect offering of penitence to God. It is the penitence which Christ's atoning act creates. It finds in Him its representative only because it is first the response to what He did alone once for all. The man who thus receives and believes the Gospel gives himself in penitence and faith in response to, and in union with, Christ's giving of Himself to the Father. He embraces every opportunity which Christ's service affords of filling up in his flesh on his part that which is lacking of the afflictions of Christ, for His body's sake, which is the Church. He lives "for Christ's sake." And his new life is perpetually sustained by the Word and Sacraments wherein the Gospel of Christ's atoning work is shown forth, and wherein he both receives afresh Christ's gift of Himself for men, and unites himself afresh with Christ's offering of Himself to the Father. Such self-identification in faith with Christ in His sacrifice is never something which he can regard as an activity willed and carried through by himself, something which is his choice of one among a number of possible ways of salvation offered to him. It does involve a decision, but it is utterly different from the human choice of a way of salvation. It is the response wrung from the human heart faced in Christ's death with the vision of its own exceeding sinfulness and God's exceeding grace; it is a man's acceptance, in the midst of God's just judgment upon him as sinner, of God's gift to him of free and undeserved redemption; it is the acceptance of the grip of Christ's pierced hand upon the hand that pierced Him. It is the soul's humbled and trembling "Amen" to the revelation of the wrath and the love of the Lord God Omnipotent.

This faith involves a death and a rebirth. If a man be in Christ there is a new creation. The life which goes to make up this world, upon whose principles this world could only crucify the Lord of glory when He came, is under sentence of death. But when a man is in Christ there is a new creation. The death of Christ was not a gesture directed towards nothing. It was an act of love done for men. Therein lies the basis of their new existence. The man in Christ has a life now which depends solely on this, that Christ died for him. His life is a new creation of the creative love of God Himself. It is a new kind of self-hood—a self with its centre in Christ and not in itself. Or rather—and this is important —it is the re-creation of self-hood as it was intended to be. It is the release of man from the prison which he has created for himself by his refusal of surrender to God. It is the birth of a human life according to the purpose of God's creation of man, human life lived in willing and loving surrender to God the Creator. And of this new humanity Christ is the Head and Representative. It is through Him that re-creation proceeds, as it was through Him that everything was made that hath been made. "He is the head of the body, the Church . . . for it was the good pleasure of the Father that in him should all the fulness dwell; and through him to reconcile all things unto himself, having made peace through the blood of his Cross " (Col. i. 18-20). And the life of this new humanity is in faith—" the faith which is in the Son of God who loved me and gave Himself up for me." In this the meaning of God's long dealings with Israel is at last made clear—" the mystery which hath been hid from all ages and generations, but now hath been manifested to his saints " (Col. i. 26); " the mystery of his will . . . to sum up all things in Christ . . . in whom we were made a heritage . . . in whom ye also (Gentiles) having heard the word of the truth, the gospel of your salvation—in whom having also believed, ye were sealed with the Holy Spirit of promise " (Eph. i. 9-13).

(c) The Dependence of Justification upon Faith

St. Paul speaks of believers being justified by faith, and denies that they can be justified " by the works of the law." The meaning is the same when he says that they are justified freely by God's grace. Corresponding to this use of the verb is his use of the noun " righteousness." He contrasts sharply what he calls " a righteousness of mine own, even that which is of the law," with " the righteousness of God by faith " (Phil. iii. 9). He makes clear how this righteousness is, in a sense, not his own when he goes on to describe his longing for it by saying that he counts all privilege to be but dung that he may know Christ, and the power of His resurrection and the fellowship of His sufferings, becoming conformed in His death, that he may attain unto the resurrection from the dead. Here righteousness is both a future hope and a present possession in foretaste. The element of hope is strongly stressed when he says, " We through the Spirit by faith wait for the hope of righteousness " (Gal. v. 5), and in other similar passages. But the preponderant stress of the epistles, as of the whole New Testament message, is upon justification as a gift of God's free grace in Christ given now to the believer. In what sense, and with what reality, does God accept as righteous the man or woman who has faith in Christ?

The man who stands believing before the Cross of Christ experiences, as I have tried to say, a double process of shattering and upbuilding, of death and rebirth. It is expressing part of that experience to say that it means the final shattering of the possibility of " a righteousness of mine own." No man can stand before the

JUSTIFICATION BY FAITH

Cross of Christ and think of himself as a righteous man. The whole attempt to achieve for oneself the status of righteousness over against God, to achieve as an autonomous moral subject conformity to the law of God's holiness written in the conscience, is there seen to be the very quintessence of man's rebellion against God. But there is a new life born there, a new mind which is the creation of Christ's redeeming love. It is, as I have tried to show, a new kind of self-hood with its centre not in the isolated ego, but in Christ. It is a life in which all self-reliance has been destroyed and the soul looks to Christ alone in penitence, in gratitude and in adoration, in which the soul is made one with Christ in His perfect love to the Father. It is the life of the new man in Christ. But this life is already righteous in the only true meaning of that term, for righteousness is nothing other than the right relation of the soul to God. The idea of righteousness as a condition or status of man apart from his relation to God is itself the product of man's alienation from God. The "righteousness" which is the achievement of man's own autonomous effort is in fact the last stronghold of man's sin against God. It is the ultimate embodiment of loveless pride. Righteousness is that relation of the soul to God wherein the soul having forsaken all reliance upon itself lives only by the grace of God, lives to give Him thanks and praise, seeks nothing but to show forth His mercy by giving up itself to His service. It is from first to last the response to God's love. That righteousness is impossible to man apart from Christ, for even though it is known to be the true righteousness, when man as an autonomous moral subject chooses it as the way by which he will seek to attain blessedness, it becomes corrupted by his own essential egotism. All man's moral life is beset by the paradox of which the enmity of the Pharisees to Jesus is the crucial expression. Man having fallen is not free to return to that relation of loving response to God for which he was created, even when he knows that the law is summed up in, "Thou shalt love the Lord thy God." But man confronted by the Cross of Christ, humbled to the dust with Him and raised with Him to the very fellowship of God in the heavenly places, is brought by God's sovereign grace back into that relation with Him for which he was made. Faith is still the condition, for God does not withdraw the responsibility He has given: but his restoration to this true relation with God has its origin in God's free grace and not in any design of man.

This restoration to God *is* justification. It is that which men hope to attain by moral struggle but which can only be the free gift of God. It is not given upon any other ground than the sovereign love of God towards His sinful children. Good works are not its condition but its fruit. For it is only when man's will is thus delivered from alienation from God that he is free to bring forth the fruits of holiness. Then real ethical activity becomes possible—for it is wholly delivered from that all-pervasive anxiety which otherwise puts the stain of egotism on all men's ethical activities. And it becomes, in a new sense, obligatory. For if God so loved us we ought also to love one another. It is after the exposition of God's free and sovereign grace in accepting them as righteous, that Paul turns to plead with the churches, by the mercies of God, to present themselves a living sacrifice to Him, and goes on to elaborate the duties that rest upon them as those who are Christ's. Their justification does not rest upon their moral effort; it is the work of God's free grace. Upon this alone can they build a true moral life, holy and well pleasing to God, because it is not the expression of man's search for his own salvation, but his response to the love of God. It is not the search for a righteousness of one's own, but the fruit of a righteousness which is the gift of God's grace through faith in Christ.

What has been outlined in very summary form is what is involved in the relation between the soul and God which is established by the atoning work of God in Christ through faith. It is not a merely theoretical statement but a transcript of something known in the experience of the Church. Yet it is manifestly not a complete account of the matter, for we do not yet see either in the Church as a whole or in the lives of any individual Christian that sinless perfection which we see in the self-giving of Christ to the Father and which ought to belong to those who are through the death and rebirth of faith made one with Him. We long for it and expect it. And we have the foretaste and earnest of it. Its power now works in us. But it is not yet fully realized. This is very apparent in the Pauline writings. Christians are told, " Ye are not in the flesh but in the Spirit, if so be that the Spirit of God dwelleth in you," yet they have to be severely warned against the works of the flesh. Their old man is dead, and yet his works have still to be mortified. They are " saints," and yet still engaged in the struggle with sin in themselves. How are these two things related?

Clearly, to begin with, God's new creation of men in Christ is subject, in this respect, to the same conditions as the original creation—namely, in respect of the freedom which it gives to men to seek their good in themselves instead of in God. We have seen that part of what is involved in man's sin against God is the loss of his freedom to serve Him, and that in Christ this freedom is restored. But it is real freedom and therefore involves the same responsibility steadily to offer to God the love which is His due and the same possibility of misusing freedom to withhold that offering. In particular, the very glory of the inheritance with the saints in light which is ours through Christ's atoning work opens up possibilities of temptation to turn this to the satisfaction of our own egotism. We are tempted to think that because we have received through the Gospel the dowry of the Spirit's gifts, therefore we possess them in ourselves, and we now inalienably *are* Christians and *have* access to the treasures of His grace. Identifying our justification with a particular spiritual experience, or with its outward rite we may conclude that we have henceforth a secure place among the redeemed, and may develop an insensitiveness and impenitence regarding our own sins which dishonour the Gospel we preach. When this happens it is manifest that we have fallen again as the first Adam did. The standing before God which is given to us as we say the Amen of faith to Christ's atoning work on our behalf is one that exists only through, and in the relation of, penitent and loving dependence upon our Redeemer. It is a relation with Him: it is not a status of our own. It is dynamic. It requires us to live always " looking unto Jesus." It exists only in an ever new giving of ourselves to the Father in response to, and in union with, His gift of Himself for us. The moment it ceases to be that and falls back into the sense of possessing a status of our own, there has been a second Fall. What exists then is no longer a self with its centre in Christ, but a self with its centre in itself, Christ's work having been made auxiliary to the soul's own search for security.

Yet it is not the same as Adam's fall. It is not an irremediable loss of the freedom of the will. For Christ's death once for all is not annulled. It is still there, re-presented to the Christian day by day in the Word and Sacraments of the Gospel. The very fact of his own sin drives him back to the Cross in fresh penitence and fresh conviction of the sole adequacy of God's grace. The sin of a man apart from Christ drives him deeper into sin. The sin of a man in Christ drives him back to his Redeemer. If a man be truly in Christ every year that passes will convince him more both of his own sinfulness and of God's grace. In truth the experience of death and re-birth is not one which is passed through and done with: it is the character of the life in Christ to its end. It is something which can only be described in terms of an event, and an event as complete and irreversible as death. Yet it is in truth something which belongs to the whole of the life in Christ from beginning to end—whether that beginning be the baptism of a child wholly unable consciously to formulate its experiences, or the conversion of an adult after spiritual experiences profound in comparison with the faint glimmerings of conscience in the majority of men and yet certainly plumbing only a fraction of the depths of the gulf that divides sinful man from God. The confession of the man in Christ is that where sin did abound, there did grace much more abound. And if it be objected that this is but an invitation to continue in sin, the answer is that such an objection rests simply on the egotism of man apart from God, and is unthinkable to the man who has died with Christ and whose life is that new creation of God's grace, a life risen with Him, and lived always and only as a perpetual receiving of the gift of God's love in Christ and an offering of life to Him in Christ.

In the last analysis the existence of sin in the Church is an inscrutable mystery. We cannot understand why, having given ourselves to God in the penitent faith which is our response to Christ's atoning work, we should ever again sin. Sin is utterly incompatible with the life in Christ. The only life compatible with membership in Christ is the sinless perfection of Jesus. Anything that falls short of that is sin, and the use of the word " imperfection " to describe it does but becloud the issue. We cannot understand the fact of sin in the Church and in ourselves, but we can refrain from denying its existence and thus destroying the possibility of forgiveness. And (for this alone makes that recognition possible) we can keep steadily in mind the fact that the righteousness which the Christian has through Christ is only and always a dynamic relationship of penitence and faith towards the living God; it can never be thought of as his own possession; it is the righteousness of God by faith. The Christian soul looks always to Jesus. He alone is its righteousness. It is because it is " in

Him" that it can dare to come before the Father. It seeks no status of its own. Its cry is "Be thou my dignity, thou my delight." Its ideal of perfect joy is never its own perfection, but always the vision of God and perfect fellowship with Him. And its life of holiness is not the effort to perfect itself, not even the effort to make itself fit for Him, but—as it were—the overflow of its love to Him.

The dynamic character of the life of faith, the fact that its whole character depends upon its constant reference to the living Christ, and the impossibility of describing it in a simple and direct "horizontal" manner, are perfectly indicated in the sentence of St. Paul which we have often quoted: "I have been crucified with Christ; yet I live" (a death and a new birth); "and yet no longer I, but Christ liveth in me" (not the old self-hood restored but a new self-hood whose centre is not in the self but in Christ): "and that life which I now live in the flesh" (for it is still an ordinary human life, as the Church is a human society) "I live in faith, the faith which is in the Son of God who loved me and gave Himself up for me" (always "looking unto Jesus").

(d) The Relation of Justification to the Life of the Church

What has been said about faith has been necessarily said of the faith of the individual. This is necessary. The new relationship with God which is established through faith in Christ crucified is the relation of a fully responsible person to his Creator. That is strikingly clear in those very passages, such as the one just quoted, in which St. Paul speaks of the new life in Christ in terms of the most complete identification of the believer with Christ. The individual is not dissolved into a larger whole. But, equally fundamentally, this faith cannot be severed from its actual living context, namely the fellowship of the Church. The new relation with God through Christ is necessarily also a new relation with all who share it. The end of the sinful assertion of the independence of the creature before God is likewise the end of the assertion of his independence of his fellow-men. On the one hand, the Gospel only comes to us through the ministries of the Church. We know the Gospel of God's redeeming grace through the fellowship of redeemed men and women. On the other hand, there is no true giving of the self to Christ which is not at the same time a giving of the self to those for whom He died. What H. R. Mackintosh called "this willingness to be lost in the great multitude of those who owe everything to Him, this eagerness to join in the doxology of the redeemed " is an inseparable part of what faith means.

God's justifying action, therefore, through His atoning work in Christ and through the faith which it calls forth in us, is the calling into being of a community which shares already here in time the life of God's saints who are to reign for ever in the bliss of His eternity. In it there is revealed the long-hidden meaning and purpose of God's calling of Israel. In it the longed-for day of God's coming has actually dawned and justification is already in foretaste a present possession. Those who are in Christ taste already the powers of the age to come. Their life as a fellowship is already a prolepsis into history of the perfect fellowship of the Kingdom of God.

It is expressing the same truth in another way to say that the Church is the extension to creatures of the life of the Blessed Trinity. In the response of penitent faith which is the soul's Amen to Christ's redeeming work, and in the life of self-offering to the Father in union with Him, the Christian is caught up into the very life of the Godhead. His unity with Christ is necessarily a unity with those who share with him the fellowship in Christ, and it is at the same time a sharing in the very unity of the Son with the Father (John xvii. 21). Justification is the means whereby we are admitted into the very fellowship of the Holiest Himself, receiving the love with which the Father loves the Son and united with the love which the Son perpetually offers to the Father. God has raised us up to sit with Christ in the heavenly places (Eph. ii. 6). This sharing in the life of God Himself is the necessary counterpart of the intensely personal and inward experience of faith. It is, at the same time, and with equal necessity, perfectly social and perfectly personal.

This is not only a matter of speculation, but is the sober truth of Christian experience. The proof of it is that God has given us " the earnest of the Spirit " (2 Cor. i. 22, v. 5; cf. Eph. i. 14). God has sealed the faith of those who hear and believe the Gospel of His redeeming work in Christ by giving to them in a manner that none can mistake or gainsay His own Spirit in their hearts (e.g., Acts x. 47; Gal. iii. 2; Eph. i. 13, etc.). The Spirit has revealed His presence by bringing forth in them His fruits; it is by Him that they cry Abba Father, and confess that Jesus Christ is Lord (Rom. viii. 15; 1 Cor. xii. 3). This gift of the Spirit is an " earnest." It is at the same time a real sharing in the life of God Himself and also a foretaste of the perfect life in Him which is to come. It is given to those who hear and believe the Gospel. The long arguments about justification in Romans and Galatians are immediately followed by passages which show that the fruit of justification is to walk not after the flesh but after the Spirit (Rom. viii; Gal. v. 16ff.). "The letter" (of the Mosaic law) is contrasted with the Spirit, the former as belonging to the old Covenant which had its end in condemnation and death, the latter as belonging to the new Covenant, which has its end in righteousness and glory (2 Cor. iii. 6). The intimate connection between justification and the gift of the Spirit must be apparent when it is seen that justification is God's acceptance of men as righteous and has as its fruit the admission of them into the communion of the Son with the Father. So also the likening of this gift to an "earnest" is a reminder of the essentially eschatological character of the idea of justification.

The sphere of the Spirit's working is the Church. This sharing in the very life of God Himself through the Spirit *is* the life of the Church. "There is one body and one Spirit." Just as it is in the Spirit that we share in the self-offering of the Son to the Father, so it is in the Spirit that we share in the fellowship of those who share this life. Our common life is a common sharing (κοινωνία) in the Holy Spirit. The Spirit gives His gifts for the purpose of building up the Body. That is their meaning. The unity and interdependence of the one Body and its members is the work of the one Spirit.

This indissoluble connection between the Spirit and the Church is one which seems very frequently to be lost sight of in current writing and speaking about the Church. It is taken for granted that the Holy Spirit is at work outside the bounds of the visible Church, and indeed, outside of any conscious connection with Jesus Christ at all, and the way is thereby opened for a doctrine of the Church which defines it in purely institutional terms while leaving room for a generous, not to say indiscriminate, acknowledgment of the presence of the Spirit outside it. In fact, the phrase "the Holy Spirit" is used to cover those parts of our thinking which we decline to bring under the discipline of strictly orthodox Christological and ecclesiological doctrine. Such thinking (or such failure to think) has the New Testament solidly against it. Its unanimous teaching is that the terms Holy Spirit and Body of Christ are correlates, that the Holy Spirit is given to believers in Christ and makes His presence known by unmistakable signs, of which the greatest is that charity which builds up the Body, and that the test of His presence is the confession, "Jesus Christ is Lord."

This indissoluble correlation of the one Spirit and the one Body rests upon the fact that the fruit of the presence of the Spirit is love. Those who are in Christ are caught up into that perpetual self-offering of the Son to the Father in the Spirit which is the life of the Godhead. This love is a gift; it is wholly the response of penitent and adoring gratitude to God's redeeming work in Christ. It finds its exercise, as love must do, in all that "builds up the Body." Upon it rests that mutual service and mutual dependence by which alone a body can live. Faction and division spring from carnality, from relying upon man rather than upon God. By these the Gospel itself is obscured—for it was Christ, not Paul or Cephas, who was crucified (1 Cor. i. 13). By the Church's visible unity, on the other hand, the Gospel is proclaimed. The marvellous unity of Jew and Gentile in a visible fellowship is the means by which the age-long purpose of God to sum up all things in Christ is now being revealed (Eph. iii. 1-13).

Unity implies continuity, for where there is unity authority will pass from generation to generation in orderly succession. The New Testament, for the reason already referred to, does not have much to say about continuity. This does not, however, alter the fact that what it has to say about unity has necessary implications with regard to continuity. The one Holy Spirit, and the one visible Church united through all the world and through all time from the Apostles to the present day, are necessarily and indissolubly correlates. There is one Body and one Spirit.

And yet one has immediately to add that while this is true in the sense that there is no rational ground upon which the two can be separated, yet in fact the irrational and absurd fact of sin *in the Church* always and everywhere upsets the correlation. The same Church to which it is said, "Ye are the Body of Christ" is also at the same time filled with faction and carnality. The Church is both holy and sinful. This is the fundamental root of the whole problem of the Church, that it is a union of sinful souls with the Holy God. We have seen that the distinction between corporeality and spirituality in the Church is not the essential one. But for sin the Body and the Spirit would be the perfect counterparts of each other. Sin is what drives them apart. It is useless to attempt to rationalize this situation in terms of the visible and the invisible Church. There is no invisible Church of souls perfectly united to Christ. It is not that some men are perfectly united with Christ and others not, and that these are mixed up together in the visible Church. It is that all Christians are both holy and sinful, both united with God by His gracious act in accepting them as righteous on the ground of faith in His redeeming work in Christ, and also at the same time liable to sin and guilty of sin. It is that they have a righteousness which is real, for it is sealed by the gift of the Holy Spirit Himself by whom they confess Jesus Christ as Lord, and yet it is not a righteousness of their own, for they have to receive it afresh every day as they give themselves to Christ afresh in penitent faith. It is a righteousness which they do not possess apart from God, but which is perpetually given them as they live the life of faith in God.

The Church is both holy and sinful, as the Christian is both holy and sinful. That is the root of the problem of the Church. And the Church is holy not because of something which it possesses in itself but because it lives in faith, the faith which is the response of God's redeeming act in Christ. Its life is lived always in this dimension of faith in the living and ever-present Lord. Its life is a perpetual receiving from God and giving to God. Its holiness, its justification, its possession of the Spirit is not something given at a point in history and then possessed once for all, like treasure stored in its vaults. It is holy, it is justified, it is indwelt by the Spirit, always and only by faith; and faith is a response new every morning to the redeeming work of Christ. Just as a man who regards his justification as an event in the past which now, because it has once happened, secures him against sin, is in fact fallen away from grace; so also a Church which thinks that it possesses the law of its own development and the resources of grace in itself, is fallen from grace. There are many more forms than one in which this fall may occur. The claim of historical correctness, evangelistic zeal, and ethical achievement are all equally—in apostolic language—carnal. " God forbid that I should glory save in the Cross of our Lord Jesus Christ " is the apostolic answer to all our denominational claims. The Church does not live by what it possesses and has inherited. It lives in the dynamic relationship of ever-new penitence and faith before the Cross of Jesus Christ, and its unity, its continuity, and all its spiritual gifts are the fruits of that.

We have, therefore, to condemn, on the one hand, the view which defines the Church as a historically continuous society which has, among its activities, the preaching of the Word and the administration of the Sacraments. We have to condemn it because it destroys the eschatological dimension of the Church's existence. The Church lives by faith in Christ, and the Word and the Sacraments are the means whereby Christ offers Himself to men as the evoker of faith and as the creator and re-creator of the Church. We have equally to condemn, on the other hand, the view which severs this faith from its necessary correlate—the unity of the whole Body. In denying that institutional continuity is the decisive "mark" of the Church we have to avoid the equally disastrous error of regarding institutional unity and continuity as an optional matter. We believe that God in His amazing mercy blesses His Word and Sacraments with fruit even in our division from one another, so that even though we are divided, we are still His Church. If we go on to acquiesce in our divisions we are of those who say, "Let us continue in sin that grace may abound." We flout His pardoning grace. Our services of Holy Communion in which we cannot share one table are as scandalous as those that St. Paul had to deal with in Corinth, however reverently we conduct them. "The bread which we break, is it not a communion of the body of Christ? seeing that we, who are many, are one bread, one body: for we all partake of the one bread" (1 Cor. x. 17). Our pride in the great traditions of our denominational forefathers is as carnal as that of the Corinthian factions in Paul, Apollos and Cephas. "For when one saith, I am of Paul; and another, I am of Apollos; are ye not men? What then is Apollos? and what is Paul? Ministers through whom ye believed; and each as the Lord gave to him" (1 Cor. iii. 4). Everyone who has concerned himself in the practical issues of Christian reunion knows the fearful strength of the corporate pride of a denominational group, the terrifying power of group-egotism when it has taken into its service memories of great and godly men, scholars, saints, and martyrs of the faith. Only one thing can subdue it, and that is the word of the Cross, before which no flesh can glory. The word of the Cross to the Church is a summons to return in penitence and faith to Him in whom alone is our righteousness, to abandon confidence in everything save His mercy, and to accept and embody in our institutional life that unity with one another which is given to us in Him.

CHAPTER SEVEN

THE METHOD OF REUNION

IN the light of the argument which we have pursued, we have now to address ourselves to the question, What is involved in an attempt to re-unite the Church? and in particular we have to consider the South India Scheme in the light of the conclusions we have reached.

One preliminary matter may be disposed of, in the first place. In attacks upon the South India Scheme and other similar projects it has frequently been stated that as the reunion of the Church must be the work of the Holy Spirit, these " man-made " schemes are to be rejected. There is as much and as little force in the argument as in the speeches of those Churchmen who sought to crush the first beginnings of the modern missionary expansion of the Church with the assertion that God would convert the heathen in His own good time, and that while Christians should pray that He should do so it was a blasphemous impertinence for them to attempt to forestall Him. It is indeed true that the reunion of the Church must be the work of God's Spirit, and there is indeed a real danger that a Scheme of Union may become the centre of an enthusiasm which is—in the Pauline sense—carnal. But if, as we have argued, the Church is divided because of sin, there are required of us both a penitent return to Christ and His atoning work, and also acts of obedience to His will. Penitence and faith must issue in acts, and among these the acts necessary to restore the visible unity of the Church have a high importance. It would be possible to set about the reunion of the Church in a purely carnal sense, out of a desire for more impressive and efficient machinery or for the sense of security which large numbers give. But it is also possible to seek reunion from a sense of the compulsion that is laid upon one by the Gospel. It was that compulsion which sent the first missionaries to Africa and the East, and I have tried to show that it is a similar compulsion which has driven the Church in South India to seek reunion. It would be a strangely un-Biblical view of the Holy Spirit which condemned as unspiritual ecclesiastical acts done under this sense of the compulsion of the Gospel.

THE METHOD OF REUNION

In the second place, it will be clear, if the preceding arguments are sound, that what is involved is the reunion of divided bodies which are, in spite of their division, nevertheless truly parts of the Church. They are not "branches." If they were it would be absurd to tie them together. They are no more "branches" of the Church than are two divorced persons "branches" of one family. They are parts of the Church broken from one another by sin but yet held still to Christ by His grace. Our Lord's metaphor of the vine and the branches is designed to emphasize the absolute necessity of union. Nothing could be more opposed to His intention than the use of it to rationalize schism.

If, then, the divided bodies are truly parts of the Church, two methods of uniting them are ruled out. One is that which treats one part as alone the Church and the others as dissident groups which have to be reunited to it. The other is that which treats all the parts as though they were quite separate and autonomous human societies which could freely decide whether and on what terms they will agree to form unions with one another. Reunion must be the restoring of the unity which has been broken, the fruit of a penitent return to Christ Himself. But that return can only mean the re-submission of all our life and thought and practice afresh to Him, for it is from Him alone that—even in our separation—we have our existence as a Church. We only know Christ through the Church, but, in fact, the Church means "the churches" with their varying traditions of belief and practice and piety. For each of us the life in Christ is also life in a fellowship shaped by these traditions. Nor is it open to us to dissolve away these externals of church life and live some sort of disembodied spiritual life without them. We are not discarnate spirits. But neither are we the mere products of our different traditions. We are persons responsible to God. Our traditions are not ultimates. They are put into our hands and we have the power and the duty to submit them ever afresh to the judgment of Christ. The task of reunion involves primarily this return to Christ to seek His judgment upon ourselves and all that we are, to give ourselves afresh to Him in penitence and faith as we face again and again the pain and tension of our differences from one another.

The fruit of that return to Christ must include fresh efforts of thought designed to clarify theological issues. But the basis of union will not be a theological statement which sets at rest the doctrinal divisions between the separated Churches. It cannot be too strongly stressed that the basis of union is a reality in the personal realm. It is the finished work of Christ for all men, and the unity with Him in the Spirit which is given to believers. Within this unity there will always be doctrinal differences. And if the Church is to live and grow in Him, there must be clear thinking about differences, and if necessary vigorous controversy, so that the Church may know if and when the Gospel itself is threatened by false doctrine. But the unity of the Church is not intellectual agreement upon doctrines; it is unity in that charity which is given through faith in the Gospel. Within that unity there is room for the vigorous prosecution of debate and argument designed to further the understanding of the Gospel, and to protect the Church from perversions and denials of the Gospel. A Church constitution must arm the Church with sufficient powers to enable it to expel from its life things which threaten to prevent the true preaching of the Gospel and the right administration of the sacraments, but it is not the purpose of such a document to provide formulæ which settle all the theological issues which divide the separated Churches. The history of the Church, and not least of the Protestant Churches, provides enough illustration of the fact that such attempts to add to the ecumenical creeds can only issue in further division and further obscuring of the true character of the Church as the new humanity in Christ.

The Scheme of Church Union in South India involves the reunion of four dioceses of the Anglican communion, claiming to have maintained unbroken the succession of episcopal consecration and ordination from the undivided Church, with other Churches, which possess a ministerial succession discontinuous with this episcopal succession. The central issue in the debate about the Scheme is in regard to the bearing of the manner of reunion upon the doctrine of the Church's unity and continuity. For the reason stated, the Scheme itself does not provide an agreed statement of doctrine such as would settle this debate. Such a statement is not yet possible. But the method of union which the Scheme sets out is, as I shall seek to show, congruous with the principles which I have tried to state in the preceding sections, and designed to safeguard the Church from wrong solutions of the problem.

THE METHOD OF REUNION

In its bare essentials the method of reunion in South India, as far as it concerns the present discussion, is based on four points:

(1) All members and ministers of the uniting Churches are accepted as members and ministers respectively of the united Church, provided that they assent to the Basis of Union and accept the Constitution. Bishops of the four dioceses are accepted as bishops in the united Church, and all the other ministers of the uniting Churches who have been ordained as ministers of the Word and Sacraments are acknowledged as such in the united Church and have the status of Presbyters therein. Similarly with deacons and probationers. B.U. 11 (p. 12).

(2) In the united Church every ordination of presbyters will be performed by the laying on of hands of the bishop and presbyters, and all consecrations of bishops by the laying on of hands at least of three bishops. Continuity with the historic episcopate is both at the beginning and thereafter to be effectively maintained. The bishops will perform their functions in accordance with the customs of the Church, these being named and defined in the constitution of the Church of South India, and including pastoral oversight, evangelism, teaching, supervision of public worship, ordination and authorization of ministers and oversight of discipline. B.U. 9 (pp. 10-11), Const. IV (pp. 44-6).

(3) The uniting Churches pledge themselves that the union will not be used to over-ride conscientiously held convictions and to impose on congregations either forms of worship or a ministry to which they conscientiously object. B.U. 16 (pp. 18-19).

(4) While at the time of the union the Church will include a large number of ministers who have not received episcopal ordination, it is agreed that the intention and expectation of the uniting Churches is that eventually every minister exercising a permanent ministry in the united Church will be an episcopally ordained minister. For a period of 30 years from the inauguration of the union, the ministers of any Church whose missions have founded the originally separate parts of the united Church may be received as ministers of the united Church provided they accept its Governing Principles and Constitution. After this period of 30 years the Church itself will determine the conditions under which it is to receive ministers from other Churches. B.U. 16 (pp. 17-18).

THE REUNION OF THE CHURCH

It will be apparent that the method of reunion is no simple and straightforward affair. That is necessary. I have tried to show that simple and straightforward solutions evade the real problem. The division of the Church of Christ by sin is something utterly absurd and illogical. The method of reunion cannot be simple.

In the first place, the method acknowledges that the uniting Churches are truly parts of the Church. Their members are accepted as members and their ministers as ministers. What is taking place is a reunion of divided parts of the Church, not the return of dissident brethren to the one Church.

In the second place, however, those parts of the Church which have left the historically continuous succession now return to it. The union is not the creation of a new "merger" by independent groups. It is the return to a broken unity. The united Church will be within the historically continuous succession of episcopal ordination and consecration. The non-episcopal Churches concerned in the union will be brought into that succession, outside of which they have hitherto lived. The union will thus seek to express not merely the desire of the uniting bodies to be one, but the fact that their unity is a unity of the whole Body of which Christ is Head, the unity of the whole building which has apostles and prophets for its foundation stones. The union is not the creation of something new, but the restoration of something which had been broken.

It is true that there are in the Scheme of Union extremely negative statements regarding the historic episcopate. The statement that continuity with the historic episcopate is to be effectively maintained is coupled with the statement that no particular interpretation thereof is thereby demanded of any minister or member. This, and other similar statements, have to be read in their relation to their context and to the whole Scheme. At the very outset, in speaking of the nature and purpose of the union, the uniting Churches say: "It is the will of Christ that His Church should be one. . . . It is also His will that there should be a ministry accepted and fully effective throughout the world-wide Church" (B.U. 1). The whole Scheme, and in particular its provisions regarding the episcopate, are to be read in the light of these basic convictions. Furthermore no discussion of details of phrasing ought to be allowed to obscure the main fact, which is that representatives of the great non-episcopal communions, whose traditions are so much bound up with resistance in the name of faith to episcopal claims, are here accepting not merely episcopacy, but the historic episcopate, the re-engrafting of separated life into the original episcopal stem; and that they are doing this not grudgingly as the "price of union," but in the belief that episcopacy "is needed for the shepherding and extension of the Church in South India" (B.U. 9). The section in the Basis of Union which deals with "The Episcopate in the United Church" refers to the wide variety of doctrines held in the uniting Churches regarding the episcopate, and disclaims—as it must do—any attempt to lay down *as part of the basis of union* a definitive doctrine in the matter. What must be clear, I think, to anyone who reads the Scheme with a sympathetic understanding of the problems that it seeks to face, is that the negative statements are intended to secure that the acceptance of the historic episcopate does not involve acceptance of the doctrine that episcopacy is the divinely appointed basis of the Church, and that it alone can guarantee valid sacraments and a valid ministry. And from the whole Scheme of Union it is equally clear, I think, that the uniting Churches are accepting the historic episcopate and returning to it as an act of obedience to Christ's will that there should be "a ministry accepted and fully effective throughout the world-wide Church." The historic episcopate, in other words, is accepted as that which has been and may be again the organ and expression of the Church's unity, its unity through time with all who have gone before and through space with all everywhere who call Christ Lord. But the return to it must be in such wise that the true nature of the Church's union, a union in Christ and in the Father through the Spirit, is not obscured. Of this union a continuous historical order and a ministry carrying the unbroken authority of the whole Church are the proper expression, but they are not the guarantee.

Of the alternatives which have been proposed to this method of reunion some do not now call for any discussion. Those, on the one hand, who have urged "simple episcopacy" as against "the historic episcopate," and those, on the other, who propose for the non-episcopal Churches a period of probation followed by episcopal re-ordination, have failed equally to understand the nature of the problem. One proposal, however, is of much greater weight and has been commended with great persuasiveness—the proposal of "supplemental ordination" as the basis of union.

This proposal has been made on several occasions from the episcopal side, in South India, in the U.S.A., and in Iran. Something of the idea, though not the name, is contained in the Lambeth Appeal of 1920. It was commended with very great earnestness to the Joint Committee by the Church of India, Burma and Ceylon, and no one present could fail to feel the spiritual power which lay behind the bringing forward of such a proposal in such circumstances. The essential basis of the proposal is that by the division of the Church not merely some but all have lost an element of the validity which should belong to the ministry of the Church. Because none of our ministries carries the authorization of the whole Church, all lack complete validity. The way of reunion, therefore, must be that each should seek from the other that which it lacks. In the words of the American proposal:

"It is proposed to make it possible for clergymen of both Churches to administer the Word and Sacraments to all members of the United Church. The rite by which this aim is accomplished shall not be regarded as ordination *de novo*, but as a supplemental ordination. The expression 'supplemental ordination' is intended to imply that he who receives it is recognized to have been truly ordained to the ministry of Christ's Church, and that by the supplemental rite he receives such further grace of orders and such authority for the wider exercise of his ministry as, according to God's will, may be conveyed through the action of the Church in and by which the rite is performed."

To this very clear exposition of the proposal it is only right to add the comment of Bishops Palmer and Western in their letter on the subject communicated to the Joint Committee:

"We must insist on the point that the essence of the problem is to find a way by which, on the one hand, Orders such as we Anglicans have inherited from the undivided Church should be given to those who have not previously received them; while, on the other hand, it should be recognized that their ordinations have made them true ministers of Christ's Word and Sacraments, and also that Anglican ministers should receive something more than an extension of jurisdiction such as could be given by constitutional enactment without any prayer or laying on of hands."[1]

[1] *Church Union News and Views*, March 1944, p. 35.

THE METHOD OF REUNION

One covets for all Christian Churches this grace of willingness to recognize that which they lack, and this willingness to seek it from others. And one must certainly agree that the recognition of the whole Church is an element in the validity of a ministry. But the more these proposals are examined in detail, the greater are the difficulties which appear.

In the first place, the rite means two different things in the two different circumstances. As Bishops Palmer and Western have pointed out, what is required in the case of the supplemental ordination of non-episcopal ministers is the conveying of orders inherited from the undivided Church. This is quite clear and understandable. By this act a minister of the non-episcopal Church would become, what he is not now, a minister recognized by Anglicans as one duly ordained in the Catholic Church. But, in the case of supplemental ordination of a minister of the Anglican communion by, let us say, a Presbytery, what is it that is conveyed? The letter quoted says, "something more than an extension of jurisdiction." What is that "something more?" It is not ordination, for the Presbyterian Churches already recognize Anglican orders as valid. Canon Broomfield says: "The acceptance by Anglican clergy, also as part of an act of union, of ordination at the hands of the Free Churches would add to the inheritance of themselves and their Church everything which God has granted to the Free Churches."[1] But is this what ordination means? It is certainly not what the ordination formulæ of the Presbyterian Churches mean. We certainly need to receive from one another spiritual enrichment through sharing the inheritances of piety, service and scholarship which we have treasured separately, but is it not a confusion of thought to say that mutual ordination is the means of this mutual sharing? Certainly the words of the service of ordination do not convey this meaning.[2] "Orders inherited from the undivided Church" can be conveyed by ordination to those who do not possess them. But the post-Reformation Churches have no corresponding orders to convey. If Anglican orders were regarded as—equally with non-episcopal—defective in that they derive only from the divided Church of the Reformation, and do not convey, any more than do others, the recognition

---
[1] Gerald Broomfield: *Anglican and Free Church Ministries*. S.P.C.K., 1944.
[2] Reference may here be made to the discussion of the nature of ordination on pp. 194-201, and in particular to the extract from the "Ordinal" of the Church of Scotland given there.

of the whole Church, then there would be mutuality in an act of supplemental ordination. But that is not the position. Anglican orders derive from the undivided Church because they derive from bishops who were consecrated by those who, in the undivided Church, had the authority to consecrate. Non-episcopal orders are derived from bodies which, in the undivided Church, had not the authority to ordain. They therefore have no corresponding authorization to offer to the Anglicans. The point at issue is the relation of "lineal descent" (in Knox's phrase) to the being of the Church. If such lineal descent is essential, then non-episcopal ministries require re-ordination, but have nothing to give in return; if it is not essential, but, as I have argued, normative and expressive, then the proper method of reunion is that of the Scheme. This method is, briefly, first, the recognition of the fact that God has graciously accepted our ministries in spite of our sins of schism, and of the fact that God's acceptance does not require our further validation; secondly, the act of obedience to His will by entering into organic union, in which union alone can the full sharing of our several inheritances take place; thirdly, the accepting and carrying forward of that form of holy order which, having been received from the undivided Church, and resting upon the largest possible area of authority in the whole Church, is the means whereby God's will may be accomplished that there should be a ministry accepted and fully effective throughout the whole Church.

One must ask, in the second place, whether the whole conception of what ordination means is not confused by regarding ordination as something which can be done more than once. It must be emphasized that since the proposal for supplemental ordination rests upon the belief that all our ministries are lacking in authority because of our separation, and that the method of reunion must be the mutual sharing of the authority which we have received in separation, it follows that on every occasion on which a union of Churches takes place, the entire ministry would undergo the rite of supplemental ordination. If, as one hopes, the union in South India provides a growing point for further union, it would follow that on every occasion on which another body joined the United Church, even if it were a small body, the entire ministries of both Churches would be ordained. One cannot but think that a Church whose ministers found themselves receiving the rite of supplemental ordination several times in a lifetime would find it very difficult to attach to ordination the values which the Church has always attached. Once again one must say that the words of our ordinals carry a different and weightier meaning than that which seems here to be implied. There is a clear distinction, surely, between ordination, which is always to the ministry of the Church of Christ, and the acts of authorization, induction and installation by which an ordained minister receives authority to exercise his ministry in a particular sphere. The latter may be repeated many times, but the former is unrepeatable. The act of union will include an act of the second kind by which the ministers of the uniting Churches will receive the extension of authority necessary to enable them to exercise their ministry in the wider sphere created by the union. Those who urge the proposal of supplemental ordination desire something which is definitely of the first kind. If this is accepted, the distinction between ordination and authorization will be very hard to maintain.

It is true, as Quick[1] points out in dealing with this matter, that ordination itself involves the two distinguishable gifts of power and authority, and that the element of authority in ordination is affected by the fact that in the divided state of the Church there is no ordination which carries the authority of the whole Church. It is true that we cannot accept the view (based on Augustine) that the validity of orders is quite independent of recognition by the Church. Yet this does not mean that we must abandon the idea that the sphere of authority in ordination is the whole Catholic Church and conclude that when a man is ordained he is ordained only to the ministry of a denomination. That would destroy the very meaning of ordination. It would require the scrapping of all our present ordinals. The Holy Catholic Church has not ceased to exist, defaced and divided though it is by our sin, and our ordination is to its ministry. It is true that owing to our divisions the authority of the whole Church is not behind our ordinations. But these divisions are but the manifestations of sin, and it is not for us to try to rationalize them and say that our ordinations are to one or other of the " branches " of the Church. The cardinal fact is that God in His mercy has not allowed our sinful divisions to destroy the operation of His grace, but has continued to give to the Church ministers empowered by His grace

[1] O. C. Quick, *The Christian Sacraments*, Chap. VII.

for the perfecting of the saints, for the work of ministering, unto the building up of the body of Christ. Our part is to recognize what He has so abundantly done, and to seek to restore that orderly unity of life which is His will for us and the fruit of the Spirit, whom He has given to us. What has been lacking in authority will be made up by the constitutional acts of the uniting Churches in the act of union and by the United Church itself, but they will be of the category of authorization, not of ordination. And for the filling up of that which has been lacking in the needed spiritual gifts, the common life of the re-united body will provide abundant means.

The foregoing discussion has referred to the first two of the four features of the South India method of reunion, and with the proposal of supplemental ordination which is an alternative to them. But this proposal would also have rendered unnecessary the other two features, those generally referred to as the Pledge, and the Thirty Year Period. To a consideration of these we now turn.

The Pledge is essentially the recognition of the principle that the basis of union is a reality in the personal realm. The uniting Churches have not reached unanimity on the doctrine of the ministry. But they have been led by obedience to the Gospel to recognize one another as truly parts of the Church, and to seek to restore their broken unity in the Body of Christ. In their sharing in the common task of evangelism, no less than in the long processes of discussion which have led to the framing of the Scheme of Union, they have learned that even though they are far from doctrinal unanimity on questions of Church order, they can trust one another as members together in Christ. They have come to see that this relationship of personal trust belongs to the very essence of that unity in Christ which they seek to express in their visible unity as one Church. And this conviction is built into the very structure of the Scheme in the passage known as the Pledge.

The situation to which the Pledge refers can be readily understood. At the inauguration of the union all the ministers of the uniting Churches are to be accepted as ministers of the united Church. Thus about half the ministers of the new Church will be men not episcopally ordained. On the other hand, about half the congregations of the Church will consist of those who have grown up and lived under the rule which requires episcopal

THE METHOD OF REUNION

ordination.[1] As we have seen, the act of union requires us to raise the question of the relation of this rule to the being of the Church, and the basis of union is incompatible with the view that this rule belongs to the divinely given constitution of the Church in such wise that apart from it there is no Church. Yet it is apparent that many who would be willing to assent to the basis of union might reasonably be unwilling for themselves to abandon that rule, and might indeed have grave conscientious difficulties about accepting permanently the ministry of men not episcopally ordained. There are similar difficulties on the side of those who have been brought up under non-episcopal ministries and with habits of worship very different from those of the Anglican Church.

There is only one way in which such difficulties can be dealt with—the way of mutual trust. The Pledge is just a statement of that fact. The following is its full text:

> "The uniting Churches recognize that the act of union will initiate a process of growing together into one life and of advance towards complete spiritual unity. One essential condition of the attainment of such complete unity is that all the members of the united Church should be willing and able to receive communion equally in all of its churches, and it is the resolve of the uniting Churches to do all in their power to that end.
>
> "But they are convinced that this can only take place on the basis of freedom of opinion on debatable matters, and respect for even large differences of opinion and practice, such as exist at present, for example, with regard to forms of worship or the conditions regarded as necessary for the valid celebration of Holy Communion. They believe that this freedom and mutual respect can be safeguarded not by the framing of detailed regulations but by assurances given and received in a spirit of confidence and love.
>
> "They therefore pledge themselves and fully trust each other that the united Church will at all times be careful not to allow

---

[1] It is perhaps not generally appreciated that the foundations of much of the Anglican work in South India were laid by men not episcopally ordained; and that their ministrations continued, without any question of re-ordination being raised, after the establishment of the Indian episcopate and even into the nineteenth century. Nevertheless, of course, the present generation of Anglican Indian Christians has grown up under the universal rule of episcopal ordination. (See *Church Union News and Views*, June 1946.)

any over-riding of conscience either by Church authorities or by majorities, and that it will not in any of its administrative acts knowingly transgress the long-established traditions of any of the Churches from which it has been formed. Neither forms of worship or ritual, nor a ministry, to which they have not been accustomed or to which they conscientiously object, will be imposed upon any congregation; and no arrangements with regard to these matters will knowingly be made, either generally or in particular cases, which would either offend the conscientious convictions of persons directly concerned, or which would hinder the development of complete unity within the united Church or imperil its progress towards union with other Churches."

This is a statement made and accepted by people who trust one another. What is often forgotten is that this trust is not something secondary or auxiliary to the nature of the Church, a sort of lubricant in its machinery. Such trust is in fact one element in the charity by which the Church lives, a mark of the presence of the Holy Spirit. The Pledge has sometimes been referred to as a "gentlemen's agreement," but that is surely an objectionable phrase, for it seems to suggest that while we cannot agree as Christians we can get on together as gentlemen. It suggests that our theological principles have been subordinated to the demands of a social code. But that is not what has happened. It is that as Christians we are led by the Holy Spirit to trust one another because—in spite of our differences—we recognize one another as being in Christ; and that we recognize that this mutual trust belongs to the very essence and constitution of the Church. Only because this is so, because we recognize in one another the fruits of the Holy Spirit, are we permitted and bound to seek the visible reunion of the Body, confident that in our obedience we shall be led into the fuller understanding of the Truth which now we see only in part.

Unfortunately the Pledge has sometimes been misunderstood because its real nature was forgotten. The promise not to transgress the long-established traditions of any of the Churches might —manifestly—be so interpreted as to prohibit all development of unity in the Church, and to constitute in effect a contradiction of the basis of union. To meet such misunderstandings the Joint Committee in 1934 sought to make plain again what its intention was. The following is the Minute of the meeting of that year as slightly amended in 1935:

"That in view of questions which have arisen, the Joint Committee thinks it right to state what is in its judgment the meaning of the provisions generally referred to as the Pledge.

"This Pledge applies to the period following the inauguration of the union when the members of the three Churches, then united in one Church, will be growing together; and the uniting Churches pledge themselves to do all in their power to assist the united Church in its advance towards complete spiritual unity, and towards the time when all the members of the united Church will be willing and able to receive communion equally in all its Churches.

"Further, they pledge themselves that because of the union no congregation shall be deprived of forms of worship or a ministry to which it has been accustomed, but every honest endeavour will be made by the authorities of the united Church that neither forms of worship or ritual, nor a ministry, to which they have not been accustomed or to which they conscientiously object, shall be imposed upon any congregation. But the Committee does not understand the pledge to imply that the fact that a minister of the united Church has previously been a minister of either an episcopal or a non-episcopal Church, will, in itself, debar him from appointment to or working in any congregation of the united Church where that congregation desires it.

"Further, the intention of the uniting Churches is that there shall be no infringement of the liberty of conscience which every worshipper and every minister now enjoys, and that in the united Church all alike shall be free to worship and to teach according to their conscience, only so that nothing be done to break the fundamental unity of the Church.

"The Joint Committee wishes further to urge upon the negotiating Churches that while the purpose for which these provisions have been inserted in the Basis of Union will not be fulfilled unless the real scope and effect of the pledge be understood by all parties, that purpose will be entirely defeated if detailed interpretations of the pledge, and precise statements as to its application to particular future and hypothetical cases, are demanded; and it appeals to the negotiating Churches to act in this matter in the full spirit of the declaration that freedom of opinion on debatable matters and mutual respect for differences of opinion and practice can be safeguarded, not by the framing of detailed regulations, but by assurances given and received in a spirit of confidence and love."

Further difficulties arose because it was thought that the words, "where that congregation desires it" in the third paragraph of the Minute implied that the desire of an individual congregation would be allowed to settle such matters apart from the will of the Church as a whole, and the Joint Committee had to explain in its Minute of 1946 that the phrase meant:

" (i) such appointments would not be made if a congregation objects on conscientious grounds, and
" (ii) as stated in II (9) of the Governing Principles of the Church, ' every pastorate . . . shall have an opportunity of expressing its judgment . . . as to the appointment of its pastor,' while the responsibility for making the appointment remains with the duly constituted authority of the united Church."

At the same time the Joint Committee gave this explanation of its intentions:

" It is understood that during the period of unification, congregations will ordinarily continue to be served by the ministries to which they are accustomed, except where pastoral needs obviously demand other arrangements. The duly constituted authority within the united Church shall be the sole judge of the urgency of such pastoral needs."

The Pledge must clearly not be so construed as to be a contradiction of the Basis of Union. It is not possible with integrity to agree that in theory a certain proposition is accepted, but that in invariable practice the Church will proceed as though it were not true. What the Pledge does is to recognize that the unity of the Church is a reality in the personal order, and that therefore the terms of the union are not to be used to over-ride conscientious conviction, but that everything is to be done for the pastoral good of the Church. Every presbyter in the Church will be capable of performing the ministerial acts which belong to his office, and where—in the judgment of the Church—the pastoral good of the Church requires it, he may be called upon to minister in any congregation. But pastoral ends will not be served by acts which over-ride deeply held convictions and coerce conscientious minorities. The union is possible—and obligatory—because the

THE METHOD OF REUNION

uniting Churches recognize in one another the fruits of the Spirit of Him who would not break the bruised reed or quench the smoking flax. This surely is the Spirit who was in St. Paul, when he was at once so adamant in his defence of Gospel principles and so tender, so willing to go to all lengths, in his application of them to the individual brother for whom Christ died. The mutual trust of which the Pledge is the expression is the gift of that Spirit by whom the Church lives.

Closely connected with the Pledge is the provision known as the Thirty Year Period. The text of this section is as follows:

> "The uniting Churches agree that it is their intention and expectation that eventually every minister exercising a permanent ministry in the united Church will be an episcopally ordained minister.
>
> "For the thirty years succeeding the inauguration of the union, the ministers of any Church whose missions have founded the originally separate parts of the united Church may be received as ministers of the united Church, if they are willing to give the same assent to the Governing Principles of the united Church and the same promise to accept its Constitution as will be required from persons to be ordained or employed for the first time in that Church. After this period of thirty years, the united Church must determine for itself whether it will continue to make any exceptions to the rule that its ministry is an episcopally ordained ministry, and generally under what conditions it will receive ministers from other Churches into its ministry. It is trusted that in its consideration of these matters it will give equal weight to the principle that there shall be a fully unified ministry within the Church, and to the no less fundamental principle that the united Church should maintain and extend full communion and fellowship with those Churches with which the uniting Churches now severally have such fellowship. It is understood that the status of those at that time already received as ministers in the united Church shall not be affected by any action which the united Church may then take."

This section is a further proof of the fact that the trust with which the uniting Churches enter upon union is not merely a trust in one another but, more fundamentally, a trust in the promise of Christ that the Holy Spirit will guide His Church into all the truth. The different practices and doctrines regarding the ministry with which the uniting Churches enter the union are not to be allowed merely to remain side by side. The united Church has the task and duty of seeking together answers to the problems which they have not been able to solve in separation. No one can as yet see how the differences with which we enter upon the union are to be resolved. But we believe that the first duty is that we should be one, and that as we obey this primary command, we shall be led by the Spirit to that clearer vision which we have not yet received. The conviction that the Holy Spirit is indeed ready to lead the Church into the truth is here no merely formal assent to a traditional doctrine. The uniting Churches are staking upon it all their inheritance. If this faith be vain, then indeed the union is a ramshackle structure that will fall to pieces at the first blow. But if it be true that having believed the Gospel, and having received the earnest of the Spirit by whom we confess that Jesus is Lord, and being bound therefore to manifest His unity in one body, we shall be led by Him into the truth we do not yet see, then we are right in leaving this issue to be settled by the Church in the light of a generation's experience as one body.

Dr. Trevor Jalland has proposed as an alternative to the South India Scheme that the non-episcopal Churches should be invited to organize themselves forthwith upon an episcopal basis, and that when they have acquired the requisite degree of conformity to the standards of the Anglican Communion in doctrine and morals, they should receive episcopal ordination and be incorporated into the Anglican Communion. He commends this plan on the grounds that " it would have allowed time for the operation of the guidance of the Holy Ghost and would not have sprung from an artificial creation of unity on the basis of a paper agreement such as the existing Scheme," and that " the Anglican Communion would in no way be compromised, if for some unforeseen cause the plan broke down."[1] There are many issues one would like to discuss with Dr. Jalland, but it must suffice here to say that the South India Scheme possesses no such insurance against possible breakdown. It is a venture of obedience and faith resting on no other security than the conviction that those who trust in God, while they may fail, will not be confounded.

It is a venture of faith in which more than South India is involved. The thirty-year period is not only to be envisaged as a period allowed for the development of full unity within the

[1] Jalland: *The Bible, the Church and South India*, p. 93.

THE METHOD OF REUNION

Church of South India. If that were all, the fruit of the thirty years would be but one more denomination. That would indeed be failure. In that case it is difficult to see how the decisions which the Church has to make after thirty years could be made. The purpose with which the uniting Churches enter upon the union is of wider range.

"The uniting Churches are agreed that in every effort to bring together divided members of Christ's body into one organization, the final aim must be the union in the Universal Church of all who acknowledge the name of Christ, and that the test of all local schemes of union is that they should express locally the principle of the great catholic unity of the Body of Christ. They trust, therefore, that the united Church, conserving all that is of spiritual value in its Indian heritage, will express under Indian conditions and in Indian forms the spirit, the thought and the life of the Church Universal.

"It is the intention and hope of the uniting Churches that all the actions of the united Church will be regulated by the principles that it should maintain fellowship with all those branches of the Church of Christ with which the uniting Churches now severally enjoy such fellowship, and that it should continually seek to widen and strengthen this fellowship and to work towards the goal of the full union in one body of all parts of the Church of Christ."[1]

It is this vision of wider union which explains the features of the Scheme which must otherwise seem illogical. It is not possible to draft a completely logical constitution for a divided Church. The only thing that can be done is to make the illogicality of division a starting-point for the task of restoring unity. The South India Scheme is full of illogicalities just because it takes account of the divisions in the Church and treats the act of union as one step only in the task of seeking the restoration of visible unity to the whole Church. It seeks to remain in communion with Churches not in communion with each other, and the tension of that effort is written right across the Scheme. The Scheme does not treat this tension as something to be accepted as a permanent feature of the Church's life. It is something to be accepted on behalf of Christendom as a means towards removing it by the drawing together of Christendom. The thirty-year period is not only a time for the

[1] B.U. 1.

Church of South India to grow together: it is a time for all the sundered parts of Christ's Church to be roused to a more active dealing with the intolerable scandal of division. The act of union is a venture of obedience to Christ's will, and of faith that obedience will open the way to more obedience. The uniting Churches have provided themselves with no line of retreat in case of failure. They do not enter upon this union as an experiment from which they could withdraw later "in the event of possible breakdown." We shall not heal our divisions on the basis of trial marriage, nor is Christ's plain command that we should be one adequately met by such tentative and conditional obedience. The union is an act of obedience and faith, and the postponement for thirty years of vital decision about Church order is the expression of that faith. The uniting Churches believe that their small and local act of obedience will help to loosen the bonds that hold the Churches apart and will hasten the fulfilment of Christ's will that His Church should be one. They are, therefore, content to accept the illogicalities and tensions of the "period of growing together" in the faith that if time is given both for the cementing of the union within and for the extension of its effects without, it will be possible to enjoy both a unified ministry within the Church and the widest possible fellowship with the rest of Christendom. In that faith they are content to postpone for thirty years the carrying out of their intention that the permanent ministry of the Church should be an episcopally ordained ministry, and to accept the tensions and difficulties which will arise from so doing.

The method of reunion in South India rests, then, upon these four points: first, the recognition that the uniting bodies are truly parts of the Church and their ministries real ministries; second, the recognition that the act of union is not the merging of autonomous groups to create a new Church with a new ministry, but the restoration of a broken unity, the return to a ministry standing in the historic succession inherited from the undivided Church with a view to the eventual restoration of a ministry accepted and fully effective throughout the world-wide Church; third, the recognition that the unity of the Church is a reality in the personal realm and that therefore many vital matters are to be secured not by detailed regulations but by assurances given and received in mutual confidence alone; fourth, the recognition that the union can only be regarded as a stage on the way to the wider reunion of the broken

THE METHOD OF REUNION

Church, and that therefore the decision of certain questions must be postponed till time has been given for growth in unity both within the Church and among those Churches with which it seeks to be in communion.

I have sought to indicate the grounds upon which this method of reunion is to be supported. The Church is a society living in time but with its life hid in God who is eternal. Its life cannot, therefore, be defined exclusively in terms of its historical continuity. Historical continuity is the fruit of that justifying and sanctifying grace of the eternal God by which the Church lives. Where this central truth has been lost historic continuity has been treated as constitutive of the Church. Where—on the other hand —this central truth has been re-discovered it has been constantly abused in an antinomian direction. The fact that God's grace has followed us even in our sin and division has been used as an excuse for continuing in division. An act of union must be an act of penitent return to Christ, and the united Church must express in the structure of its life that holy order which was broken by sin, and which is the visible expression of the Church's unity through all time and through all the world. The acceptance of the historic episcopate as the Anglican Communion has preserved it is—for those of us who have hitherto stood outside of it—an act of return to a form of that holy order larger than, and prior to, that in which we have been brought up. When, in the providence of God, the time comes for reunion with the great Catholic communions of West and East, there will be the opportunity for a further great step in the restoration of a ministry accepted and fully effective throughout the world. This, too, must proceed on the same principles: it must secure, on the one hand, that the order of the Church expresses not merely the will of those who unite but the unity of the whole Church, built upon the foundation of apostles and prophets; it must secure, on the other, that such return to a broken unity is not the seeking of a guarantee of God's grace, but the response to the gift of His grace. For the unity of the Church is and must always be the work of the Holy Spirit. And it is the Church that—even in its division and sin—is the sphere of His working.

PART 3

Heads of Agreement

CHAPTER EIGHT

THE STANDARD OF FAITH

THE section on "The Faith of the Church" in the Basis of Union is as follows:

"3. The uniting Churches accept the Holy Scriptures of the Old and New Testaments as containing all things necessary to salvation and as the supreme and decisive standard of faith; and acknowledge that the Church must always be ready to correct and reform itself in accordance with the teaching of those Scriptures as the Holy Spirit shall reveal it.

"They also accept the Apostles' Creed and the Creed commonly called the Nicene, as witnessing to and safeguarding that faith; and they thankfully acknowledge that same faith to be continuously confirmed by the Holy Spirit in the experience of the Church of Christ.

"Thus they believe in God, the Father, the Creator of all things, by whose love we are preserved;

"They believe in Jesus Christ, the incarnate Son of God and Redeemer of the world, in whom alone we are saved by grace, being justified from our sins by faith in Him;

"They believe in the Holy Spirit, by whom we are sanctified and built up in Christ and in the fellowship of His Body;

"And in this faith they worship the Father, Son and Holy Spirit, one God in Trinity and Trinity in Unity.

Notes—(i) The uniting Churches accept the fundamental truths embodied in the Creeds named above as providing a sufficient basis of union; but do not intend thereby to demand the assent of individuals to every word and phrase in them, or to exclude reasonable liberty of interpretation, or to assert that those Creeds are a complete expression of the Christian faith.

THE STANDARD OF FAITH

(ii) It is understood that it will be competent to the united Church to issue supplementary statements concerning the faith for the guidance of its teachers and the edification of the faithful, provided that such statements are not contrary to the truths of our religion revealed in the Holy Scriptures.

(iii) The act of union will not debar any teacher of the united Church from using for the instruction of the faithful any confession of faith which had been employed in any of the uniting Churches before the union, and which is not inconsistent with the doctrinal standards officially set forth by the united Church."

The same paragraphs are reproduced *mutatis mutandis* in the Constitution of the Church of South India, except that Notes (i) and (iii) are omitted.

This section has been criticized along two principal lines:

(a) the position assigned to the Bible as the supreme and decisive standard of faith is criticized because the authority of the Church in the interpretation of Scripture is not made clear;

(b) the disclaimers in the second part of Note (i) are held to destroy the value of the Churches' acceptance of the Creeds. Confirmation of this criticism is found in the fact that the use of the creeds in worship is not obligatory.

In approaching the discussion of these criticisms, and of the whole question of standards of faith, it is important to be aware of the pre-suppositions with which one enters it. The critic examining this section of the Scheme from the outside searches for loopholes through which error might enter the Church. Having found them he is apt to conclude that they were provided for the express purpose of admitting error. There then rises before him the horrific vision of the proposed union as the very embodiment of all heresy, against which he must fight with all his powers, and merely factual statements about the nature and purpose of the union cease to have any force for him. The difficulty is partly created by the fact that discussion has been so largely carried on without personal meeting. But it raises a fundamental question about the nature of the Church's security against error. The creeds are, at their heart, confessions of faith. They are the articulation of faith's response to the apostolic *kerygma*. Their elaboration in successive stages has been necessitated by the need to guard against error. But error is hydra-headed, and the Truth is not a proposition but a Person to be known only in personal faith. No creed has been framed that can guard the Church in perpetuity from error. It is only the presence of Him who is the Truth, the Church's living Lord, which can do that. When the discussion of credal statements in the form of propositions is divorced from the experience of personal meeting in the life of faith, worship and service, it is inevitable that there should be this misunderstanding. What is important in examining one another's position is that we should attend to what the other has tried to affirm rather than reconstruct his thought for him on the basis of what he has omitted to deny.

At the outset of a discussion of the question of the standard of faith one must press this question of the nature of the Church's security against error. It is often asserted that if God has granted to men a revelation of Himself, He must have done it in such a way that we can be infallibly certain of what that revelation is. This belief is important just because it is so often regarded as a self-evident axiom not requiring proof. It is not discussed but it is assumed, and it governs the course of the discussion. It is assumed, in other words, that there is somewhere—in the Bible, in the Creeds or in the teaching of the Church—a standard by reference to which the individual may know with infallible certainty what is the truth, and that it would be inconsistent with the character of God if this were not so.

About this assumption two things must be said: the first is that it is in plain contradiction to the facts of God's self-revelation in Christ. There is nothing in the Gospels which removes the responsibility which rests on every man to recognize and accept the truth for himself. We do not find there infallible revelations and signs over-riding men's fallible insights but precisely the opposite—tender and challenging and demanding appeals to men's own fallible insight and stumbling faith. Nothing less than a man's own faith, it seems, would content our Lord. It would have been easy for Him to give to the Jews a sign that would have proved Him beyond doubt to be the promised Messiah. But He refused. When challenged to produce authority for His deeds He replied with a question which proved His adversaries incapable of recognizing true authority, because they feared men rather than God (Mark xi. 27-33). To such as these He produced no "authority."

The authority with which He met men, with which He taught, with which He cast out devils, with which He healed on the Sabbath, was in Himself alone. It was the personal authority of Truth, for He is the Truth. It was the authority of God, the Creator of men, who has made men to recognize Himself. His contemporaries in the days of His flesh were familiar with the rabbinical method of teaching which found authority for its pronouncements in the sayings of those who had gone before. Jesus taught in a quite different way. He taught " with authority, and not as the Scribes." Scribal teaching required no fresh decision of faith on the part of the hearer. He had already accepted the authority of the law, and he left it to the lawyers to tell him how the law applied to each new situation. The teaching of Jesus required a fresh decision of faith in Himself, and its character was such that the righteousness which it described could only be the fruit of faith. The Sermon on the Mount cannot be turned into a legal code with sanctions and rewards. It is the law which can only be accepted as such on the basis of faith in Christ, and which can only be fulfilled as the fruit of the death and rebirth of faith. The authority with which Christ confronted men in the days of His flesh is the same as that with which He now confronts men in His Church. It is the authority of the Truth, demanding of men the personal response of faith. When the Church claims to have a deposit of infallible truth which requires only the submission of her members, and which is untouched by the errors and misunderstanding of men, she has lost the only true authority. The truth of the Gospel cannot be possessed apart from personal faith in the living Christ.

Secondly, it must be said that the assertion that God's revelation must be capable of being infallibly known rests not upon God's revelation but upon man's own sense of insecurity. The psychological basis of the absolute conviction with which this assertion is made is just that sense of fallibility and impotence which is so large a part of man's self-consciousness. That sense of insecurity and consequent anxiety is the mark of our human nature involved, as it is, both in the determinism of the natural world and in the freedom of personal responsibility. It is the ground from which all idolatries spring, and the secret of their tremendous power; for it is the essence of all idolatry that it seeks to provide men with the assurance that the forces controlling their destiny have been brought down on to the plane of human society and human action where they can be, to some extent, controlled. The experience of seeking to commend the Gospel to those accustomed to idolatry cannot fail to accentuate in the mind of the evangelist the contrast between the Gospel of the sovereign grace of the living God, and all religious systems which claim in some way to have included God within a human system. God is the living and active God, and He is only to be known in personal faith and obedience. The conviction that He must have provided some safeguard against error other than that which is known in the act of faith itself rests upon the same human anxiety which is the basis of idolatry.

Such a statement is, of course, liable to misunderstanding. It is misunderstood if the nature of faith in Christ as Redeemer is forgotten; it is likewise misunderstood if faith is severed from its context in the life of the Church. Both of these misunderstandings have been the cause of disastrous confusion in the Church. Nevertheless, at the outset of a discussion of the authority by which the Church believes we need to remind ourselves that if, in the last analysis, we seek for the seat of authority in another direction than that indicated by the Gospel record of the authority which Jesus wielded, we shall go astray. The Church as the Body of Christ must exercise only the kind of authority which Jesus exercised, and it must be its task to evoke in men that same kind of personal faith which Jesus evoked. The Gospel does not provide, and the Church ought not to seek, any escape from the personal responsibility of every man for his faith. Indeed, the Church which fails to give to its members the opportunity and encouragement to accept personal responsibility for their faith will *pro tanto* sever itself from the only source of authority, and will destroy in itself the capacity for stating what is the faith.

The criticisms made of the South India Scheme involve the two questions: What are the Church's standards of faith? and, What is the relation of the Church and of the individual member to those standards? The two questions cannot be separated from one another, but we may distinguish them in a general way for purposes of discussion.

A. The South India Scheme is criticized because it states that the Bible is the supreme and decisive standard of faith, and because it does not state that the tradition of the Church has authority in the interpretation of Scripture. It is regretted by the

THE STANDARD OF FAITH

critics that the framers of the Scheme have departed from their earlier statement which began with a reference to " the faith which the Church has ever held in Jesus Christ the Redeemer of the world," and then proceeded to refer to the embodiment of " that faith " in the Scriptures and the ecumenical creeds. It is even urged that by its present wording the statement departs from " catholic " principles because in the pre-Nicene period the Scriptures occupied " only a subordinate place in relation to the common witness of the Church's tradition " and because " just as no law is self-interpretative, no document can be decisive."[1] The issue which these and similar criticisms raise can be stated in a rough preliminary summary as follows. On the one hand there is the view that Christianity is essentially a traditional pattern of belief and life, and that the Scriptures, being the earliest written embodiment of that tradition, possess a very special—possibly unique—authority. But, in this view, not only are the Scriptures part of the tradition and therefore not to be placed over against it, but also there are other unwritten elements in the tradition, ante-dating the Scriptures. Among these the traditions of liturgical practice and the traditional ministry are of an importance at least equal to that of Scripture. On the other hand there is the view which finds in Scripture " the supreme and decisive standard," the norm by which the Church must ever be ready to correct itself, but which thankfully acknowledges that the faith is continuously confirmed in the experience of the Church. Here, therefore, Scripture and tradition are related to each other in a different way. The wording of the Scheme as it stands, in spite of a slip in editing,[2] is quite clear on this issue: it excludes the possibility of treating the Scriptures merely as the earliest expression of the continuous faith of the Church, and treats the faith of the Church as a response, continuously confirmed in its experience by the Holy Spirit, to the revelation of God's saving acts which the Scriptures record.

Stated thus, the issue is another form of the issue which was the subject of the preceding chapter—the nature of the Church's continuity. The phrase used in the earlier editions—" the faith which the Church has ever held "—meant, in its context, the faith which

---

[1] Jalland: *The Bible, The Church and South India*, p. 52.
[2] As Bishop Palmer has pointed out (*South India*, p. 7). The phrase " that faith " which formerly referred to " the faith which the Church has ever held," is now left without a proper antecedent.

is first of all faith in Christ rather than belief in propositions. It is clear that the uniting Churches have no intention to depart from this faith. But the phrase has sometimes been treated as though the faith referred to were the *quod* of the Vincentian Canon,[1] as though "the faith which the Church has ever held" were a series of doctrinal statements providing the final standard by which the beliefs of Churches and individuals are to be tested. But "the faith which the Church has ever held" in the sense of the "what" of all Christian belief, cannot provide the standard which is required as a basis for reunion unless the word "Church" is first defined. And that means that one must begin by begging the all-important question. All the beliefs held at all times by all the bodies in all lands calling themselves Christian Churches hardly together constitute a manageable standard of faith. One must begin by defining the word "Church" in terms of the faith one wishes to establish, and then define the faith as what the Church —so defined—has always believed. In fact the appeal to the Vincentian Canon is usually made by those for whom the term "Church" is defined in terms of historical continuity with the Apostles. Where this happens it is simply the logical completion of the destruction of the New Testament idea of the Church which was discussed in the previous chapter. Where it does not happen the Vincentian Canon loses all value as a standard of faith by which the beliefs of existing Churches might be judged. In either case the true relation between the Church and the faith is denied. Faith is the response to God's revelation in Christ; by it the Church lives. The Church has the duty of confessing before men the faith by which she lives, but in making her confession she must be aware that she who confesses is sinful and fallible. No one can state the truth who is not aware of the fact that he may also speak untruth. The Church will confess truly when she keeps her eyes on the object of her faith—the revelation in Jesus Christ. The standards of faith, therefore, by which the Church's confession is to be judged is not the confession itself, but the revelation to which faith is her response.

Again, this is a question of the nature of the Church's continuity. One cannot discuss the question, What is the standard of faith without also discussing the nature of the Church's relation to its standards. And one cannot discuss that without again

[1] *Quod ubique, quod semper, quod ab omnibus creditum est.*

reminding oneself of what we have called the eschatological dimension of the Church's existence. The ultimate standard of faith is the revelation of God in Jesus Christ. When we appeal from the present to that revelation we are not appealing from a later to an earlier phase in the development of a society called the Church. We are appealing to the Church's living Lord, who is alive in the Church to-day, whom alone we must obey, but who has made His nature and will clear to us by a work done for mankind at a certain point in history. To that point in history, therefore, we must go, not because it is earlier than the point at which we live but because it is the place where Christ has revealed Himself and wrought redemption for us. We do not go to the Bible to find the earliest forms of the traditions and rules of the Church. If we were doing that, the criticisms of those who point to the still earlier traditions of liturgical practice would be sound. We go to the Bible to meet Christ, our present and living Lord.

Let us freely admit at once the frequent and disastrous misuse of the appeal to Scripture to provide infallible justification for the detail of ecclesiastical polity as well as for many things much less important and for purposes much less noble. Let us also admit at once the fact that the Scriptures of the New Testament are documents written by the Church in the Church for the Church, that the fixing of the canon was accomplished long after other elements in the Church's tradition were fixed, and that the most recent criticism of the four Gospels themselves has shown how profoundly the experience of the Church has modified this material in the course of its oral transmission. That is all indubitable, and it is a reminder to us that the Bible can only be understood in the Church. It is of the very essence of the revelation in Christ that this is so. If God's purpose of salvation could be accomplished by providing each one of us with an infallibly correct statement of the truth about Him expressed in the form of propositions, then Christ would have written a book. There would have then been no need for a Church (though there might be churches, for man is a gregarious animal). It would be sufficient for each individual to know and accept what the book contained. But Christ wrote no book, and expounded no system of doctrine or ethics. He lived a perfect human life, drew to Himself friends, knit them into a fellowship of faith in Him, and—after His resurrection—in His atoning death, and gave to them a common rite whereby they should remember His death for them and enjoy His living presence. They were to be the nucleus of that fellowship in which all men were to be made one in faith alone. Salvation is in that fellowship and nowhere else.

But, as I have already tried to show, that fellowship is not something which possesses within itself the law of its own development. It is a society living in history by reference to something beyond history—by faith in the eternal and ever-present God, which faith is the response to His redeeming act once for all at a point in history. It must always be controlled, therefore, by reference to what happened at that point in history. Thus, while the fixing of the canon of the New Testament was the work of the Church, it was not that the Church chose a collection of books which best expressed her doctrines, but that she chose those books which had the highest claim to be true records of the testimony and teaching of those who had been " eye-witnesses and ministers of the Word." The basis of the Church's claim against the heretic was the uninterrupted tradition of public teaching in the great apostolic sees. The Church choosing the canon was not like a book-lover selecting a library on the basis of his tastes; it was like a court sifting evidence in order to obtain the most reliable account of what really happened. The controlling fact was that Christ had lived, taught, done mighty works, died, risen again and appeared to His disciples. The appeal was to those who could claim either to have seen and heard and handled these things, or to have been in direct contact with those who had. The canon of scripture is the result of that appeal. The selection of the canon is the work of the Church, but it is the expression of the fact that it is the actual event of God's work in Christ which is the supreme and decisive standard for the Church.

The critical study of the Gospels themselves has shown much of the influence of the community in shaping the material as it is presented. But it has not weakened, but rather strengthened, the impression which the Gospels give of the presence of a finally controlling tradition as to the essential facts of Christ's work, and of the fact that the fundamental pattern of the Gospel narrative is that of the first Christian preaching, the proclamation of the event of God's work in Christ by which the Church is brought into existence. It is that event which provided, and must always provide, the supreme and decisive standard of faith, because that

THE STANDARD OF FAITH

event is the occasion and basis of faith. The Christian faith is faith in the living God evoked by, and based upon, what God has done for men at a point in time. The supreme and decisive standard of faith must, therefore, be the testimony of those who were eye-witnesses of what God did.

If this be a true statement of the grounds of the appeal to Scripture, it provides at the same time a safeguard against certain wrong types of appeal. In the first place, it guards against the idea that Scripture is a corpus of uniformly infallible oracles any part of which may be appealed to in isolation from the rest. It makes clear the principle that Scripture is to be interpreted in the light of Christ Himself.

In the second place, it guards against the view that the New Testament, being the record of the earliest chapters of the history of the Church, provides the plan upon which the Church must at all times model the details of its life. Quite evidently if the Church is a living organism it cannot submit to being permanently fixed to the ways of life and government which marked its first appearance. There is, however, a permanent and natural tendency for the Church to seek for infallible norms in its own past. We shall discuss in a moment the question of the relation of the present to the past in the life of the Church, but we may admit at once that there is force in the Catholic criticism of the Reformers' tendency to seek to reproduce in the life of the Church in the fifteenth and sixteenth centuries the exact polity of the Church of the first. We must add, however, that while there is at least an intelligible principle behind the attempt to find the permanent pattern of the Church's life in the first century, there is none whatever in trying to find it in the third or fourth.[1] It can be intelligently held that the Church must be permanently controlled by the pattern of its first foundation. It can also be intelligently held that, since the guidance of the Holy Spirit is promised to the Church, the Church as it is now is the only norm of what the Church ought to be. That is the Roman position. But it cannot be intelligently believed that the Holy Spirit so guided the Church that it had by the fourth century developed the pattern which is the true norm for all subsequent centuries, unless there is some more ultimate standard in the light of which the pattern of the fourth century can be seen to be normative for all time. In that case what is required is

[1] E.g. Jalland: *The Bible, the Church and South India.*

that that more ultimate standard should be publicly acknowledged. In fact, however, the appeal to Scripture is not an appeal to the first chapter of church history. It is an appeal to the events in which the Church's living Lord wrought the salvation by which she now lives. The erroneous views which we have been considering all rest upon a failure to remember the eschatological dimension of the Church's existence. The Church is not merely a historically continuous institution bound by the terms of its original articles of association. It is a fellowship in the living Christ through the Holy Spirit, living the daily renewed life of faith in the Redeemer but embracing the whole company of the faithful in all ages and in all lands. Its appeal to the Scriptures is an appeal to the living Christ Himself, in order that it may know, in the circumstances of the present, what His living Spirit has now to speak to it concerning His will. Its unity with those who have gone before does not consist in its being bound to the details of their practice; it consists inwardly in its obedience to the same living Lord whom they obeyed, and outwardly in the maintenance, so far as that obedience permits, of continuity with them in one visible institution.

But if the supreme and decisive standard of faith is in this sense the Holy Scriptures, it is at the same time true that the Scriptures are only to be understood in the Church and in the Spirit. They are "flesh," until the Spirit takes them and quickens them; and it is the Church which is the sphere of His working. This point now needs to be developed more fully.

The Scriptures are decisive because they are the testimony of the witnesses to God's saving act. We believe on their testimony. We do not generate the knowledge of what God has done for us in Christ out of any religious resources of our own. We receive it from the Bible. Its testimony is the only basis of our knowledge. In that sense we believe on the authority of the Bible. But when we confess Jesus as Lord, we do not do so just because the Bible tells us that He is Lord. We so confess because the Holy Spirit moves us to do so. Flesh and blood cannot communicate this faith to us. It is the work of God's own Spirit in our hearts. We know about Jesus because the Bible tells us. But when, like Thomas, we cry to Him, "My Lord and my God," we are not repeating a confession of faith because we have been told to do so. We are speaking in the Spirit, because Christ Himself has laid hold on our own spirits by His Spirit so that we can do no other than yield ourselves to Him. We confess not because the Bible tells us we ought to, but because the Spirit lays hold on us personally and we can do no other.

But when we have begun to speak about the Holy Spirit we have begun to speak about the Church. The Church is the fellowship which lives by the common sharing of the Spirit. Through it we meet with Him. We have spoken of the meeting with Christ in the Bible in purely individual terms, but this is simply a necessary artificiality for the sake of orderly statement. In fact, this meeting is always in the context of the fellowship of His people. It is in the Church that the Bible was written and preserved, often at the cost of martyrdom, and it is as the Bible of the Church that it comes to every man to-day. The man who buys a farthing Gospel portion from a colporteur in an Indian village knows that he is buying the scripture of the fellowship which confesses Christ as Lord and preaches Him as Lord, and that the invitation to read the Scriptures is part of an invitation to join the fellowship. What the apostolic Scriptures mean to him will be largely dependent upon what the apostolic fellowship has been able to communicate to him of the radiance of Christ's living presence. And his confession of Christ as Lord will be at the same time the occasion of his public reception into the company of those who confess, the fellowship of the Holy Spirit. The acceptance of the redemption wrought for him in Christ will be at the same time the acceptance of the fellowship of Christ's redeemed people.

We must say, therefore, that the Bible can only be understood in the fellowship of the Church—and the Church means the whole company of Christ's people in all ages. Any attempt to sever the authority of the Bible from its context in the life of the Church is based on a misunderstanding of the Bible. No man has a right to treat the Bible as the revelation to him privately of a way of salvation which he is free to follow with or without the company of others. The Bible is the story of the people of God, and, in particular, the eye-witness accounts of those events of divine self-revelation by which God has purchased a people for Himself. It comes to us in the hands of that people and as the title-deeds of its existence.

But this does not mean that the Bible ceases to have the finally normative authority in relation to the traditions of the Church.

THE REUNION OF THE CHURCH

The Bible is to be understood in the fellowship of the whole Church, but the traditions of the Church are to be judged in the light of the Bible. The Church is the sphere of the presence of the Holy Spirit, but the gift of the Holy Spirit is the fruit of the hearing and receiving of the Gospel. The Church cannot, therefore, regard the promise of the Holy Spirit as delivering her from the obligation of submission to the authority of those Scriptures in which the events which are the content of the Gospel are set forth. The Church is liable to error and has erred. When she treats her own traditions as finally normative, she delivers herself over in a kind of bondage which Christ never imposed to a law which is not the law of God. She is to live always in penitent and alert obedience to her living Lord, and she has the revelation of His nature and the record of His mighty acts done for her redemption in those Scriptures which she has treasured from the days of those who were witnesses of them. These, therefore, are her supreme and decisive standard of faith, and to these she must ever turn, knowing that as she exposes herself afresh to the Gospel of which the Scriptures are the record, she will receive afresh the guiding of the Holy Spirit as to the present will of her Lord.

One further word may be said regarding criticisms which have been made of this part of the section entitled, "The Faith of the Church." It is objected that while the statement of the Church's duty to reform itself in accordance with the teaching of Scripture, as the Holy Spirit shall reveal it, is "unexceptionable as a general statement . . . it might cover a claim to revise the ecumenical creed without reference to the rest of Christendom. It is not stated to whom this 'revelation' will be made nor by whom it will be judged. As the Scheme stands, the doctrine of the united Church is left at the mercy of the letter of the Scripture text, as interpreted arbitrarily by individuals or at best by its own local Synod."[1] Bishop Palmer[2] has pointed out that in the wording of the Scheme the word "Church" cannot here mean simply "The Church of South India," and has also pointed to other parts of the Scheme which ought to have been considered as evidence of the attitude of the uniting Churches towards the rest of Christendom. The statement is here made in a general way as a truth which must govern the life of the Church always and everywhere. The

---
[1] *The Unity of the Faith*, pp. 4-5.
[2] *South India*, pp. 6-7.

question as to how much liberty one part of the Church can rightly claim to "correct and reform itself" apart from the rest is one upon which much debate has centred. It is surely sufficient to say that while, on the one hand, the framers of the Scheme of Union would not assert the right of the Church of South India to re-write the ecumenical creeds without reference to the rest of Christendom, their critics, on the other, would not presumably wish to assert that a local Church must even in the smallest matters await the unanimity of Christendom before attempting any reform. The Scheme does not attempt to adjudicate upon this question, and its silence ought not to be interpreted as assent to the most extreme sort of particularism which its critics can think of.

B. We now turn to deal with the second question raised by the criticisms of the Scheme of Union—the question of the relation of the Church and the individual member to the standards of faith. If what has been said is true, we must go on to say that there are two responsibilities which nothing in the Gospel removes. There is first the responsibility of the individual before God for his faith. No man can evade this responsibility. Even the man who professes to have no independent judgment and to accept in blind submission whatever the Church teaches, is responsible for his decision so to do. He has, at the last day, to answer the question whether this was the right stewardship of the talents which God gave him, whether this was the right response to the redemption won for him by Christ, whether this was his due part in the whole life of the fellowship of the Church. Likewise the man who professes to believe nothing except what he can see for himself to be true is responsible for the results of that decision if it cuts him off from riches of wisdom treasured in the Church in which he might have become sharer had he been willing patiently to learn. This personal responsibility before God is—as I have tried to show—part of what is necessarily involved in the life of the Church. The attempt to evade it destroys the true character of the Church.

There is, second, the responsibility of the Church to declare to each generation what is the faith, to expose and combat errors destructive of the faith, to expel from her body doctrines which pervert the faith, and to lead her members into a full and vivid apprehension of the faith. As a human society the Church must have the power to do this and the responsibility to do it. If it fails to do this it ceases to have any recognizable identity of its own. This is always a fresh task in every generation, for thought is never still. The words in which the Church states its message in one generation have changed their meaning by the time the next has grown up. No verbal statement can be produced which relieves the Church of the responsibility continually to re-think and re-state its message. No appeal, whether to ecumenical creeds, to the universal belief of the Church, or to the Scriptures, can alter the fact that the Church has to state in every new generation how it interprets the historic faith, and how it relates it to the new thought and experience of its time. This act of confession has to be the work of the living Church indwelt by the living Spirit. In this sense the Roman criticism of the appeal to the Vincentian Canon has force in it. Nothing can remove from the Church the responsibility for stating *now*, what is the faith. It belongs to the essence of a living Church that it should be able and willing to do so.

This issue has never been exposed with more piercing clarity than in the famous case of 1904 when the small remnant of the Free Church of Scotland which declined to enter into union with the United Presbyterian Church successfully sued the United Free Church, which had been formed by the Union, for the entire property of the Church. The Free Church claimed that the act of Union involved departures from the doctrinal standard expressed or implied in the fundamental documents of the Free Church, and that by such departure the majority had lost its identity and continuity as a Church and therefore forfeited its right to the property of the Church. The defendants' case rested upon the claim that there is inherent in the character of the Church the right and duty to state from time to time what is the faith which it confesses, and to be itself the sole judge of the conformity of such statements to its fundamental standard of faith. Their attitude may be indicated by two extracts from the speeches of Principal Rainy at the time. One may be permitted to interject the reminder that these speeches enunciate principles for which the Church had just suffered the loss of the whole of its property. They have that claim to serious attention. And one may add the remark that when ecclesiastical principles are put forward as of sufficient weight to justify the perpetuation of Christian disunity one must ask that those who put them forward show proof that they also count them of greater weight than the securities of property and establishment. Here are Rainy's words at the opening of the Assembly which followed the announcement of the judgment of the House of Lords:[1]

> "We have to maintain as of old the spiritual views of the Church of Christ, the liberty and independence which belong to the Church of Christ, the liberty and independence which are valued because they are necessary to obedience. We cannot obey our Master unless we keep ourselves free to obey Him. We claim for Churches as well as for individuals to have a conscience, and we ask that we may have leave not to go against our conscience in managing our own affairs, committed to us by our Lord.
> "Moderator, if there is anything to which this principle applies; if it applies to settling of ministers, if it applies to arrangement of our constitution with reference to its ways and workings, if it applies to discipline, to questions of receiving members and of exercising discipline on members or ministers, surely as much or more than any of these it applies to the Confession of our Faith. And surely it is implied in that relation that as our Confession of Faith itself declares that we are not infallible and that no Confessions are infallible, as we claim to be living under the wise providence and administration of Christ, and as we claim still more—humbly we may claim it, but our hearts would be sore indeed if we could not claim it—that we are living under the promise of the Holy Spirit of God, and that under His influences we pursue our calling, surely it is implied in that relation that it is part of our calling to learn whatever Christ makes apparent to us through His word, whether our fathers had learned it or not. The idea with which some of these distinguished men seem to be content, the idea of a Church consenting to be held absolutely and for ever by the faith of men who died two hundred or two hundred and fifty years ago—good men, no doubt—that idea is simply to be denounced as thoroughly ungodly. It is an ungodly idea, and the Church or the tribunal that cherishes it is unawares proceeding on fatally wrong principles. Moderator, I very much desire to be restrained from saying anything that is unsuitable to the importance and solemnity of the occasion, but I do feel that in this matter it is essential that we should speak out. The Christian faith is to believe in a living and present God, a living

---

[1] P. Carnegie Simpson, *The Life of Principal Rainy*, II, pp. 365-6.

and a present Saviour, a living and a present Holy Spirit, to whom we hold relations while we live and till we die."

And here is his summary of the situation at its close:[1]

"To make one comprehensive affirmation is a course that has been forced upon us by a negation just as general: for the judgment of the Lords proceeded on the view that they could make no distinction in doctrines more or less important. Their business was to hold the Church bound (for the purposes of any civil suit in which she might be engaged) to retain what she had at the outset of her history declared, in the sense in which the civil court understood it—and that the attempt to do otherwise entails the forfeiture of identity and of the civil rights which accompanied it. That laid on us the obligation to declare plainly our position. Our faith as a Church is not grounded in the wisdom of our fathers—no human councils authoritatively bind it. Our orthodoxy is not guaranteed by civil restraints. We are as a Church subject to the Church's Head; we receive His revelation in the Word; and looking for the promised grace of His Holy Spirit, we are free because we must hold ourselves ready to obey One only. But this assertion of freedom is not of the kind that fosters arrogance: rather it is akin to reverence and godly fear. And there is much in the constitution of our Church tending to deliberation and caution in the exercise of it. Besides, we are thoroughly persuaded that Christians of former days, and sister Churches of our own day, have attained under the same Master to great knowledge and certainty of Divine truth, which we share with them. Therefore, while we have something to learn, we have much also to hold fast. We are conscious, by God's grace, of our possession of a great body of doctrine, which through the Word, and also through the providence of God in the history of the Churches— through the fidelity of martyrs and fathers—through the great return to Scripture of the Reformation, through many particular conflicts and revivals, became clear and dear to our fathers, and has become so also to us. In particular, we are Scottish Presbyterians; we value the life and the traditions we inherit, though we refuse, and we need to refuse, to place them in the room of our living Head or of His Word. We own some benignant purpose of God in the genealogy of Church life in which He has cast our lot, and in the peculiar influences which are derived to us from past history. We are not insensible to this, we are

[1] *Op. cit.*, pp. 438-9.

not tired of it; but it must not run into idolatry. We desire to draw from our history, for ourselves and those who come after us, all the good it has carried with it. We are not ashamed of our fathers. But they taught us that one is our Head, even Christ, and that this holds not only for the individual Christian, but for the Church, for that peculiar society which He created and has promised to sustain. That the Church, every branch of it, in this relation, bears itself and performs its part most imperfectly we sadly believe and know. Nevertheless, it is the Church's life to claim this relation, to assert it, and to guard it through whatever trouble and persecution may arise."

One may add also this paragraph, embodying the fruits of this and former battles for the crown rights of Christ in His Church, from the Articles Declaratory of the Constitution of the Church of Scotland:[1]

"V. This Church has the inherent right, free from interference by civil authority, but under the safeguards for deliberate action and legislation provided by the Church itself, to frame or adopt its subordinate standards, to declare the sense in which it understands its Confession of Faith, to modify the forms of expression therein, or to formulate other doctrinal statements, and to define the relation thereto of its office-bearers and members, but always in agreement with the Word of God and the fundamental doctrines of the Christian Faith contained in the said Confession, of which agreement the Church shall be sole judge, and with due regard to liberty of opinion in points which do not enter into the substance of the Faith."

In Dr. Simpson's summary of the whole matter, "The Church has a Master, *and that Master is living*; therefore, the Church must be free to obey whatever His living voice says to her, whether of truth to confess or of duty to do."[2] Surely this claim and this right belong to the very essence of the Church.

But if this be so, then one must add that the Church can only use this liberty which she must claim, can only keep herself free to obey her living Lord, if she encourages every one of her members according to his ability to lay hold upon the faith for himself. This brings us to a consideration of the Note in the Scheme which disclaims on behalf of the uniting Churches the intention "to

[1] The Church of Scotland Act, 11 and 12. Geo. V. Schedule, para. V. See Bell, *Documents on Christian Unity*, pp. 170ff.
[2] *Op. cit.*, II, 423-4. Italics in original.

demand the assent of individuals to every word or phrase in the Apostles' and Nicene Creeds, or to exclude reasonable liberty of interpretation, or to assert that these Creeds are a complete expression of the Christian faith." No part of the Scheme has been more severely criticized than this. It is assumed without argument by the critics that these clauses have been inserted to make it possible for the Church to embrace error. One must reply that they have been inserted to make explicit the only condition upon which the Church can embrace the truth. The promised guidance of the Holy Spirit does not remove from the Church the necessity that every member should seek to lay hold for himself upon the truth as it is in Jesus. Rather, everything that the New Testament teaches about the Spirit emphasizes the close relation between a living personal faith and His presence. It is the duty of the Church to press upon every member the duty of strengthening and deepening his apprehension of the faith. But it is the condition of all honest human thinking that it must be free to accept the responsibility of deciding between truth and error. The Church has the absolute duty and responsibility to safeguard its life and witness from false teaching, and there are occasions when this duty can only be discharged by removing a teacher judged to be teaching false doctrine. But the Church can only discharge this duty as the true embodiment of the Holy Spirit if she is—through all her members—awake and alert to the truth. It is true that there are Churches which have so evaded the duty of articulate confession that they have become, like jelly fish, incapable of moving in any direction but that of the tide; but there are also examples of Churches which have so identified faith with blind submission to authoritatively prescribed formulæ that they have become but petrified fossils, having the form of a Church but not its life. To insist that reasonable liberty of interpretation be safeguarded is not to destroy the power of the Church to confess the faith, but to safeguard the condition of its so doing. It is asked, " Who is to judge what is and what is not reasonable? " Of course, the Church must judge. Nothing can remove its responsibility to do this. In this affirmation, the uniting Churches publicly state the aim which they hold before themselves in discharging that responsibility. When they claim that they do not intend to exclude reasonable liberty, it is implied that they have the power and intention to exclude unreasonable liberty. As to

THE STANDARD OF FAITH

their discharge of the responsibility which that power gives them, they will be judged by God. And they look for His will in His revelation.

The statement that the uniting Churches do not intend to demand the assent of individuals to every word or phrase in the Creeds has been taken to mean that they regard some " clauses "[1] or " parts "[2] as of minor importance, and they are challenged to say which ones they refer to. Now, of course, if one starts with the assumption that the South India Scheme is " a pantomime horse "[3] then one is likely to regard this clause merely as a loose cover for every sort of heresy. But may it not also be treated as the honest statement of an intention which we all share? Fr. Williams writes, "No one, I hope, wants to excommunicate individuals who have difficulties about certain articles of the Faith."[4] Some people have wanted to do so, but let us assume that we do not want to do so. How, then, are we to state this intention of ours? What form of words can be devised which shall take away needless causes of offence from before the feet of those of groping faith and tender conscience who desire to confess their faith in Christ with us, without opening the way to every sort of error? Notable attempts have been made to produce such a statement. The members of the Archbishops' Commission on Doctrine in the Church of England recorded, apparently unanimously, the following convictions:

" 1. The Christian Church exists on the basis of the Gospel which has been entrusted to it.

" 2. General acceptance, implicit if not explicit, of the authoritative formularies, doctrinal and liturgical, by which the meaning of the Gospel has been defined, safeguarded, or expressed, may reasonably be expected from members of the Church.

" 3. Assent to formularies and the use of liturgical language in public worship should be understood as signifying such general acceptance without implying detailed assent to every phrase or proposition thus employed."[5]

---

[1] *The Unity of the Faith*, p. 5.
[2] *A Voice from India*, p. 9.
[3] The phrase is one of Mr. T. S. Eliot's better-known contributions to the discussion of the subject. *Reunion by Destruction*, p. 21.
[4] *A Voice from India*, p. 9.
[5] *Op. cit.*, pp. 38-9.

THE REUNION OF THE CHURCH

The words "every phrase or proposition" open the door to error even more widely than those used in South India. Yet responsible Churchmen found themselves bound to use them in trying to make clear their considered views upon this matter. The Declaratory Articles of the Church of Scotland already quoted are more carefully worded. It will be noted in these that the Church "has the inherent right . . . to define the relation (to the Confession of Faith) of its office-bearers and members, but always in agreement with the Word of God and the fundamental doctrines of the Christian Faith contained in the said Confession, of which agreement the Church shall be sole judge, and with due regard to liberty of opinion on points which do not enter into the substance of the Faith." This represents probably the most careful attempt that has anywhere been made to express in a Church document the point we are here concerned with. The essential point is that it places the responsibility finally and absolutely upon the living Church. It is the Church which must decide what is and what is not of the substance of the Faith, what is and what is not in agreement with the Word of God and the fundamental doctrines of the faith. No formula can remove the responsibility from her. But she cannot discharge that responsibility except she encourage in all her members the personal appropriation of the faith for themselves, and for this she must have due regard to liberty of opinion in matters which do not enter into its substance.

Certainly this makes it possible for the Church to err. One might say that the removal of such provisions would make it certain that the Church would err. But may one not reasonably plead that critics should wait until the Church of South India has actually fallen into manifest heresy before concluding that their consciences forbid them to have communion with her members? There are many members of the Church of England profoundly disquieted by the thought that as the law now stands her standards of doctrine and worship are in the keeping of the House of Commons. They are aware that the time may come when it will be the duty of the Church to assert, at whatever cost, its freedom in these matters. Would it not be unfair if critics from outside, who view the situation with the single-minded abhorrence which is the privilege of the outside critic, should conclude that they can have no fellowship with a Church which permits the present situation to continue? If it is to be a question of excommunication—for that is what is at stake—must we not plead that for such a sentence it is not sufficient to prove that the accused has placed himself in a position where it is possible for him to commit the crime?

But it is suggested that there is a difference between the consideration which every Church must show in practice towards the consciences of individuals and a deliberate attempt to state in writing the intention of the Church to allow reasonable liberty of interpretation. What is the difference? If the critics desire that we should exclude reasonable liberty, and should demand of every member assent to every word and phrase in the Creeds, let them say so. They have not yet said so. If they do not desire this, do they mean that while it is right to allow liberty of interpretation it is wrong to admit that you allow it? One hopes not. Then, do they mean simply that the Scheme has failed to find the right way of stating the true place of liberty of interpretation? In that case, let them produce a better form of words, for it is quite certain that the present wording is far from perfect. But they have not so far offered one. They must surely be asked to do so, if the defects in the present one are to be shown to provide adequate grounds for excommunication.

But it is urged that the heretical intentions of the uniting Churches are shown by the fact that they do not intend to demand of every congregation the use of the Creeds in public worship. "If a congregation decides that it cannot conscientiously recite the ecumenical creed, the inference is that it does not hold that Faith. If its refusal is not based on conscientious grounds, it still denies the right of the Catholic Church to receive the assurance that it does, in fact, hold the Catholic Faith, and so violates the fellowship of the Church."[1] Is it really possible that those who write thus are so unaware of the reasons for which great parts of the Church, holding the orthodox faith, do not use the Creeds in public worship? And is the Catholic Church always to take Lear as her model in her dealings with her daughters? We have it on the authority of St. James that the Catholic Church could obtain in Hell all the assurance that is here desired (James ii. 19). And one must ask whether the recital of a creed to satisfy ecclesiastical authority as to one's own orthodoxy would really be an act of worship. All the three uniting Churches in South India

[1] *The Unity of the Faith*, p. 6.

make a regular practice of reciting the Creed in worship. In the Anglican and Methodist Church it is, I believe, universal. In the South India United Church it is normal. Many of us regret its absence in the normal worship of our mother-Churches. The Gospel is the heralding of God's mighty acts, and the proper response to the Gospel is that the congregation should rise and joyfully affirm their faith in God and in the mighty works that He has wrought for them. That act of corporate confession is, perhaps especially in a pagan land, one of the high " moments " of the whole act of worship. One can safely predict that it will find its place in the universal custom of the united Church. But if it is to be regarded as a compulsory punctuation of public worship for the purpose of taking regular assurances of the orthodoxy of the congregation, one must confess that it would be regarded with repugnance. There are times when the Church has the right to demand assurances regarding the belief of its members and ministers. The Scheme of Union provides for them. The Church has also at all times the duty of guarding its common life from errors destructive of the faith, from interpretations of the faith that transgress the bounds of " reasonable liberty." That duty the Church of South India will have power to discharge. The statement by the uniting Churches at the time of their union of their intention to safeguard reasonable liberty of interpretation, is not designed to facilitate the entrance of error. It is designed to secure the widest possible diffusion of that personal faith which issues in the love of God with all the heart and mind and strength, and by which the Church lives and is edified and empowered to commend to every new generation Him who called Himself not tradition but Truth.

    I turn in conclusion from this note in which the uniting Churches say what they do not intend to do, to a brief reminder of the things they positively affirm. They begin with the Scriptures, where the facts of God's saving revelation are recorded. They accept them as the supreme and decisive standard. They acknowledge that they—like all the Church—need always to be ready to correct themselves in the light of that revelation. There may be, there certainly are, many things in their common life, and in the Scheme of Union, which are contrary to God's will. They profess themselves ready to accept correction in the light of the teaching of the Scriptures as the Holy Spirit shall reveal it. In

THE STANDARD OF FAITH

seeking thus to find His will, they acknowledge the duty of the united Church so to regulate its acts as to maintain fellowship with the Churches with which they are now in communion, to give full weight to the pronouncements of bodies representing the whole Church, and to take part in' the deliberations and decisions of an Ecumenical Council if such should in the mercy of God be called together.[1] They may perhaps claim that by the struggles and prayers that have attended the birth of the united Church they have some hope of being saved from forgetting the rest of Christendom and thus meriting the contemptuous expectations of some of their critics.[2] They go on to acknowledge that the faith which they hold is that to which the ecumenical creeds bear witness, and that which the Holy Spirit has continuously confirmed in the experience of the Church of Christ. Thus they claim to be propounding no " new creed."[3] It is the faith of the historic Church which they confess, faith in Father, Son and Holy Spirit, one God. But for the supreme standard by which all things are to be judged, including the most venerable pronouncements of the Church, they look to the one place where God has revealed Himself in the Word made Flesh, to that revelation of which the Bible is the record and witness. For it is by that revelation that the Church lives.

[1] *Scheme of Union*, p. 14. B.U. 13.
[2] *The Unity of the Faith*, pp. 4-5.
[3] As they are accused of doing. Thornton, *The Judgment of Scripture*, p. 5.

CHAPTER NINE

THE MINISTRY

THE following are the paragraphs of the "Basis of Union" dealing directly with the ministry.

"The uniting Churches believe that the ministry is a gift of God through Christ to His Church, which He has given for the perfecting of the life and service of all its members. All members of the Church have equally access to God. All, according to their measure, share in the heavenly High Priesthood of the risen and ascended Christ, from which alone the Church derives its character as a royal priesthood. All alike are called to continue upon earth the priestly work of Christ by showing forth in life and word the glory of the redeeming power of God in Him. No individual and no one order in the Church can claim exclusive possession of this heavenly priesthood.

"But in the Church there has at all times been a special ministry, to which men have been called by God and set apart in the Church. Those who are ordained to the ministry of the Word and Sacraments can exercise their offices only in and for the Church, through the power of Christ the one High Priest.

"The vocation of the ordained ministry is to bring sinners to repentance, and to lead God's people in worship, prayer, and praise, and through pastoral ministrations, the preaching of the Gospel and the administration of the Sacraments (all these being made effective through faith) to assist men to receive the saving and sanctifying benefits of Christ and to fit them for service. The uniting Churches believe that in ordination God, in answer to the prayers of His Church, bestows on and assures to those whom He has called and His Church has accepted for any particular form of the ministry, a commission for it and the grace appropriate to it."[1]

Chapters IV and V of the Constitution deal with the functions and responsibilities of bishops, presbyters and deacons, and Chapter VI with "the ministry of the laity." Little has been found to

[1] *Scheme of Union*, pp. 6-7.

criticize in the description of the functions of bishops and presbyters.[1] As regards the sections on functions of deacons (where it is said that the ministry of the diaconate may be undertaken—either for life, or for a period preparatory to ordination to the presbyterate), and those on "the ministry of the laity," there is much that might have been discussed but has not been. There will come into the united Church men and women who have been performing many ministries in the Church, ordained elders, unordained deacons, stewards, wardens, lay preachers, class leaders, Sunday School teachers, catechists and evangelists and many others. It is symptomatic of a certain unreality in our thinking about the Church, or—more precisely—of that divorce between our doctrine of the Church and our doctrine of the Holy Spirit to which reference has already been made, that this great part of the ministry of the Church is so often simply omitted from discussion. A Presbyterian must certainly confess that the eldership as it has been understood in the Reformed Churches receives inadequate treatment in the Scheme. But it may perhaps be claimed as a merit of the Presbyterian tradition that it has kept clear the distinction between fundamental standards and subordinate standards, and that it has always claimed freedom to modify the latter in obedience to the former. The act of union will involve drastic modifications in matters very deeply embedded in our traditions and made explicit in our subordinate standards. We enter it because we believe ourselves bound so to do by our fundamental standard—the Word of God. We believe that it will follow upon the discharge of that duty that we shall be enabled in fellowship to give and receive what is best in our several traditions regarding all these forms of ministry.

We have to concern ourselves here with criticisms made of the provisions of the Scheme in regard to the ministry, criticisms made on the ground that these provisions destroy or compromise what is essential to the being of the Church itself. Much has been written along these lines which it would be best to pass over in silence were it not that some have derived their view of the Scheme

[1] The Report of the Archbishop of Canterbury's Committee of Theologians finds that " the duties and functions of presbyters as set forth in these parts of the Scheme are satisfactorily stated." Further, the Committee " welcomed the positive conception of the Episcopate therein set forth, and it is of the opinion that (subject to the provision of satisfactory forms of service for the Consecration of Bishops) the Scheme and the intentions of the Church provide adequately for the continuance and carrying on of the Episcopate as the Anglican Communion has received it." *Op. cit.*, pp. 24-5.

from reading it. It is said, for instance, that in the Scheme " only the priesthood of all members of the Church is conceived to be a ' gift of God.' What is called ' a special ministry ' is stated to have existed in the Church at all times as a matter of history, but it is not stated that it owes its authority either to God or to the Apostles. It would seem from this that the ' special ministry ' is regarded simply as a product of human needs and experience "[1] and again that " in the South India Scheme . . . the ministry becomes a piece of organization which is so constructed as to meet the wishes and convenience of those who are to live under it."[2] The uninstructed reader might be excused for mistaking these expressions of strong emotion for factual statements. Nothing in the Scheme justifies these travesties of its own plain statement that " the ministry is a gift of God through Christ to His Church." But there are three primary criticisms of the Scheme in regard to the ministry which require to be considered. They are:

(a) that episcopal ordination is the guarantee of a valid ministry (that is, a ministry certainly possessing Christ's authority) and that by recognizing the competence as presbyters of men not episcopally ordained the Scheme surrenders something vital to the existence of the Church;
(b) that the Scheme does not regard the ministers of the Church as priests;
(c) that the position of the bishops in relation to the Synod deprives them of their proper power and responsibility as guardians of the apostolic faith and practice.

The first of these three is the most fundamental and will be discussed at some length. The other two must be considered only briefly.

(a) *The Ministerial Commission*

I have neither space nor competence to add one more to the many discussions of the doctrine and history of the Apostolic Ministry, and I must therefore begin by defining precisely the area of discussion. What we are to discuss is the view that the authority and commission of Christ reside in the episcopate *alone*, and that

---

[1] Jalland, *op. cit.*, p. 34.
[2] Thornton: *The Judgment of Scripture*, p. 6.

therefore a Church which fails to believe this truth and to rely exclusively on this authority is to be excommunicate. It is to be noted, first, that the point is not in regard to episcopacy as a manner of government but to the episcopate as the repository of the commission which Christ gave to His Apostles. Episcopacy has existed in almost every possible variety of form. The essential point is not one or other of these varieties, but the possession of the commission from Christ through the Apostles. Perhaps the nearest modern approach to the earliest form of mon-episcopacy is the Presbyterian minister, surrounded by his elders and sharing with them the duty of *episcope*, but having himself alone the right to administer the sacraments. But, according to the view we are considering, the Presbyterian minister does not—as a matter of historical fact—possess that apostolic commission which is the guarantee of the Church's continuance. That commission is now, as a matter of fact, held by the men whom the Church now calls "bishops." Secondly, it is to be noted that the argument does not rest on the claim that the Church is one organic whole from apostolic times until to-day. This claim has already been discussed at length and will not be referred to here. This is the claim upon the basis of which the Roman Church excommunicates the Anglican equally with the non-episcopal Churches. What is appealed to here is not the unity and continuity of the Church as one organic whole,[1] but the continuity of the episcopal ministry as the guarantee of the Church's existence. It is only upon the basis of this claim that it is possible at the same time to assert the duty of excommunicating non-episcopal Churches and to deny the right of Rome to excommunicate episcopal. Anglican writers who undertake the discharge of this exacting war upon two fronts have to prove that the plenitude of Christ's authority rests in such an exclusive manner in the hands of the historically continuous episcopate that where—on the one hand—a part of the episcopate separates itself from the rest of Christendom, there the Church still exists, but that where—on the other hand—a Church acts without the authority of the episcopate, it places itself in a position where it must be excommunicated. The plenitude of Christ's commission therefore rests in the bishops, and is retained by them even when they separate themselves from the rest of the Church.

[1] To this extent the arguments of Dr. Burn-Murdoch, *Church Unity and Continuity*, are irrelevant to the position which he seeks to establish.

THE REUNION OF THE CHURCH

Ubi episcopus ibi ecclesia[1]

Such a claim must rest on both historical and theological grounds. In the first place it has to be shown as a matter of history, not that a principle of continuous succession in ministerial office operated in the Church from the beginning (that would support the Roman claim, not this one), but that there was from the beginning a continuous chain of ministerial authority from the Apostles to the bishops *distinct from the unity and continuity of the Church as a whole*. On the other hand, there must be exhibited a theological view of the nature of the Church, of redemption, of life in the Spirit, which is coherent with this view of the nature of Christ's commission.

The most impressive recent attempt to establish this position, and to justify therefore the rejection of such schemes of union as that in South India, is the collection of essays on *The Apostolic Ministry* edited by the Bishop of Oxford. It would be presumptuous to attempt in a few paragraphs to deal in any way with so massive a work, or to attempt to speak of the many profound and suggestive things which it has to teach on the Christian ministry. All that can be done is to consider how far this work succeeds in proving the case which we are considering.

(a) We shall take first the historical case. Ignoring, for the moment, matter in which the writers are not unanimous, we may define the case which they seek to prove as follows: there were in the apostolic and sub-apostolic ages of the Church two totally distinct institutions, the apostolate and the eldership. The elders were the Christian equivalent of the *zeqenim* of the Jewish synagogue. Their collective function was the oversight (*episcope*) of the local congregation, and some or all of them may at some times have been called *episcopoi*. They performed for the Christian Churches the functions which the elders of the Jewish synagogues performed. They had "a collegiate, not a personal authority, for specific purposes within a local society."[2] They had no power to ordain. On the other hand "above—or perhaps better, alongside —and outside this Judaic organization of self-government in the New Israel, are the 'apostles,' the men 'sent' in His own person

---
[1] Cf. Newman: "Catholics believe that their orders are valid because they belong to the true Church; Anglicans believe they belong to the true Church because their orders are valid." *Essays Critical and Historical*, ii, p. 87. Quoted in *The Apostolic Ministry*, p. 30.
[2] Dix, *op. cit.*, p. 286.

by our Lord Himself, to fulfil His own mission, equipped with His own authority and power by the gift of His own Spirit."[1] The word apostle is to be understood in terms of the Jewish *shaliach*, one who has received—so to say—a power of attorney for his principal, in virtue of which " the envoy's action unalterably committed his principal."[2] The Apostles alone possessed this commission from Christ, and they did not transmit it to the local *zeqenim*. They could not do so because these " had not yet developed any personal organ to which such a personal commission could be transferred."[3] They transferred it to other " apostolic men," who continued in the sub-apostolic age an apostolate quite distinct from the ministry of the local *zeqenim*. It was only as this latter developed in the direction of mon-episcopacy that the two ministries could become fused by the transfer to the local *episcopoi* of the " power of attorney " which had hitherto belonged to the quite separate office of the apostolate.

It will readily be seen that if this picture of the historical events can be substantiated, it provides just the kind of justification which is needed for the view that the modern episcopate possesses a plenary commission from Christ in virtue of which it is possible for it to take part in a separation from the main body of the Church and still claim to possess the full nature of the apostolic Church.

Of the arguments which are used to support this historical picture one is bound to say that however possible and even probable some of them may be, they fall very far short of proof. Nothing can quite compensate for the fact that there is no single case recorded in the literature of the first century in which an apostle indisputably transmitted his apostolic authority to a successor. The many plausible suggestions made regarding some who were called apostles but were not part of the apostolate (e.g., 2 Cor. viii. 23), regarding others who were part of the apostolate but were not called apostles (e.g., Acts xiii. 1-3 and Farrer, *op. cit.*, p. 144), and regarding the many who were part of the apostolate but of whom we possess no shred of evidence as to how they were admitted to it, are still only suggestions. Nor does it inspire confidence to find that in what one would suppose to be a crucial

---

[1] Dix, *op. cit.*, p. 237.
[2] Dix, *op. cit.*, p. 228.
[3] Dix, *op. cit.*, p. 273.

instance, where Paul defends his apostleship and denies that of the "pseudo-apostles," his complete failure to refer to what are, *ex hypothesi*, the real credentials of an apostle is explained by "the heat of the conflict."[1] I shall, however, refer here only to two points.

(i) The argument requires us to assume that our Lord's words of commission to "the disciples" (John xx. 19-21) were addressed to the Apostles alone, and to them as individuals and not as in any sense representatives of the Church which was to be. The contrary views of (for example) Hort,[2] are not referred to. It is assumed that the apostolic commission is something which can only be held by individuals as individuals, and that a corporate body—such as the early presbyteries—could not receive it. The ten disciples who were in the room when He gave His commission received it as individuals. It was thus henceforth to pass on to other individuals. It was in no sense the commission of the whole Church. St. Thomas, on this assumption, did not receive it, since he was not present at the time. His subsequent meeting with the risen Lord is described in some detail as the background to the words "Blessed are they that have not seen and yet have believed," but nothing is said of a commission to him. It is difficult to understand how a reference to this could be omitted if a commission of this character was really given to him.

(ii) The main point of the argument is the interpretation of 1 Clement. It is true that after devoting ten closely reasoned pages to the evidence of Clement Dom Dix remarks airily that "nothing crucial turns on it" since "the whole of the rest of the evidence is unanimous that the 'apostolate' as distinct from the local 'episcopate' did continue for a while after the first, properly 'apostolic' Christian generation."[3] One tries to remember what the rest of the evidence is. It is given a few pages later:

> "What happened to the office of *shaliach* at the end of the apostolic age? Did it disappear? That is the key question; for if it continued then as a *personal* commission, this *cannot* have happened without the personal action of the original apostles. I submit that the documents available between

---

[1] Farrer, *op. cit.*, p. 130.
[2] *The Christian Ecclesia*, pp. 29-32.
[3] *Op. cit.*, p. 262.

A.D. 70 and A.D. 100—1 and 2 Timothy; Titus; 3 John; the Apocalypse (the *Didache*, if we like to place it here); and 1 Clement—all of which represent the 'apostolate' as continuing to be exercised in this period in some form, are amply sufficient to prove the point. The Pastorals and 1 Clement specifically assert that it continued by the deliberate provision of the original apostles."[1]

Here the point as regards Clement is taken as proved. We have to examine the proof offered in a moment. As regards "the whole of the rest of the evidence," the Pastorals and 3 John are evidence either for what happened while the Apostles were still alive, or for what could be represented in the next generation as having happened while the Apostles were still alive. They cannot be used as evidence for the commissioning by the Apostles of attorneys to act for them after their death. As regards the Apocalypse, Dom Dix's only reference is to ii. 2, which scarcely supports him here, and he does not otherwise indicate what support he draws from it for his thesis. As regards the *Didache* he elsewhere devotes some pages to it but gives no hint whatever that he finds in it such support. The crucial evidence for his theory is 1 Clement § 44.

He translates Clement as follows: "(i) And our apostles knew through our Lord Jesus that there would be strife concerning the name of the *episcope*. (ii) For this cause, therefore, having received a perfect foreknowledge, they appointed the aforesaid *episkopoi* and *diakonoi* and afterwards they made a further enactment that if they should fall asleep, other approved men should succeed to their (own) liturgy. (iii) Those therefore who were appointed by them, or afterwards by other men accounted apostles (*heterōn ellogimōn andrōn*) with the common consent of the whole Church, and who have blamelessly liturgized for the flock of Christ . . . these men we consider to have been unjustly thrown out of their liturgy."[2]

We have to note:

(a) That in (ii) "if they should fall asleep" is taken to refer to the apostles, not to the bishops and deacons. The second part of the sentence thus refers to a quite different theme from the first. The theme of the first part of the sentence is the provision made

---

[1] *Op. cit.*, p. 267.
[2] *Op. cit.*, p. 256.

by the Apostles for a ministry of *zeqenim* in the Churches. The theme of the second part is, on this reading, provision made for the perpetuation of the apostolate, which is—*ex hypothesi*—a quite separate institution.[1]

(*b*) The word "liturgy" is used in the second part of this sentence to refer to the work of the apostolate, while in the rest of the paragraph it refers to that of the *zeqenim*.

(*c*) We are required to adopt the "bold translation" of *ellogimōn andrōn* by "men accounted apostles." This is defended on the ground that the primary meaning of *ellogimos* is something "included in a list." If that is accepted, then the meaning given here rests on the assumption that the "list" in question is the apostolate. The defence therefore begs the question.

The arguments adduced by Dom Dix against the generally accepted reading of the passage only have force if one comes to them with the complete dichotomy of apostolate and local ministry already established in one's mind, or if one accepts the assumption, which he makes but does not justify, that the only alternative in the mind of Clement to appointment by an apostle was "purely local appointment,"[2] an alternative to which there is no reference in the context.

It is, of course, true that when the existing evidence is so scanty, every reconstruction of the pattern of the early centuries must depend in large measure on hypothesis and probability, and that it is very easy to produce objections to any proposed reconstruction and very difficult to produce anything better. Dom Dix sets out very fully the objections to his interpretation of the passage and leaves it to the reader to weigh the probabilities for himself. But surely we have to remind ourselves that we are not dealing here merely with discussions among fellow Christians about Church history; we are examining grounds upon which the duty is professed to perpetuate the division of the Body of Christ. We are

---

[1] The most recent edition of 1 Clement to which I have had access (Ed. Lowther Clarke, S.P.C.K., 1937) translates: "So, for this reason, since they had perfect foreknowledge, they appointed the aforesaid persons, and subsequently gave them permanence, so that, if they should fall asleep, other approved men should succeed to their ministry."

Lightfoot translates: "and afterwards they provided a continuance that if these should fall asleep other approved men should succeed to their ministration." Of the proposal to take "if they should fall asleep . . . their ministration" as referring to the Apostles themselves, Lightfoot's comment is that "it is enough to say that it interrupts the context with irrelevant matter."

[2] *Op. cit.*, p. 261-2.

dealing not with academic questions, but with the question, "Where is the Church?" and therefore with the question, "What must we do to be saved?" The gravest issues which the human mind can conceive are at stake. We are often reminded that the word "valid" means, fundamentally, sure and reliable. It would be difficult to imagine anything that conformed less to that description than the historical arguments which are here offered to prove what is and what is not a valid ministry. The death of Christ for sinners, His rising from the dead and ascension to the right hand of God, His gift of the Holy Spirit to believers to the end that we might be built up in one Body—these are the mighty certainties upon which we rest all that we have and are, and which we proclaim to every man who will hear. When a man speaks to us of things which he deems so vital to the redemption of the world that he can place them alongside the Gospel, and demands in their name the excommunication of great parts of Christ's Church, he must speak a language of like assurance. There are places where historical probability is all we have a right to look for; but here, surely, we are in a realm where probability is not enough. Here we need something as sure as the Cross and the empty tomb.

(b) We turn to consider the theological grounds upon which this view of the apostolic ministry rests. It is one of the merits of the book under discussion that it emphasizes again and again the fact that the necessity of episcopacy is to be proved on theological grounds; that those who would defend episcopacy must know what its theological meaning is. From this point of view—and from any point of view—the most important part of the book is the noble chapter on "Ministerial Episcopacy." Here the fundamental nature of the ministry is set forth, if one may be permitted to say so, with rare penetration and balance. The fact that the ministry is both *in* the Church and *to* the Church; the evils resulting from viewing either of these two aspects of the ministry in isolation; the eschatological character of the existence of the Church and therefore of the ministry, and the reference of the ministry to Christ's ascension to the right hand of God—these all receive their due emphasis in Fr. Hebert's exposition. What has to be asked is whether this exposition of the nature of the ministry points to the doctrine of the episcopate which the book sets out to establish—the doctrine that episcopacy is "the authentic guarantee of (the Church's) claim to be the Body of Christ among men."[1] Fr. Hebert in answering this question says that the double character of the ministry, as on the one hand representing the prophetic, priestly, and royal character of the Church, and on the other, having the dominically given responsibility for the Gospel, the Sacraments and the flock, requires an office in the Church "firstly representing in each place Christ's relation to the Church, secondly expressing the unity of the Christian ministry both in place and in time, and thirdly entrusted with the commission which our Lord gave to His *shelihim*."[2] It is left to the Church to arrange all matters of detail, but "there must always be at the centre the essential office of the apostolic ministry, namely that which bears the name of bishop."[3] The crucial question is with regard to the third point, in so far as it is separated from the first. We have to ask whether the nature of the ministry as expounded requires an office not only representing Christ to the Church but also holding a personal commission from Christ by a line of succession distinct from the continuity of the Church as a complete organism.

Two points have to be noticed. The first is that in the attempt to substantiate this position use is constantly made of a kind of argument which seems strangely foreign to the New Testament. The New Testament most explicitly teaches that the ministry is a gift to the Church of the ascended Lord. The forms of ordination given by Hippolytus make very explicit, as do (for instance) Presbyterian ordinals of our own day, the fact that ordination is fundamentally an act of the living and ascended Christ in response to the prayers of His Church; that the Church acts, in this matter, as the hands of the living Christ. But in the present volume a very different note is struck. Thus Dr. Kirk writes that "it is only as (the Church) can claim that her ministry derives *from the Lord Himself in the days of His flesh* . . . that she can pursue her victorious yet dreadful pilgrimage undaunted";[4] and again that the successors of the apostles exercised the plenitude of Christ's power "*looking back to Christ* as its source, not by way of 'the Church' but by way of the apostolic line of descent."[5] This is surely far from the New Testament doctrine of the ministry. It amounts in

[1] Kirk, *op. cit.*, p. 46.
[2] Hebert, *op. cit.*, p. 527.
[3] *Ibid.*, p. 528.
[4] Kirk, *op. cit.*, p. 52. Italics mine.
[5] *Op. cit.*, p. 49. Italics mine but inverted commas original.

THE MINISTRY

effect to treating the apostolate as the extension of the Incarnation. It removes the Ascension and Pentecost from the determinative position which the New Testament gives them in relation to the ministry. It detaches the apostolate completely from the Church, as the Body of Christ and the dwelling-place of the Spirit. Perhaps the most remarkable illustration of the effect of this detachment occurs in the passage where Dr. Kirk is explaining that non-episcopal ministries are real but not valid. He writes, "To say that a thing is valid, or *de jure*, implies that we are morally bound to respect its claims; if we admit a particular ruler to be king of his country *de jure* it would be immoral of us to abet any who were planning to overthrow his régime. But when we admit a man to be ruler *de facto* only, we are not by that admission committed to any particular attitude towards him. We assert his might only; and might never creates rights or carries them with it. Similarly, to say that non-episcopal ministries are 'real' ministries, or ministries *de facto* (and if this is what is meant by the word 'real,' we do not quarrel with it for a moment), does not in itself commit us to any special behaviour towards them—to what is called 'interchange of pulpits,' for example, or to intercommunion."[1] This is a very remarkable argument, for the king concerned in this case can only be our Lord Himself, since it is made clear in the context that the whole difficulty arises from the fact that non-episcopal ministries have clearly been owned by our Lord and show the fruits of His presence. Nothing could more clearly illustrate the error in which this kind of argument is bound to become involved. In the New Testament the Church is the Body of the living Christ, and the ministry is the gift of the living and ascended Christ to the Church. In the view here set forth the ministry is defined in purely legal terms as a body of men entrusted with a power of attorney on behalf of Christ, looking back to Christ in the flesh as the source of their authority. From this the remarkable conclusion follows that the (acknowledged) acts of the Church's living Lord in pouring forth upon non-episcopal ministries gifts which "produce results such as the validly ordained minister ought to produce"[2] are to be regarded as analogous to the acts of a man who has successfully but unlawfully usurped the kingship of a country. Dr. Kirk's triumphant refutation of the wording of the

[1] *Op. cit.*, pp. 44-5.
[2] Kirk, *op. cit.*, p. 37.

Anglican *Memorandum* of 1923 provides the *reductio ad absurdum* of his own.

This leads us to the second point, closely related to the first. At the beginning of this volume Dr. Kirk lays it down as an axiom that "every theory of Church order must start from (the distinction) between the gifts of God and ecclesiastical enactments."[1] One can only say that on a reading of the New Testament this is not a self-evident truth. If one begins from there one has begun by begging the one vital question, namely the relation of this visible temporal ecclesiastical institution to its living and eternal Head. By accepting that as an axiom one has settled the whole question without argument, and it is not surprising that the required conclusions follow without difficulty. It is upon the basis of this supposed axiom that a distinction is made between authority from above and authority from below. In the usual use of this distinction the spatial metaphor used has no reference at all to the "vertical" dimension of the Church's existence—to its present relation, that is, to the living God. When a bishop is consecrated according to the ordinal of the "Catholic" Church the act is regarded (on this view) as being "from above," not because the descent of the Holy Spirit is invoked, but because the authority is given by those who are already bishops. On the same view the ordination of a minister according to the custom of the Congregational Churches is "from below," not because it is believed that the Holy Spirit is not present, but because the ordaining congregation consist of persons who are not themselves bishops or presbyters. In either case nothing is said about the relation of the act to the living and ascended Christ. What is said concerns solely the relation of the act to previous similar acts in the life of the Church. But the crucial question is, what is the relation of ecclesiastical acts to the will of the living Christ? Or, to put the matter more precisely, in what manner is the authority and grace of Christ given to His ministers in the ecclesiastical acts of ordination and consecration. The phrases "from below" and "from above" tend—in their ordinary usage—only to obscure the real issue.

Let us begin with the fundamental facts upon which Fr. Hebert's exposition is based, that the ministry is both an organ of the Body of Christ and also the representative to the Church of Christ its

[1] *Op. cit.*, p. 16.

Head. The historical thesis set forth by Dom Dix and others is that this double character of the ministry was—in the first decades of the Church's history—represented by two quite distinct institutions, the eldership and the apostolate; and that while these two institutions later became fused, yet the ministry can only perform the function of representing Christ to the Church if it possesses an authority derived from Christ in the days of His flesh by a line of succession which is *not* " by way of the Church."

Now it is clear that in the days when the Apostles of Christ were founding the first Churches, their function as the representatives of Christ to these Churches was clear and unmistakable. They were not officers of the local Churches, but their fathers in God by whom these Churches had been begotten. Something similar (though not identical) is found in the position of the missionary who comes for the first time to a new country, or of an evangelist by whose labours a new village is won for Christ. The infant Church in such circumstances no more appoints the missionary or the evangelist than does a new-born babe appoint its parents. It is not remarkable that the New Testament faithfully records this situation. What is remarkable is that even at this stage of the Church's life St. Paul could write " apostles " alongside of prophets, teachers and the rest of them, in his list of those whom " God hath set in the Church." So highly does he value the truth that the Church is the Body of Christ.

But the infant Church grows. The time comes when men from the village are appointed elders; from the new Church pastors are chosen, trained and ordained. But that does not mean that they have a totally different function from the missionary or evangelist. They are, indeed, representatives of the local church. But they are at the same time representatives of Christ to the Church. They have a commission from Him which requires that while they serve the flock they have also the authority to rule and teach. That belongs to the character of the ministry as the Church has always understood it. It is given to them in ordination. Ordination is an act of the Church done in faith towards her living Head, in the faith that He hears her prayer and " bestows upon and assures to those whom He has called and the Church has accepted for any particular form of the ministry, a commission for it and the grace appropriate to it."[1]

[1] *Scheme of Union*, p. 7.

Ordination is thus a point at which the relation between the two dimensions of the Church's existence becomes vividly clear. In it the Church acts in her true character as a society constituted by the union of her members in faith with the ascended Christ. In this faith she sets before Him the man whom she believes that He has called, and she lays her hands upon him in the act of prayer that Christ Himself may bestow upon him the commission and the grace that are required. And in the faith that He hears and answers, acting as His instrument, she commits to the ordained man the authority to act as minister of Christ to the Church. The prayer is the prayer of the whole Church and the hands are the hands of the whole Church which is His Body—not only of those now present, not even of those now living, but of all who have gone before everywhere and always. It is the hands that bear the unmistakable authority and commission of the whole Church that must be laid on the head of the ordinand, in token that the prayer that is offered is in truth the prayer of the whole Church— is indeed, " through Jesus Christ our Lord," a part of the one undiscordant offering of perpetual prayer which is made by Christ and by the Church in Him. The double nature of the Church is here made vividly clear. The Church appoints, ordains, commissions. It does so " in the name of Christ." But that is not a mere formula, nor does the Church act as the attorney of an absent Principal. Her act is a prayer to Him to act (for He alone can give what is to be given), and her prayer is an act which is thenceforth recognized as an act of the Body of Christ in all its consequences (for His will is to be done upon earth).[1] The man so

---

[1] I venture to append, for those who do not know it, the ordination prayer from the " Ordinal " of the Church of Scotland:

" Almighty God, most merciful Father, Who of Thine infinite goodness hast given Thine only Son Jesus Christ to be our Redeemer and the Author of everlasting life, and hast exalted Him unto Thy right hand, whence, according to Thy will, He hath sent down the Holy Spirit and given gifts unto men; we thankfully acknowledge Thy great mercy in bestowing upon us these inestimable benefits; and, we humbly beseech Thee, SEND DOWN THE HOLY SPIRIT UPON THIS THY SERVANT, WHOM WE, IN THY NAME, AND IN OBEDIENCE TO THY MOST BLESSED WILL, DO NOW, BY THE LAYING ON OF OUR HANDS,

Here the Moderator lays his hands upon the head of the Ordinand, the other Ministers also laying on their right hands.

ORDAIN AND APPOINT TO THE OFFICE OF THE HOLY MINISTRY IN THY CHURCH, COMMITTING UNTO HIM AUTHORITY TO DISPENSE THY WORD AND SACRAMENTS, AND TO BEAR RULE IN THY FLOCK. Impart to him such fulness of Thy grace as shall fit him more and more for the work to which he has been called. Give him counsel, understanding, and utterance,

THE MINISTRY

ordained is not merely the representative organ of the Church. He is the representative of Christ to the Church, possessed of the authority to speak and act for Him to His Church. But his commission does not come to him "from the Lord Himself in the days of His Flesh."[1] It comes from the Church's living Lord who having ascended upon high led captivity captive and gave gifts unto men. It therefore comes from the same Source as that from whom the whole Church from the Day of Pentecost onward derives her divine life.

There is no dispute about the fact that the apostolic ministry must possess a commission to represent Christ to His Church. What is in dispute is the manner in which the commission is given. What is here denied is the belief that this commission can only[2] be given by transmission through those who look "back to Christ as its source not by way of 'the Church' but by way of the apostolic line of descent,"[3] and that only this succession, distinct from the continuing life of the Church, can provide the Church with the guarantee of its claim to be indeed the Body of Christ.[4] This claim must, if it is pressed to all its practical conclusions, issue either in a total disconnection of the doctrine of the ministry from that of the Church, or else in a total disconnection of the doctrine of the Church from that of the Holy Spirit. That is to say, firstly, that if the Church be defined as the Body of Christ animated and indwelt by the Holy Spirit, as the communion of created souls in the Spirit with the living Christ, then the ministry which is constituted exclusively by the possession of a commission derived by transmission from Christ in the flesh, belongs to a quite different order of being and exists by quite different principles. The two being quite separate and distinct one or the other has to be given the primacy, and either one will be compelled—with many Protestant groups—to regard the ministry as a legal-

---

that he may boldly proclaim Thy word and will. Make him a light unto them that sit in darkness, a watchful and loving guardian over Thy fold, and a follower of the Good Shepherd Who gave His life for the sheep. Enable him to guide aright the people of his charge, and in all things to fulfil his ministry without reproach in Thy sight, so that he may abide steadfast to the end, and be received with all Thy faithful servants into the joy of His Lord.

"These things we ask through Jesus Christ our Lord, Who taught us to pray: Our Father . . ."

[1] Kirk, *op. cit.*, p. 52.
[2] It should be remembered that we are here discussing the question from the theological point of view. We are not discussing the historical question.
[3] Kirk, *op. cit.*, p. 49.
[4] *Op. cit.*, p. 46.

istic irrelevance, or else one will be compelled, with Dr. Kirk, to adopt the appalling alternative of having to recognize the works of the Holy Spirit *de facto* but to refuse to recognize them *de jure*. On the other hand, secondly, if the Church be defined in terms of its possession of the apostolic ministry, non-episcopal bodies being denied the title of Church, then one becomes committed to a doctrine of the Church divorced from that of the Holy Spirit. The constitutive fact of the Church is now not a communion with the living Christ in the Spirit, but the existence in its midst of men who have received a commission from Christ in the days of His flesh many centuries ago. The episcopate is the extension of the Incarnation, and the Church is constituted by the relation of its members to the bishop. Thus Dom Dix writes that "the apostolicity of the whole Church consists not in the exercise of a metaphorical apostolate by the laity, but in the spiritual communion which exists between all the members and the apostle. He lives in their lives and they in his, and through and in him they exercise the apostolate."[1] Truly "the *shaliach* is as him that sent him"! for here the relation between the Apostle and "the laity" is described in almost the same words as are used by our Lord to describe His relation to His Church. The Apostle is here in the place of Christ in a manner which makes Christ's living presence unnecessary. The idea of an apostolate of the laity—of a commission given to the whole "people of God" (the *laos*, including the ministry), in the discharge of which every member has the duty to share—is dismissed as a metaphor. The Church receives its mission to the world not by its union with Christ in the Spirit, but by its relation to a ministry which is derived by authorization from Christ in the flesh. Pentecost need not have happened.

One may quote as an extreme contrast to the view we are criticizing some words of an Orthodox theologian:

> "There is no direct evidence to show that in founding new ecclesiastical communities the Apostles personally ordained definite hierarchs for them. Rather, a *possibility* was provided for establishing a hierarchy, and this in time was done by the Church herself. Out of the fullness of her abiding Pentecost the Church created a hierarchy in accordance with the Divine Spirit dwelling in her, and with the general principle of the successive transmission of Grace. In the Old Testament Church

[1] *Op. cit.*, p. 176.

hierarchy was established at the command of God through the prophet Moses; in the Christian era Hierarchy arose through the prophetic spiritual activity of the Church. The Church is logically *a priori* to hierarchy and not *vice versa*. The conception of hierarchy as a direct and unbroken succession of ordinations beginning with the Apostles is typical of a later age—the age of Irenæus, Tertullian, and Cyprian. It is, however, too pragmatic in character, and cannot be regarded as *historically certain*. . . . It is supposed that the mere fact of successive ordinations establishes once for all a hierarchy which rules over the Church in the capacity of ecclesiastical oligarchy. Although this idea is prevalent among Orthodox theologians as well, it is not consistent with the Orthodox conception of the Church as an organic unity of its different members—the union of all in freedom and love (*sobornost* or commonalty). From this point of view, all gifts, including the Grace of Ordination, were given to the *whole* Church as a body, and consequently the Church was able to differentiate various organs for the fulfilment of specific functions and to *establish* hierarchy. This did not require a *direct* succession of ordinations going back to the Apostles; such a succession is only a supposition and cannot be proved. The whole idea of hierarchy must be interpreted in accordance with the organic conception of the Church, which implies that hierarchy exists in and for the Church, and is not *over* it; it is an organ of the Church, endowed with special powers."[1]

This, surely, goes too far in the other direction, both historically and theologically. The Apostles are, in a sense, logically prior to the Church. In another sense the Apostles were the Church in embryo. Yet it belongs to the nature of the Church always and everywhere that it is apostolic—that is to say, missionary. The apostolic ministry is not something which the Church has produced in the course of its history, though its forms have developed in the course of history. The apostolic ministry was there from the beginning. The Church has been—as it has been said—a vertebrate organism from the very beginning. But this is not the whole truth for the ministry is not only an organ of the Church, but also the representative of Christ to the Church. It can be both these things because the Church is not a historical society existing indepen-

[1] Sergius Boulgakoff: "The Hierarchy and the Sacraments" in *The Ministry and the Sacraments*, 1937, pp. 102-3.

dently of Christ and free to have or not to have dealings with Him. It exists in Christ and derives its life at every moment and in all its parts from Him. The apostolic ministry is, therefore, *both* continuous with, and a part of, the continuous organic life of the body, *and* at the same time the bearer of a commission from Christ to the Church; and it is both these things because the Church is the Body of Christ and lives in the dynamic relationship of faith in Him and in the power of His Spirit. Thus the clue to the double character of the ministry does not lie in the existence of a double historic succession—the succession of validly transmitted " power of attorney " from Christ in His flesh, on the one hand, and the continuous succession of the Church's life, on the other. It lies in the double character that belongs to every part of the Church's life —sacramental, evangelistic, ministerial. This—as I have suggested—is what is made clear in ordination. Here the prayer of the whole Church in every time and place is offered up to the Father in and through Christ, and here the gifts of God's Spirit are poured down in and through Christ upon the Church so that the Church, acting as His Body, commissions and empowers the man set apart for the sacred work. And both in the upward and in the downward movement Christ acts through the ministerial organs of His Body—organs which have been part of its structure from the beginning.

If this be a true account of the ministerial commission, it must at once be added that the picture is marred almost beyond recognition by our sinful division. The hands that are stretched forth to ordain and the prayers that ascend in the act of ordination no longer represent the one undiscordant prayer of a people made one in Christ. Yet Christ in His infinite mercy does not disown them. He treats even these mutilated limbs as His own Body and fills them—so far as they are able to receive Him—with His Spirit. That, surely, is the cardinal fact of the situation, beyond comparison the most vital truth upon the basis of which we must erect our thinking. But what follows from it? Shall we continue in sin that grace may abound? Shall we treat the unity and continuity of the Church and the ministry as matters of small account? It must be sadly confessed that we of the non-episcopal communions have often been content so to do, and that as a result our sense of the transcendent authority of the ministerial commission has been woefully weakened. I think all of us would confess that for the recovery of a truer doctrine of the Church and ministry we are very deeply indebted to the Anglican Communion. The South India Scheme of Union is but one small act of obedience to this recovered insight into the nature of the Body of Christ. Those who are entering into the union would claim, I think, that it is only in the restored unity of the One Body that we shall fully recover in practice that rich and full and balanced view of the ministry that is exemplified in Fr. Hebert's essay. And when it is proposed to visit the united Church with the penalty of excommunication on the strength of a claim that the sole authenticity of a ministerial commission derives from Christ in the days of His flesh and not by way of the Church which is His Body, we have to reply that this claim can neither be proved from the historical evidence nor reconciled with the credal affirmations of the Church. The ministerial commission is from the living Christ in and over the Church which is His Body.

(b) The titles " Priest " and " Presbyter "

It has been objected that the use in the Scheme of Union of the Biblical word " presbyter," and the absence of the word " priest," indicate that the united Church is departing from the faith of the Church as held and taught in the Anglican Communion regarding the nature of the ministry.[1] The objection has been so completely dealt with by Bishop Palmer[2] that I shall not attempt to add anything to his treatment of it, except to say that where proposals for union between Anglicans and others are being discussed, the position of the Anglican communion naturally cannot be regarded as by itself the supreme and decisive standard.

(c) The Bishops and the Synod

The South India Scheme envisages a form of Church government in which episcopal, presbyterial and congregational authorities have their due place, and in which personal and conciliar elements are combined in a proper harmony. In each congregation there will be a " Pastorate Committee," in each diocese a Diocesan Council, and for the whole Church a Synod which will be its supreme governing and legislative body. Provision is made whereby any proposition which directly concerns the faith of the

---

[1] See *The Unity of the Faith*, pp. 8-9, and *Priesthood and South India*, Mascall.
[2] *South India*, pp. 20-2.

Church, the conditions of membership and rules governing excommunication, the functions of ordained ministers and the worship of the Church, must be considered both by the whole Synod and by the bishops sitting separately. In the event of a divergence of opinion between the majority of the bishops and the majority of the Synod as a whole, provision is made for a very elaborate process of consultation, including if necessary twice repeated reference to the Diocesan Councils and back to the Synod—a process which would probably take some years. If the difference remains in the end unreconciled it will be possible, by the votes of two-thirds of the Diocesan Councils and by a majority of three-quarters in the Synod, for the views of the majority of bishops to be over-ridden.[1] The bishops thus have the power of interposing a very heavy brake upon precipitate action, but the final responsibility is not exclusively theirs but is borne by the Synod as a whole. It is clear that it would be necessary that almost the whole Church should adhere steadily for a long period to views contrary to those of the bishops before their views could finally be over-ridden. But the final responsibility does rest with the Church as a whole acting through the organs described.

It has been pointed out that " in view of the extreme remoteness of the contingency contemplated "[2] objection to these provisions may seem theoretical, but it is replied that "we are dealing not with probabilities but with principle."[3] Many who support the Scheme of Union yet regret that—as a matter of principle—the responsibility for guarding the purity of the Church's doctrine—"one of the oldest and gravest responsibilities of bishops"[4]—is not entrusted exclusively to them. Others, apparently, regard the matter as one of sufficient gravity to justify excommunication.

I believe that this is a matter upon which more discussion is needed. I will here say only three things:

(1) It is important that the principle involved should be clearly stated. If it is the " principle " which we examined in the earlier part of the chapter, that episcopacy is the sole guarantee of the Church's existence, then it must be rejected. If it is the principle that the Church should not depart from a very ancient practice in the manner of its government, it is a matter upon which the

---

[1] *Scheme of Union*, pp. 67-9.
[2] Archbishop of Canterbury's Committee of Theologians: Report, p. 29.
[3] T. Jalland, *op. cit.*, p. 66.
[4] E. J. Palmer, *op. cit.*, p. 23.

Church of South India must—along with the rest of the Church—hold itself ready to correct and reform itself in the light of its supreme and decisive standard.

(2) It is important to call to mind here what was said earlier regarding the duty of the Church to lead every member—according to his or her ability—into a full and responsible and personal faith. Only as the Church does this will she be enabled to remain, in any vital sense, orthodox, and to nurture and train men able to accept the special responsibilities of the ministry. It is difficult to believe that this is adequately done where all opportunity of effective discharge of that responsibility is lacking. Education without corresponding responsibility is the sure means of producing—whether in Church or in State—an irresponsible spirit of destruction.

(3) The fact that the re-consideration of this matter is urged upon the South India Church by its friends makes it almost certain that it will be re-considered in course of time. But when it is put forward as one amongst the grounds for treating the Church of South India as excommunicate,[1] one must ask whether this is really responsible churchmanship. When one calls to mind, as one must do in all sympathy, the position of the bishop of the Church of England in his relation, on the one hand, to the organs of the modern secular state, and, on the other, to those members of his flock who are ready to threaten him with schism if he fails to comply with their requirements, it is indeed difficult to believe that there are in the relation of the South Indian Bishop to the Synod of the Church adequate grounds of "principle" for the proposed excommunication. It may be that this is a matter upon which the Scheme is wrong, though I do not myself believe that it is. But I am sure that we do not really honour the "crown rights of the Redeemer" or safeguard His divine commission to the Church by trying to put it right under such threats of excommunication and schism.

[1] *The Unity of the Faith, loc. cit.*

CHAPTER TEN

THE SACRAMENTS

THE provisions of the Scheme of Union with regard to the Sacraments have received less adverse criticism than have its provisions regarding the standard of faith and the ministry, and it is therefore unnecessary for the purpose of the present book to devote more than a short chapter to their consideration.

The following are the principal passages in the Scheme relevant to the subject:

Basis of Union § 4

"The uniting Churches believe that the Sacraments of Baptism and the Supper of the Lord are means of grace through which God works in us, and that while the mercy of God to all mankind cannot be limited, there is in the teaching of Christ the plain command that men should follow His appointed way of salvation by a definite act of reception into the family of God and by continued acts of fellowship with Him in that family, and that this teaching is made explicit in the two Sacraments which He has given us. In every Communion the true Celebrant is Christ alone, who continues in the Church to-day that which He began in the upper room. In the visible Church, the celebration of the Lord's Supper is an act of the Church, the company of believers redeemed by Christ, who act as the local manifestation of the whole Church of Christ in heaven and on earth. It has in experience been found best that one minister should lead the worship of the church, and pronounce the words of consecration in the service of Holy Communion. From very early times it has been the custom of the Church that those only should exercise this function who have received full and solemn commission from the Church to do so; this commission has ordinarily been given by the laying on of hands in ordination.

"The only indispensable conditions for the ministration of the grace of God in the Church are the unchangeable promise of God Himself and the gathering together of God's elect people in the power of the Holy Ghost. God is a God of order; it has been His good pleasure to use the visible Church and its regularly constituted ministries as the normal means of the operation

THE SACRAMENTS

of His Spirit. But it is not open to any to limit the operation of the grace of God to any particular channel, or to deny the reality of His grace when it is visibly manifest in the lives of Churches and individuals.

"In the united Church the Sacraments will be observed with unfailing use of Christ's words of institution and of the elements ordained by Him."

Basis of Union § 8

"It shall be a rule of order in the united Church that the celebration of the Holy Communion shall be entrusted only to those who have by ordination received authority thereto. But it is desirable that, with the ordained presbyter, there be present to assist him in the administration of the Lord's Supper others appointed by the Church for this purpose.

"*Note*—After union certain exceptional arrangements will continue until permanent arrangements can be made by the united Church. The Synod of the united Church will have full authority to make what provision is needed for the administration of the Sacraments in all its congregations."

In the *Constitution*, Chapter III, § 1, the first condition of membership is to "have been baptized with water in the name of the Father and of the Son and of the Holy Spirit." And in Chapter X there are listed the following nine parts of the service of Holy Communion which the Church desires to have a place in every service, it being understood that as the Church grows together in unity the Synod will be able to issue more detailed forms of service for general use:

(i) *Introductory Prayers.*
(ii) *The Ministry of the Word*, including readings from the Scriptures, which may be accompanied by preaching.
(iii) *The Preparation of the Communicants* by confession of their sins, and the declaration of God's mercy to penitent sinners, whether in the form of an absolution or otherwise, and such a prayer as the "Prayer of Humble Access."
(iv) *The offering to God of the gifts of the people.*
(v) *The thanksgiving* for God's glory and goodness and the redemptive work of Christ in His birth, life, death, resurrection and ascension leading to a reference to His institution of the Sacrament, in which His own words are rehearsed, and to the setting apart of the bread and wine

THE REUNION OF THE CHURCH

to be used for the purpose of the Sacrament with prayer that we may receive that which our Lord intends to give us in this Sacrament.

Note—It is suggested that this section should begin with the ancient phrases and ascription of praise known as the *Sursum Corda* and the *Sanctus*.

(vi) *An Intercession for the whole Church*, for whom and with whom we ask God's mercy and goodness through the merits of the death of His Son.

(vii) *The Lord's Prayer*, as the central act of prayer, in which we unite with the whole Church of Christ to pray for the fulfilment of God's gracious purposes and to present our needs before the throne of grace.

(viii) *The Administration of the Communion*, with words conformable to Scripture indicating the nature of the action.

(ix) *A Thanksgiving for the Grace received in the Communion*, with which should be joined the offering and dedication of ourselves to God, unless this has been included earlier in the service. This Thanksgiving may be accompanied by an appropriate hymn.

The mere quotation of the Scheme is a sufficient treatment of some of the criticisms. Dr. Jalland, for instance, after studying (but not quoting) the provisions of Chapter III, gravely informs his readers that "it might perhaps be inferred from this that at any rate for the future Baptism is to be regarded as indispensable, though this is not formally stated."[1] It is unfortunate that such a statement must inevitably convey to the reader an impression which is the reverse of the truth, an impression which is further confirmed when Dr. Jalland writes, "Nowhere can we find it stated that candidates for the three sacred orders are required to be confirmed or even baptized. No doubt precedent for ordination without the pre-requisite of Confirmation may be found in out-of-the-way places, but we challenge anyone to show that any precedent can be found for the omission of the requirement of Baptism."[2] The most charitable thing that can be said about these sentences is that, in the words of the Archbishop's Committee, they "involve the overlooking . . . of the explicit requirements" of the Constitution. Again, Dr. Jalland tells his readers that in the Scheme the Sacraments "are declared to be 'means of grace

[1] *Op. cit.*, p. 41.
[2] *Op. cit.*, p. 63.

THE SACRAMENTS

through which God works in us' and are recommended on the ground that each of these rites traces its origin to 'the teaching of Christ,' though here again we find a certain elusiveness in the forms of expression chosen to convey this relatively simple idea."[1] The Scheme does not "recommend" the sacraments: it refers to Christ's "plain command" in the matter. Dr. Jalland would have done well to quote the passage in full and let his readers judge for themselves of its "elusiveness." I refer to these remarks of Dr. Jalland with regret,[2] and only for the reason that those who read this and similar criticisms of the Scheme without having the Scheme itself before them, must inevitably be given a totally false impression of it.

The serious criticisms of the substance of the Scheme in regard to the Sacraments may be subsumed under two heads. There is, firstly, criticism that the Scheme does not provide sufficiently explicit teaching regarding the doctrines of Baptism and the Eucharist, that nothing is said of the precise meaning and effect of Baptism, of the purpose with which the Eucharist is to be celebrated, or of the necessity of sacramental grace for salvation.[3] These points have been so conclusively dealt with by Bishop Palmer that I do not propose to traverse the ground again.[4]

There is, secondly, criticism regarding what is said about the place of the minister in the celebration of Holy Communion, both in the general statements in the Basis of Union, § 4, and in the "Note" regarding "exceptional arrangements" after the inauguration of the union. As is well known, there lies behind these passages as they stand in the final edition of the Scheme a controversy regarding the question of Lay Celebration which seemed at one time likely to destroy altogether the possibility of union. Something must, therefore, be said about this controversy and about its outcome.

Two distinct matters were involved in the controversy, a matter of pastoral need, and a matter of Church principle. The Church in South India is a growing Church, and in some areas it is growing with great rapidity. Most of those who are coming into the Church belong to the castes regarded in Hinduism as untouchable.

---
[1] *Op. cit.*, p. 61.
[2] Cf. Jalland, *op. cit.*, pp. 34, 48, 61-2, with the relevant parts of the Scheme.
[3] *The Unity of the Faith*, pp. 6-7.
[4] *South India*, pp. 11-12.

THE REUNION OF THE CHURCH

They come from a background of extreme poverty, of illiteracy, and of traditional subservience to the castes above them. The shepherding of these multitudes is a gigantic task, and requires a process of training and selection of teachers, evangelists and pastors which will take several generations adequately to complete. But in the meantime the sheep must be fed and shepherded. Over practically the whole of the vast area of South India which the uniting Churches occupy the task of shepherding the individual village congregation has fallen on the grant-aided teacher catechist. He both runs the school and also conducts daily and weekly services, instructs the young, leads in evangelism and supervises the life of the congregation. It is, of course, at present quite unthinkable that each village congregation should support a pastor for itself. These congregations consist for the most part of families whose total income in cash and kind is of the order of £5 per annum per family. They live in poverty of a kind which the Western European can with difficulty imagine. They give, in proportion to their means, liberally, but if their givings are to bear any sort of relation to the expenses of the Church it is impossible to have more than one pastor for a score or so of villages. The pastor, therefore, can only pay infrequent visits to each village. It is thus at all times extremely difficult to secure for the village congregations, which are the real basis of the Church, the regular celebrations of Holy Communion which are so vital for their growth in grace. Yet to solve the problem by reducing the standard of training required for the ordained ministry is a course which most Indian Christian leaders are rightly reluctant to contemplate. On the contrary, all responsible opinion is urging the need for higher standards.[1]

In almost all parts of the Church the problem has simply been solved by leaving the village congregations with infrequent celebrations of the Sacrament. But in certain parts of the Methodist Church and of the South India United Church licence has been given by the Synod or Council concerned to unordained Christian workers—such as senior evangelists—to administer the Sacrament in certain defined localities and for a defined period. The South India Provincial Synod of the Methodist Church passed in 1939 the following very clear statement of its position in the matter: "The Provincial Synod, in granting licences renewable annually

[1] E.g., Ranson: *The Christian Minister in India.*

to pastors[1] to administer the Sacraments, hereby declares that it does not regard the administration of the Sacrament by laymen as an essential part of our Church organization, but as a temporary expedient to meet special and exceptional needs that have arisen chiefly in mass movement areas." The Methodists, therefore, were entirely opposed to the suggestion that the practice of lay administration should be regarded as something to be included in the permanent structure of a united Church. They were only anxious to secure that the needs of the newly converted Christians were met.

In the South India United Church the majority of the Councils had never permitted lay administration and many were, of course, strongly opposed to it on principle. Some Congregationalists, however, felt that there was a matter of principle at stake in addition to the practical issue which has been explained. They urged on grounds of doctrine and of history that the fundamental Biblical truth that the Church is a Holy Priesthood could only be safeguarded if permanent provision were made for the celebration of the Sacraments by duly authorized laymen, that only thus could a falsely sacerdotal view of the ministry be excluded, and that, in fact, Congregationalists could not abandon the practice " without abandoning their very *raison d'être*."[2] It was upon this question of principle that the enterprise of union seemed for a while to be in danger of foundering.

There was an extensive interchange of thought in correspondence and in two short booklets to which reference may be made,[3] and the Joint Committee appointed a Sub-Committee to deliberate in the matter. It was one of the many occasions on which it was found that difficulties which seemed insoluble on paper were capable of solution in the context of the personal meeting of Christians responsibly engaged in the common life of the Church. The Committee found that the desire for lay celebration was due primarily " to a deep-rooted fear that the doctrine of the Priest-

---

[1] The highest grade of evangelist in the Hyderabad Methodist District, but not an ordained minister.
[2] J. S. Whale in *The Ministry and the Sacraments*, p. 214.
[3] *The Lay Celebration of the Lord's Supper*, a Congregationalist Point of View, H. C. Lefever. C. L. S. Madras.
The Lay Administration of the Lord's Supper, a Methodist Point of View, A. M. Ward. C. L. S. Madras.
I venture to commend these two booklets as models of the way in which theological controversy should be conducted. *O si sic omnes!*

hood of all believers is not adequately safeguarded by the Scheme of Union." They therefore felt that what was needed was "to make clear the theological issues and to draw out more fully the true doctrine of priesthood." They produced together a statement[1] on the subject which is now largely incorporated in the Scheme of Union, and on the basis of this it was possible for the request for a permanent provision for lay celebration to be dropped.

It will be readily understood that to those who were participants in these events it seemed clear that God's good hand was guiding them, and there was a profound sense of thankfulness that what seemed an impassable obstacle had been surmounted. I suppose, however, that everyone concerned would be willing to admit that the resultant changes in the Scheme are not all above criticism. I should myself feel that the phrase, "It has in experience been found best that one minister should lead the worship of the Church" is open to some of the criticism which has been levelled at it. Nevertheless the position to which the Sub-Committee was led, and on which the three Churches found that they could come together, is a clear and defensible one, and I submit that the criticisms made of it are certainly not of such gravity as to justify the perpetuation of disunity.

In the first place, as the basis of all that follows, is " the heavenly High Priesthood of the risen and ascended Christ, from which alone the Church derives its character as a royal priesthood."[2] In Him all priesthood exists and there is no priesthood apart from participation in His risen and ascended life. In this priesthood the whole Church is called to share. A doctrine of the ministry, or a practice with regard to the ministry, which makes it appear that priesthood is the exclusive possession of the ministry violates the most essential element in the character of the Church and justifies the most energetic protest against such falsehood. In the service of Holy Communion the congregation acts "as the local manifestation of the whole Church of Christ in heaven and on earth."[3] They meet as a holy priesthood. "The Eucharist is emphatically a sacrifice offered by the Church in its corporate unity, and not a sacrifice offered by a celebrant on behalf of the

---

[1] The original statement is given in Ward: *op. cit.*, pp. 38-40.
[2] Scheme, pp. 6-7.
[3] *Ibid.*, p. 7.

THE SACRAMENTS

Church."[1] Those of us who rightly press for the recognition of this truth must ask ourselves whether we have really grasped it ourselves. Does the common life of our Churches, the activities of all our members in evangelism and service, really bear the marks of a holy priesthood? Does the kind of worship which leaves the minister to say every word, including even the " Amen " to his own prayers, not constitute a very false sort of sacerdotalism? And does not the demand for lay celebration as an *indispensable* evidence of adherence to the doctrine of the priesthood of all believers imply the belief that the celebrant is *exclusively* the priest, and thus rest upon precisely the very error which it is sought to resist? The truth is that we shall worthily express in the life and worship of the Church the truth that the Church is a holy priesthood, firstly by forms of worship which fully recover the primitive sense of the activity of the whole congregation in the act of worship, including the act of consecration of the elements in the Holy Communion; and secondly by a common life of witness and service which is a true participation in the work of Christ's risen life.

In the second place—if this be firmly grasped—we can see that the rule that the celebrant at Holy Communion shall be an ordained minister is a *rule of order*.[2] The essential matter is that the dispensing of the Sacraments shall be so ordered that it visibly expresses the truth that what is done is the act of Christ in His Church—the whole Church in earth and in heaven. Thus while in the Presbyterian Churches the duty of administering the sacrament of Baptism is confined very strictly to ordained ministers, yet Baptism given otherwise is not simply regarded as null and void. But it would be a grave sin against the order and unity of the Church for anyone to baptize who was not a minister, except in circumstances of a very exceptional kind. So also with regard to the Eucharist. We do not know precisely when or how or by whom it was first established in the Church that the celebration of

[1] Gregory Dix, *The Idea of the Church in the Primitive Liturgies*, p. 127. Quoted Ward, *op. cit.*, p. 25.
[2] Cf. Bishop Palmer: " I will withstand anyone to the face who wishes to say that for this Sacrament, or for the forgiveness of sins, a priest is essentially and indispensably necessary. There is no evidence for that in the Bible, and there is much against it. . . . At the same time, I will not cease to say that the Church was quite right in making the rule by which the celebration of the Eucharist is confined to the priest, a very good rule of order—probably the best that could be made—but not an essential condition of the celebration of the Sacrament." Sermon in Westminster Abbey, 29th June, 1933, quoted Ward, *op. cit.*, p. 31.

the Sacraments should be confined strictly to those who have been ordained for the permanent exercise of that ministry, but it belongs to the whole nature of the Church, and of the Sacraments, that some such rule of order in the matter must have become established from a very early stage, even if not from the very beginning. It is not an accident of history, but of the essence of the Church, that this ministry should be both conjoined to the permanent exercise of pastoral responsibility in the Church, and also connected with a succession of authority binding the Church in all ages and places into one. Yet it remains still a rule of order, derivative from and subordinate to the fundamental truth that the whole Church is a sharing in the heavenly High Priesthood of Christ.

From this it follows that, on the one hand, the proposal that permanent provision be made for lay celebration of the Sacraments as a witness to the truth of the priesthood of all believers is rejected; for on analysis, it is seen not to be a witness to this truth, but to rest upon its opposite, to obscure the true nature of the Church's priesthood. It follows, on the other hand, that the arrangements which are now in operation to meet exceptional needs by the granting of temporary authority to certain unordained evangelists for the celebration of the Sacraments will not be suddenly terminated. Congregations must not be deprived of the means of grace by any such sudden change. The Synod, as the organ of the living Church, will have the authority both to sanction these exceptional arrangements for as long as is necessary, and also to take all necessary steps to see that provision for regular celebrations of the Holy Communion is made as soon as possible without further breach of the Church's rule.

On this point no one can accuse the Scheme of ambiguity. It is absolutely explicit that the restriction of the duty of celebration to Bishops and Presbyters is a rule of order. It will be apparent from all that has been said before that this part of the Scheme stands or falls along with the rest, for it depends upon the fundamental doctrine of the Church's nature. If a validly ordained celebrant is the absolutely indispensable condition of a sacrament, so that without this there is no sacrament, then this fact must determine the whole doctrine of the Church. In that case one will be committed to a view which bases the Church entirely on valid ministerial succession. When this is accepted the whole Biblical view of the nature of the Church is lost. The statement of the

THE SACRAMENTS

Scheme that "the only indispensable conditions for the ministration of the grace of God in the Church are the unchangeable promise of God Himself and the gathering together of God's elect people in the power of the Holy Ghost"[1] is not entirely satisfactory. But it does not merit the abuse which has been directed at it. It would have been supposed that to those who were accustomed to giving some place in their thinking to the doctrines of election and of the Holy Ghost, these words would have conveyed some intelligible meaning. But it seems not to be so.[2] Fr. Williams sarcastically asks: "Is the average Church service, it may be with a rather ordinary, uninspired and uninspiring clergyman celebrating or preaching, and a rather dull and unresponsive congregation, a 'gathering together of God's elect people in the power of the Holy Ghost?' I always thought that faith and humility and obedience to our Lord's command . . . were the things that really mattered, not a mysterious and unexplained something called 'being gathered together in the power of the Holy Ghost.'" But this will not do. Does Fr. Williams mean that our own faith and humility are the conditions of the validity of a sacrament? And does his doctrine of the Holy Spirit have nothing at all to do with the ordinary humdrum life of a congregation? Does it seem quite inexplicable to him to talk even of a very ordinary gathering of Christians for worship as "being gathered together in the power of the Holy Ghost?" I agree that the phrase is far from perfect. It would probably be best to accept the suggestions of the Archbishop's Committee of Theologians, or else to re-write the whole paragraph. But the phrase does nevertheless direct attention to the fundamental realities of the sacramental life—the promise of God Himself in Christ, and the living Church which is the Body of Christ, in-dwelt by the Holy Spirit. The sort of criticisms to which I have referred surely do less than justice either to the Scheme or to its critics for they seem to represent a theology of the Church which has removed the doctrine of the Holy Spirit altogether from the determinant position which properly belongs to it.

The wording of the final edition of the Scheme, with its em-

---

[1] Scheme, p. 6.
[2] E.g., Williams, *A Voice from India*, p. 11.
Thornton, *The Judgment of Scripture*, p. 6.
Jalland, *op. cit.*, p. 48. This latter may incidentally be studied as the *reductio ad absurdum* of a method of exegesis which appears to be increasingly popular.

phasis upon the priesthood of the whole Church as a participation in Christ's heavenly priesthood, does not justify the statement of Fr. Mascall that " the restriction of the celebration of the Eucharist to an ordained minister . . . is only a matter of convenience."[1] It is hardly fair that Fr. Mascall should quote only the later sentences of the section on the sacraments, omitting all reference to the earlier sentences, of which the Archbishop's Committee " strongly approved." But in any case one can believe that this restriction is a rule of order dating from the very earliest years of the Church's history, and yet repudiate the suggestion that it is " merely a matter of convenience." It is a rule which expresses and is congruous with the fundamental nature of the Church as the Body of Christ, but it is a rule of the Church. When, therefore, there are circumstances in which obedience to the Church's calling and priestly vocation demands it, and only then, the Church has the power and duty to make exceptions.

[1] *Priesthood and South India*, p. 7.

PART

4

CHAPTER ELEVEN

SOUTH INDIA AND THE ECUMENICAL MOVEMENT

THE foregoing chapters have been to a large extent negative and destructive in character. While I have sought to defend the South India Scheme on positive grounds against both Catholic and Protestant objectors, the argument has inevitably been dominated by the fact that an influential group of thinkers is seeking to urge upon the Anglican Communion the duty of excommunicating the South India Church. This is a matter of actual ecclesiastical action, a living issue which must be settled in the near future. I have sought to overthrow the reasoning by which this course of action is commended. It is all the more necessary, therefore, to add that there is a constructive theological task to be performed, more important and much more difficult than any such effort of destruction.

There is widespread conviction that the time for such a constructive effort is upon us. The ecumenical movement has made possible real and searching conversation between the different communions and confessions. To speak particularly of the divisions of Western Christendom, many Catholics in the Church of England are showing a real eagerness to grasp elements in the Protestant tradition (elements which Protestants themselves are often forgetting) which form part of the wholeness of Christian faith and life and which have been lost or obscured in the Catholic tradition. There is a recognition that " there were truths asserted at the Reformation; there were questions asked which demanded an answer," and that the breach will not be healed until an answer is given.[1] There is also evident among some Protestants an increasing consciousness of what Protestantism has lost of the wholeness of the Christian faith and life, especially in the some-

[1] A. G. Hebert, *The Form of the Church*, p. 102.

times shocking impoverishment of its sacramental life, and in its failure to embody in its common life a true doctrine of the relation of material things to the life in the Spirit. While giving thanks for this increasingly fruitful intercourse between these long-separated traditions one is bound to confess—as a Protestant—that one is often disappointed by the failure of Catholic writers to grasp, for instance, what the Reformers meant by justification, or what the preaching of the Word means as the central act in public worship. I have no doubt that my own understanding of what Catholics seek to affirm is equally dim. The fault in both cases lies in large part in our tragic failure to be true to the best insights of our own traditions. Just for this reason it is of the utmost importance that the task of mutual understanding and synthesis should not be cut short by easy solutions. The recent report on "Catholicity" rightly attacks the method of synthesis on the basis of the Highest Common Factor.[1] The danger of this method is that it should lead us to abandon the effort to answer the really great questions which were raised at the Reformation and to be content to agree on the basis of our often very enfeebled and distorted versions of the faith.

But here we have to remind ourselves again of the real context of the effort of mutual understanding—namely the common life in the Body of Christ. The Church is not primarily an association based on agreement about theological propositions. It is a unity of persons in the Body of Christ, represented locally by congregations in which Christ is present in the midst in Word and Sacrament, and through which He reaches out to save the world outside. The question of the reunion of the Church is only grasped in its true significance here—in the congregation and the parish. What matters is that there should be in each place one congregation which represents to that place Christ in His saving power, and which is not a special cultural or economic or social group, but just regenerate humanity. The search for mutual theological understanding and synthesis is not something which is to be completed before the reform of local church life is begun. Theological thinking is a function of the Church, and the two cannot in that way be separated. The danger of which all who are taking part in the work of the Faith and Order movement are conscious

---

[1] *Catholicity. A Report to His Grace the Archbishop of Canterbury.* Dacre Press, 1947, p. 44.

is that the process of theological synthesis should become a matter of the study and the conference-room, divorced from the actual life of the congregation and the parish. The two processes—the search for theological synthesis and the effort to bring the actual (local) life of the Church into conformity with its true nature—must proceed together, reinforcing and illuminating one another.

In an earlier chapter I have sought to show[1] that the South India Scheme has to be understood in the context of the actual life of the Church in that area. It has its basis not in study or conference-room but in the life of the local Church. In that sense it can truly be said that the effort of the Joint Committee has been primarily an effort to register a unity which is already there. It is because the Church, under the principles of comity, has been led in the discharge of its evangelistic task to be *locally* one, that it has had to seek to go on to conform its whole structure to that fact. Naturally there has been a real effort of theological comprehension and synthesis, but no one, I think, imagines that South India has produced anything of very special value in that direction. The Scheme is the result of the actual growth and development of the life of the local Church, not of an effort of theological synthesis. If God so wills it the united Church may become a place where this constructive work can be very fruitfully done; it must certainly be attempted. But much misunderstanding of the Scheme arises from the fact that the critic, living in a situation where the local Church exhibits the disunity of Christians at its maximum, and conscious of the difficulty of the task of theological synthesis, and of the extreme danger of premature solutions, regards the South India Scheme as just such a premature solution and condemns it accordingly. But the South India Scheme is not an essay in theological synthesis; it is a scheme for ecclesiastical union, the result of a real situation of the Church *vis-à-vis* the world which is in many respects the opposite of the situation in Great Britain. I have said that in the effort to recover the " primitive wholeness " of the Church's faith and life, we cannot separate the task of theological reflection from the whole context of the Church's common life, or say that the former must be completed before its expression in practice can be begun. In fact, we find that in the West the theological effort has far outrun its expression in church life. But in the younger Churches the opposite has happened: the theo-

[1] Chapter I.

logical effort has sometimes been allowed to be almost forgotten in the concentration on practical evangelistic and pastoral problems. That weakness is writ large across the South India Scheme. It is one of the deplorable features of human history that not only does it display a maddening reluctance to conform to rational patterns, but that it has a way of displaying contradictory forms of irrationality at different times and places. The weakness that besets the ecumenical movement in the West is the precise opposite of that which besets the South India Scheme, and it is this difference in the actual character of the Church situation which has—I believe—been the cause of much of the hostility which the Scheme has evoked. One may put the point sharply by saying that if the South India Scheme were now proposed as a basis for union between the Churches in Great Britain many of the criticisms made against it would be valid, for it assumes as its background a pattern of local church life which is not that of Great Britain. And one may hazard the statement that the issue of reunion in Britain must first be tackled in the realm of local church life in its relation to the life of the local community.

But—it will be rightly argued—this is an over-simplification of the issue. You cannot allow geography so completely to dominate theology. It is true that the task of theological synthesis and the recovery of a true church life have to proceed together, and that, in fact, they are always liable to get out of step. But it is impossible to admit that the West can start from one end and the East from the other and that we can agree to differ until we find that we have met. If it is false to suppose that the task of theological synthesis is to be completed before you start the task of ecclesiastical reformation, it is nevertheless true that you must have some theological basis for the action you take, and that you cannot simply say, "Let us unite in order that we may learn to agree."

In the last analysis the basis of agreement is something which it is impossible exhaustively to define in a series of statements. It is something of complete simplicity, as comprehensible by an old peasant woman in a South Indian village as by a doctor of divinity. It is just being in Christ and recognizing one another as in Christ. But that elemental fact has to be made explicit in more elaborate statements as to its basis in the revelation to which the Scriptures witness, its explication in the ecumenical creeds, its effectual signs in the sacraments and its visible incorporation in the historic Church unified round the apostolic ministry. On every one of these matters Christians have disputed, and a patient and resolute effort of mutual understanding is needed if we are to grasp the truth about them in all its fulness with all our minds. But the explicit basis of union should not attempt to provide a resolution of these differences. It is sufficient that it guard from distortion what is essential to our being "in Christ." This is not to cut short the process of theological synthesis by accepting an easy highest common factor. It is to secure the conditions under which alone real progress in the task of theological synthesis can be made. It is only when varying insights are held in some sense within the unity of the common life of the Church that their opposition is fruitful of new and richer insight. When each is made the basis of a separate ecclesiastical organization the result is merely that familiar struggle of rival groups which the Apostle had to reprobate in the Corinthian Church. The attempt to find the basis of Christian unity in a completely articulated theological system is part of the essence of sectarianism. The Catholic theologians whose report I have already quoted have wise words on this subject. Of the apostolic church they write:

> "Only a Church which was not afraid of 'tensions' and which was able to discern without prejudice the 'wholeness' of the revelation in Christ, would have dared to set side by side four differing Gospels, the Epistles of St. Paul and St. James, the apostolic history of Acts and the eschatology of the Apocalypse, and to acclaim them all as normative."[1]

Later on they speak of "the spontaneity and vitality which such contained tensions always bring to theological and ecclesiastical thinking" and add that, in contrast to the Papal Communion, "the much smaller and more theologically homogeneous Protestant bodies on the Continent, each modelled largely upon the thought of a single master-mind, had no such inner possibilities, as is shown by the increasing stagnation of orthodox Protestant thought abroad after about 1570."[2] It is precisely with such thoughts as these in view that the framers of the South India Scheme deliberately stated that room was to be made in the united Church for widely different and even mutually contradictory

[1] *Catholicity*, p. 15.
[2] *Ibid.*, p. 35.

opinions, within the framework of a firm adherence to " the fundamentals of the faith and order of the Church Universal."[1] It is quite unjust to assume that those who have laboured for this comprehensive union have done so because they fail to see the theological importance of the points of difference, and to dismiss the Scheme as a premature and shallow attempt at theological synthesis. They have laboured for this union because they believe that the unity of the Church is a reality more deeply founded than the unanimity of a theological school. They will take into the union their diverse views and will continue to press them vigorously within the fellowship of the united Church. They believe that as they do so they will be in a better position than they are now to forward the task of theological synthesis and to re-discover the wholeness of the Christian life of faith, worship, fellowship and service. It is not that diversity is wanted for its own sake. These tensions are painful and will be hard to bear. Nor is it that one supposes that the wholeness of the Christian pattern can be achieved by tying the broken pieces together by the merely external bonds of a new organization. That would be wrong—even though God in His mercy might still bring much good out of it, as He has done out of the Elizabethan attempt to clamp the pieces together in the bonds of state control. It is that, amid all that is arguable and uncertain, the central and simple fact of redemption into Christ makes outward division intolerable, and it is this central certainty which makes us sure that even through these tensions and disagreements we shall be led forward into unity of heart and mind and into the full riches of the inheritance of the Church.

But it will be argued that there is possible a real and constructive conversation among Christians apart from actual union. The history of the ecumenical movement shows, it will be said, that we can advance a long way along the path of theological synthesis short of actual reunion, and that it is wrong to cut short this process by a premature act of union which forecloses some of the issues which the ecumenical movement has left open. One must ask, what is the issue that will be foreclosed? The answer is that only one will be—the issue as to whether non-episcopal ministries are real ministries. The South India Scheme, without making any comments on questions of validity or regularity, and while itself

[1] *Scheme*, p. 2.

committed to the maintenance of the historic episcopate, is nevertheless equally committed to the view that non-episcopal ministries are real ministries of the Word and Sacraments within the universal Church. And if the Church of South India is to be treated by the Anglican Communion as excommunicate it can only be because a decision has been made that such ministries are not real ministries. In either case that issue has to be settled. If it is not settled the future of the ecumenical movement must be permanently precarious. For the process of mutual understanding and synthesis which the ecumenical movement has made possible has been based upon a tacit acceptance of one another as Christians by the members of the different Churches. Its starting-point is the acceptance of the fellow-Christian of another Church, *in his Church*, as a fellow-member in Christ. "It accepts him in Christ not in spite of, but because of, his allegiance to another Church. It sees him thereby as reflecting Christ not as an individual with different views, but as the bearer of a different Church life."[1] But that starting-point already involves a theological judgment the full implications of which, even if they remain unnoticed for some time, must eventually be faced. It seems that South India has provided the point at which these implications will have to be faced. The South India experiment might perhaps have been permitted to take place with the benevolent neutrality of the rest of Christendom but without involving the raising of these wider issues at the present stage. But it has not been so. South India has been made an ecumenical issue, and that being so the issue cannot be evaded. If South India is to be excommunicated by the Anglican Communion it can only be because that Communion has decided that it cannot regard the non-episcopal Churches as parts of the universal Church, that apart from the historic episcopate there is no Church. If that decision is made, the consequences for Anglican participation in the ecumenical movement will eventually have to be faced. If, on the other hand, the South India Scheme is recognized as a valid attempt, within the conditions of a particular part of the world, to restore the visible unity of the Church, then one cannot help feeling that the whole process of theological and ecclesiastical reintegration within the ecumenical movement will receive a new impetus.

[1] *Towards the Conversion of England*, p. 97.

THE REUNION OF THE CHURCH

I have already alluded to the danger that besets the ecumenical movement, the danger that it should settle down to being only an affair of the study and the conference-room, remote from the real centre of the Church's life in congregation and parish. We ought to accept no goal short of the reunion of the Church, made visible in a local congregational life which gathers up into itself the full and many-sided richness of the whole Christian tradition. The attempt to achieve theological synthesis apart from the actual reunion of these tragically divided bodies must deflect attention away from the central task. The South India Scheme is not a premature attempt to cut short the necessary processes of theological synthesis. It is an example of what will have to be done if that process is not to be arrested. It is a reminder to all who are concerned in the ecumenical movement that the goal is organic reunion, and that nothing must be allowed to deflect attention from that goal. I do not believe that it can be repudiated without imperilling the whole future of the ecumenical movement.

I have spoken in this chapter about the relation of the Anglican Communion to South India. I am conscious of the presumption of this, but my excuse is that it is the Anglican Communion which has most actively concerned itself with the Scheme. I do not forget that to many in the non-episcopal Churches the Scheme is exceedingly distasteful. That they have been (in Britain) less vocal in their dissent has been due partly to theological and ecclesiastical tradition and partly to a strong reluctance to do anything which looks like interfering with the growth of one of the younger Churches. I have tried in the course of the argument to meet some of these objections too, though I am conscious of failure to do so with any adequacy. I would plead with those who oppose the Scheme from the Protestant side to consider again whether our return to the unity of the one Body must not be also a return to that continuous ministerial succession by which the Church is visibly united through time and through space. And I would plead with those Catholic critics who advocate the excommunication of the Church of South India because it acknowledges the reality of the non-episcopal ministries to consider again whether the ground they are occupying really holds out any hope at all for the restoration of the Church's visible unity. So long as episcopacy is accepted and cherished as the organ of the Church's continuing unity from the Apostles in Palestine to the Christian Churches in every land to-day it will offer a centre round which the Church may be visibly re-united.[1] But the claim that episcopacy—by itself and in isolation—is the sole organ of the Church's apostolicity, will be rejected as emphatically by the great Roman and Eastern Churches as by the non-episcopal. The tragedy of the position which I have criticized is that in the attempt to justify itself against Rome and the East it is compelled to excommunicate the rest, yet by this dual warfare it can gain the acceptance of neither. What might have been a stepping-stone for mutual traffic between separated bodies is turned into a fortified and isolated island inaccessible to either side. I submit that the method of reunion adopted in South India, however grave may be the defects of the Scheme as it stands, provides a starting-point from which further advance is possible as the process of mutual understanding and re-integration advances. If, as we are bound to pray, the process of mutual comprehension, of reformation, and of recovery advances far enough to make reunion with Rome and with the East a matter of practical possibility, we shall surely have to follow the same method—the recognition of one another as truly parts of the Church, and the return of those who have stood outside of it to a form of order and of authority larger than, and prior to, that in which we have lived. However far-reaching may be the transformation required both of the Protestant Churches and of the Roman and Eastern before union can be a matter even of discussion, there ought to be nothing to prevent our looking now towards the restoration to the whole Church of a visible unity with a central organ of unity such as Rome was for so many vital centuries of the Church's history. I cannot but believe that the first steps towards that goal must be rather in the direction that South India has taken than in the direction of those who find in the Church polity of Cyprian the last and unalterable word about the nature of the Church. The long story of the Church's division is not only the chronicle of human sin. It is also the story of the still unfinished work of the Holy Spirit in taking of the things of Christ and showing them to us in ever greater fulness. The test of every scheme of reunion is that it should help to gather up and express in one visible fellowship the full riches of the inheritance of the Church in all ages, that all who bear Christ's name may be " strong to apprehend with all the saints what is the breadth and length

[1] As, for instance, in Ramsey: *The Gospel and the Catholic Church.*

and height and depth" of the Truth as it is in Jesus. But this comprehensiveness will be achieved not as we seek it for its own sake, but as we return to the central simplicity of the Gospel and learn " to know the love of Christ which passeth knowledge." Our deepest need is not synthesis but repentance. It is as we learn to know nothing save Jesus Christ and Him crucified and to have no ground of glorying save His Cross, that the broken and distorted pattern of His divine life in us will be visibly restored, and we shall be "filled unto all the fulness of God" (Eph. iii. 18-19).

INDEX

ACTS, ii:38-41, p. 41; ii:39, p. 31; viii:12ff., p. 41; ix:18, p. 41; x:45, p. 32; x:47, p. 41; xi:17, p. 32; xi:18, p. 37; xiii:1-3, p. 153; xv:5, p. 32; xvi:15, p. 41; xvi:33, p. 41; xviii:8, p. 41; xix:4-6, p. 41; xxii:16, p. 41
Amos, 30
Anselm, 24
Apocalypse, 155
Apostles, 151-6, 161, 164-6
Atonement, 16, 45-8, 61, 86-8, 94-7
Augustine, 113
Authority, 127f.

BEVAN, EDWYN, 75
Bible, 27-9, 75, 102, 125, 128, 131-6, 142, 144, 146
Boulgakoff, Sergius, 165
Broomfield, Canon, 111
Burn-Murdoch, Dr., 56, 71, 151

CALVIN, 29
Catholicity, 182, 185
Church, The, Its task, 10, 19; in Paganism, 12; in N.T., 17, 25; founded on Gospel, 18f., 46, 62; the *ecclesia*, 23; Mother, 28f.; Israel of God, 31f.; Temple, 45, 55; Body of Christ, 48, 51, 160, 182; One, 55f.; "Incarnation of God," 61-4; its body and soul, 64ff.; as sacrament, 66-70; of two dimensions, 70-8; its individualism, 80; its sin, 81f., 84; sphere of justification, 85, 97f.; a holy priesthood, 176f.
Church in South India, 12-15, 17, 20f., 137, 144, 145f., 173-5
Church, Methodist, 146, 174f.
Church of Scotland, The, 141, 144
Church, The Roman, 56ff., 81f., 151, 189
Churches, Eastern, 189; Presbyterian, 111, 151, 177; Western, 9, 11; Younger, 9
Clement, I, 154ff.
Colossians, i:18-20, p. 92; i:26, p. 92; ii:10f., p. 36; ii:11, p. 40; ii:14f., p. 38; iii:3, p. 48; iii:4, p. 48
Comity, Mission, 11ff., 20f.
Congar, M. J., 17, 56ff., 78ff.
Corinthians, I, i:1-3, p. 44; i:4-9, p. 44; i:10-ii:16, p. 45; i:13, p. 100; i:17, p.39; iii:3, p. 54; iii:3f., pp. 18, 48; vii:19, p. 36; x:18, pp. 33f.; xii-xiv, p. 51; xii:3, p. 98; xii:13, pp. 40, 69; xv:1-4, p. 87; xv:3f., p. 61
Corinthians, II, i:22, pp. 45, 98; iii:6, p. 99; v:14f., p. 89; viii:23, p. 153
Creeds, 124-6, 137, 142, 145f. 147
Cyprian, 165, 189

DENOMINATIONS, 16f., 20
Deuteronomy, vi:5, p. 93; x:16, p. 42; xxx:6, p. 42
Didache, 155
Disunity, 23, 24f., 54, 103, 186
Dix, Gregory, 70, 152ff., 161, 164, 177
Dodd, C. H., 32

ECUMENICAL MOVEMENT, THE, 181, 182f., 186-8
Eldership, The, 152f., 161
Elijah, 30
Eliot, T. S., 143
Ephesians, i:9-13, p. 92; i:13-iv:30, p. 45; ii:6, p. 98; ii:11, p. 36; ii:11-22, p. 38; ii:12, p. 31; ii:17, p. 39; iii:1-13, p. 100; iii:18f., p. 190; iv:3, p. 50; iv:5, p. 40; v:26, p. 40
Episcopacy, Mon-, 151, 153
Episcopate, The, 82f., 107-9, 123, 150-8
Eschatology, N.T., 73-8

FAITH, JUSTIFICATION BY, 76, 84-103; Standard of, 124-47
Farrer, 153f.

GALATIANS, i:8, p. 39; ii:20, pp. 48, 57, 89, 97; iii:1ff., p. 43; iii:2, p. 39; iii:7, p. 33; iii:16, p. 34; iii:23-9, p. 40f.; iv:26, p. 34; v:1-6, p. 33; v:5, p. 92; v:6, p. 40; v:16ff., p. 99; vi:12, p. 34; vi:13, p. 40; vi:13f., p. 43; vi:14, pre-title p., p. 101
Gavin, F., 33
Gospel, The, 17, 20, 26, 28

HEBERT, A. G., 157f.
Hebrews, ix:26-8, p. 60; ix:28, p. 87; xi:6, p. 57; xii:2, p. 95
Hindus, 28
Hort, 154

Hosea, 35

IRENÆUS, 165
Isaiah, 30
Israel of God, The, 27-43

JALLAND, DR. TREVOR, 120, 129, 133, 168, 172f., 179
James, ii:19, p. 145
Jeremiah, iv:4, p. 42; xi:16, p. 32
John, i:13, p. 47; i:14, p. 63; iii:16, p. 48; vi:63, p. 60; vii:38, p. 69; xii:20-32, p. 30; xii:24, p. 30f.; xii:32, p. 31; xv:16, p. 27; xvi:7, p. 60; xvii:21, pp. 59, 98; xx:17, p. 60; xx:19-21, p. 154; xx:21, pp. 22, 39; xx:28, p. 134
John, I, i:1, p. 26; iv:11, p. 80; iv:20, p. 81
John, III, 155
Johnston, George, 36
Judaisers, 32f.

KINGDOM OF GOD, THE, 30
Kings, I, xix:15-18, p. 30
Kings, II, v:12, p. 28
Kirk, Dr., 152, 158ff.
Knox, John, 112

LAITY, 149, 164, 178, 180
Lefever, H. C., 175
Life in the Spirit, 48f., 98ff.
Lightfoot, 156
Luke, xviii:13, p. 66

MACKINTOSH, H. R., 97
Mark, xi:27-33, p. 126; xiv:58, p. 36; xv:34, p. 88
Mascall, 167, 180
Matthew, vii:29, p. 127; viii:5-13, p. 30; x:1-8, p. 39; xv:21-8, p. 30; xxv:40, p. 80
Ministries, 82, 107
Ministry, The, 148-69
Missionary Movement, The, 9f., 19

NATIONAL CHRISTIAN COUNCILS, 12
Newman, 152

ORDINAL, CATHOLIC, 160; Church of Scotland, 162f.
Ordination, 148, 161ff., 165; Supplemental, 109-14

PALMER, BP., 110f, 136, 167f., 173, 177
Peter, I, iii:18, p. 60
Philippians, iii:1-9, p. 36; iii:3, p. 40; iii:9, p. 92; iii:20, p. 72
Protestantism, 78f., 181f.

QUICK, O. C., 113

RAINY, PRINCIPAL, 138ff.
Ramsey, 189
Reformation, Protestant, 78f.
Reunion, Missionary impulse, 9, 104; bound up with evangelization, 19; method, 104-23; basis, 122f.; goal, 189f.
Romans, ii:28f., pp. 34, 40; iii:22, 24, 25, 26, p. 34; iii:25, p. 89; iii:25f., p. 86; iv, p. 42; iv:1-10, 11, 12, p. 34; iv:10-12, p. 40; v:8, p. 89; vi:1, p. 103; vi:4, p. 89; viii, p. 99; viii:9, p. 94; viii:15, p. 98; ix-xi, p. 34; ix:6-8, p. 35; ix:25f., p. 35; x:1-12, p. 35; x:14, p. 39; x:20f., p. 35; xi:1-12, p. 35; xi:17f., p. 32; xi:13-24, p. 35; xi:32, p. 35

SACRAMENTS, THE, 58, 67-70, 102f., 170-80
Scottish Church case, 1904, 138-41
Shaliach, 153f.
Simpson, P. Carnegie, 139ff.
Sin, 24, 62, 66, 81, 84, 87f., 90, 95f.
Solitariness, 52f.
South India Scheme, 14, 21, 22; Basis, 52; Method, 104-23; The Pledge, 114-19; 30 Year Period, 119-22; Standard of Faith, 124-47; The Ministry, 148-69; Bishops and Synod, 167-9; Sacraments, 170-80; Result of Growth, 183f.
Spirit, The Holy, 45, 47, 48, 51, 58, 98-102, 104, 116, 119f., 133ff., 142

TAYLOR, VINCENT, 85
Temple, Wm., 26
Tertullian, 165
Theologians, Archbishop of Canterbury's Committee of, 168
Thornton, Lionel, 41ff., 147, 179
Timothy, I and II, 155
Titus, iii:5, pp. 40, 155
Traditions, 105, 129

UNITY, THE CHURCH'S, 15f., 24, 25, 35, 50-2, 53f., 59, 100f. 106

VINCENTIAN CANON, 78, 130, 138

WARD, A. M., 175f.
Western, Bp., 110f.
Whale, J. S., 175
Williams, Fr., 143, 179

Zeqenim, 152f., 156

www.ingramcontent.com/pod-product-compliance
Lightning Source LLC
Chambersburg PA
CBHW070338230426
43663CB00011B/2375